921   Graham, Fred
GRAHAM
           Happy talk   NNF

7/90

$19.45

DATE		

Other books by Fred Graham

The Self-Inflicted Wound
The Alias Program

HAPPY TALK

W·W·NORTON & COMPANY

New York London

HAPPY TALK

CONFESSIONS OF A TV NEWSMAN

FRED GRAHAM

Printed in the United States of America.

The text of this book is composed in Janson,
with display type set in Bodoni Ultra Extra Condensed.
Composition and manufacturing by the Haddon Craftsmen, Inc.
Book design by Jacques Chazaud.

First Edition

Library of Congress Cataloging-in-Publication Data

Graham, Fred, 1931–
Happy talk.

Includes index.
1. Graham, Fred, 1931–   . 2. Television journalists
—United States—Biography. 3. Television broadcasting
of news—Political aspects—United States. 4. CBS News—
History. I. Title.
PN4874.G664A3 1990   070.92 [B]   89-8838

ISBN 0-393-02776-7

W. W. Norton & Company, Inc.
500 Fifth Avenue, New York, N. Y. 10110
W. W. Norton & Company Ltd.
37 Great Russell Street, London WC1B 3NU

1 2 3 4 5 6 7 8 9 0

This book is for my children,
Grier, David, and Lys Graham,

in hopes that it will bring pleasure
and understanding.

Contents

CONTENTS

HAPPY TALK

1

Real Anchormen Don't Part Their Hair

The Can Man was in trouble, and so was I. His problem was a lack of vision. Mine, I knew, was much more fundamental than that.

The Can Man's difficulty was that his eye-holes were in the wrong place. Technically, his outfit was a thing of wonderment. His body and head were encased in a "can," a tube of beige burlap chopped off at the knees so that he could romp around before the television cameras without tripping. His burlap can was topped just above his hairline with an impressive display of papier-mâché edibles—celery, tomatoes, turnip greens, and a banana— all thrusting forth as if from the top of a can brimming with foodstuffs.

It was the first week in April 1987, and I was meeting the Can Man for the first time. He was the creation of my new employer, television station WKRN in Nashville, Tennessee. Once or twice a year a disk jockey from the radio station upstairs was trotted down into our TV studio encased in the Can Man suit, to be videotaped in promotional commercials used to solicit donations of food for the poor. People liked the klutzy getup and generous idea. The Can Man had become a warm and fuzzy fixture on the local scene.

Unfortunately, either the disk jockey's eyes were uncommonly close-set, or the eye-holes in the burlap had been cut too far apart. In either event, as the Can Man bounded about the brightly lit set in time to enthusiastic Nashville music, he found it impossible to maintain his view of the teleprompter. Unable to read his lines as they rolled up across the camera lens, the Can Man kept blowing his part. Nobody could fault his panting enthusiasm about vittles for the poor, but through the wideset eye-holes the Can Man could not get it right.

A technician tried to point out to the director that, since viewers couldn't see his lips anyway, it would be easy to record the Can Man's voice, play it back as he romped through his act, and fake the whole thing. Television has no scruples about such trickery, but it does have a rigid pecking order that puts the director in command of such decisions.

At WKRN/Channel 2, this division of power parted along the lines of redneck versus yuppie. The studio hands tended to be beer-bellied, single-gallus types who could have dropped in from a coon hunt. They had become my instant comrades and protectors as soon as I straggled into Nashville from the devastation of CBS. But I had not yet become accustomed to looking out toward the cameras and viewing a studio crew that might have been guarding a still.

The director, a jive-talking black yuppie, wasn't

about to do a public turnabout on a studio technician's tip. So the Can Man continued to flounder along. With every bad take from the Can Man, my teleprompter rehearsal time was slipping away, and so was my morale.

That I had any morale at all was a triumph of optimism over reality. There I was, a somewhat shopworn refugee from CBS News, sitting alone at the floodlighted anchors' desk, which loomed like a pulpit over the vacant studio floor, empty because the cameras had been pulled over to the side to photograph the struggling Can Man. Behind me was a fascinated newsroom staff watching the highest-priced anchor in town waiting to practice reading the teleprompter.

My practice sessions with the teleprompter were the first shadow over a glittering return to my hometown two weeks earlier, after a quarter century as a high-profile journalist in Washington. My homecoming in the spring of 1987 had seemed a master stroke of good timing. CBS News, where I had been the law correspondent for fifteen years, was in turmoil, wracked by brutally executed layoffs, angry resignations, public bickering, and general unhappiness. I had maneuvered a timely exit by signing on as the star anchor of the ABC station in my hometown.

Nobody had asked if I could read a teleprompter. When it turned out that my skills were wanting, there was nothing to do but spend the two weeks before I actually went on the air practicing.

For the new anchor to require work on the teleprompter was as if Leonard Bernstein needed to brush up on waving his baton. The teleprompter is the basic tool of the television anchor—a device that allows him to appear smart and eloquent enough to earn six figures for telling the news to everybody else. They call it the "idiot box" only half in fun. With its adroit use, the emptiest intellect can appear wise and profound. It explains, as well as any of the technological hocus-pocus of TV, television's basic illusion—the magical capacity to make an electronic reconstruction of life seem real.

A teleprompter uses something like a two-way mirror to flash the anchorman's lines on a pane of glass in front of the camera lens, while the camera peers through the nonmirror side of the glass at the anchor. It is done by leaning the mirror side of the glass forward at a forty-five–degree angle from the bottom of the camera lens out toward the anchor. The words are flashed on the mirror side of the glass from an upturned TV screen jutting out from the lower lip of the camera. The anchor sees the words roll up in front of the lens. The camera sees only the anchor, looking eloquent.

Like any illusion that depends upon technology, when things go awry, a teleprompter can be perverse. One of WKRN's anchors had been its victim. As he read earnestly into the camera one day, the teleprompter caught fire. Smoke billowed up from the TV monitor jutting out from the lower lip of the camera lens—but the words continued to crawl up the screen (the words are always stacked in short lines of just two or three words across, to spare the anchor a back-and-forth, shifty-eyed look), and the anchorman kept on reading.

As the puffs of smoke intensified and thickened around the camera lens, so did the look of determined nonchalance on the anchorman's face. Somebody ran up beside the camera and tried to fan the smoke away with a sweater. Finally, a studio tech rushed forward with a fire extinguisher and sprayed suds into the innards of the upturned TV monitor. The anchorman peered earnestly through the smoke, cribbed from the script on his desk, and completed the show.

As limited as my own experience had been in reading a teleprompter on the air, I had also come a cropper once while reading one on the "CBS Morning News." My problem was familiar to those who live by the idiot box; a malfunction of the teleprompter operator.

The operator's job is to work a switch that rolls the copy across the camera lens as the anchor reads it. The only trick is to time the roll with the natural speed of the anchor's reading, and the only required skill is the ability to read.

One morning I found myself on the air with a tele-prompter operator who was illiterate.

CBS had a rule: all the technicians who worked in its studios had to be able to operate all the equipment. But over the years, people tended to gravitate to jobs that fit them. Nobody had noticed—or had cared to mention—that for as long as anyone could remember, a certain cameraman had never done a stint at the teleprompter. But one morning, when I was scheduled to deliver a commentary about a legal subject, absences due to sickness and vacations on the early shift led the unsuspecting studio floor director to assign that cameraman to work the teleprompter for me.

I led off with jaunty confidence, until I got to the bottom of the first page. At first, it didn't move up at all. Then, as I stammered around, it suddenly lurched upward, and I chattered as fast as I could, trying to keep up.

It slowed down again, and so did I, hoping that new words would climb into view before I read all the words in sight. But the slower I read, the slower the tele-prompter ran. I slowed down. It slowed down. Finally, out of words, I stopped. It stopped.

Experienced victims of teleprompter operators always keep turning the pages of script before them as they read the copy on the screen—so that if the operator slips into a trance they can find the place and read on. I had not done this. My only recourse was to assume my most authoritative look and complete my commentary, ad lib.

As soon as we went off the air, Lesley Stahl, who had been anchoring in New York, placed a worried call. She was afraid I had suffered a seizure and might need medi-cal attention.

All I had suffered was a brief fit of anger, which quickly passed when I discovered that the teleprompter operator felt worse than I did. Nobody had noticed before that he couldn't read, and he was mortified to have it surface in such a spectacular fashion. He was, however, a competent cameraman, and we quietly agreed that he would remain in that role from then on.

For those who master the art of reading it, the tele-prompter becomes magic. The anchor speaks with ef-fortless confidence, faking an occasional look at his notes for realism, spicing his eloquence with a well-placed smile or toss of the head. Television abounds with leg-ends of anchors with IQs at room temperature who earn vast salaries on the strength of looking good while read-ing other peoples' words on the idiot box.

The trick, of course, is to learn to read it while appearing to be just talking. That is accomplished mostly by spending so many hours reading into the idiot box that it does, almost, seem natural. Any local television journalist logs enough teleprompter time in the course of learning the trade to do it with ease.

I was in difficulty because I had become a network correspondent without so much as a day's experience working at a local TV station. Almost all network correspondents serve a local apprenticeship on their way up. I had become a national legal correspondent through a series of flukes; first practicing law in Tennessee, then writing about law for the *New York Times,* and finally interpreting it on a major television network.

Network correspondents rarely read from teleprompters. They work in the field, recording their stories on videotape for later use on the evening news. Their on-camera stints are memorized and then recorded—as often as it takes to get it right. I was miserably aware that somewhere among the blooper files of CBS a sadistic CBS tape editor had squirreled away a cut of me, surrounded by gawkers at the Watergate hearings, mumbling sheepishly into the camera, "Take thirteen. . . ."

Before I left CBS, several of my colleagues offered free tips on how to read a teleprompter.

A favorite was, "Always imagine you are talking to only one person."

I tried imagining that I was explaining things to my wife. That worked fine, as long as I knew she was at home, watching. When she was away, it seemed phony to talk to her and disloyal to talk to anybody else. There were other suggestions, including one Douglas Edwards had received when he became television's first anchor, back when they created the "CBS Evening News." Somebody advised Edwards to learn braille. Then he could communicate with his viewers through a tele-prompterless-camera—while reading his lines with his fingers. Neither he, nor I, considered that a viable solution.

In hard fact, I would have to learn to use the teleprompter by doing it, and the viewers of Channel 2 and I were in for some painful moments in the process.

Unfortunately, I had an additional problem—I could not see.

Actually, my eyes were perfectly normal—for a fifty-five year old. The abnormal part was that a man in the prime of his middle years was trying to learn to be a television anchorman. Most people afflicted with middle-aged eyes wear bifocals. But not if they are attempting to outdo the yuppie sex symbols on the other stations for Nielsen ratings.

I had quietly placed an emergency order for contact lenses. In the meantime, each time I confronted the teleprompter screen, my only recourse was a determined squint.

Even before the Can Man's performance, the reality of my situation had begun to dawn on me earlier in the day. It was brought on by the occasion of my first post-network haircut.

I had come up with a clever thought: Why not find out which barber in town styles the hair of the most dashing anchor on a competing station and at least begin my career with a state-of-the-art Nashville anchorman's haircut? Using my award-winning investigative skills, I

asked the reporter with the best haircut in our news-
room who styled the hair of a mustachioed anchor on
Channel 4 who looked, distressingly, like a younger Tom
Selleck.

The hair stylist turned out to be a very hip young
woman named Kim, who took one critical look at my
silver-haired coif, and began to snip away. I eased into
my usual barber-chair trance. . . .

One evening in Washington about three months earlier, I had invited a local TV anchorman to dinner. My
purpose was to try out a vision that was taking shape in
my mind of a television-age Tom Paine. That took some
explaining.

Every newspaperman has two fantasies tucked in the
recesses of his consciousness. One is a dream to practice
his profession in the fashion of Tom Paine, the Colonial
pamphleteer who personified independent, strong-
minded, go-to-hell journalism. The other is a vision that
someday, perhaps, that brand of journalism could be
practiced in a reporter's autumn years by going to his
roots and running a local newspaper.

My fantasy was a television version of that dream.
The answer was local TV news. Local markets had luck-
ily avoided much of the viewer shrinkage that had diminished network news. Cable channels didn't offer local
news, so viewers who wanted it had no choice but to
switch to their local stations.

Local stations had bottom-line reasons to appreciate
their newspeople. Advertisers supported news, because
compared to the game shows and reruns otherwise offered on the station's time, local news had class. The

bank's commercial might well pop up on the local news between a house fire and the latest rape, but that offered more dignity than having it sandwiched between the adolescent innuendoes of "The Newlywed Game." As a result, many stations were expanding their news. Some were even working to improve its quality.

It seemed to me that the future of television news was in local TV. Even some top people in the networks were speaking of the network evening news shows as dinosaurs that would not make it into the twenty-first century. Already there had been talk by the president of NBC news about dropping the NBC evening news in favor of shorter segments. Anchored by Tom Brokaw, these segments would be integrated into local news programs. There was nervous talk among network people that some of the big-city network affiliates could make a bundle if they would drop the network evening news, put together their own mix of local, national, and international news, and keep all of the ad revenues for themselves. If one local affiliate tried it and got rich, others would quickly create their own do-it-yourself evening news programs. Many experts predicted that the network news operations would eventually become video versions of the AP and UPI wire services, providing segments for local TV programs.

If network news was destined to decay, local TV would have to pick up the slack to keep the public informed—and that was the genesis of my television-age Tom Paine vision.

I tried my Tom Paine idea out on Gordon Peterson, a local anchorman in Washington of class and maturity. Maturity, in Peterson's case, meant that he was only ten years younger than I. Over a high-priced dinner and reassuring wine, I told Peterson about my hometown, and WKRN/Channel 2.

It was a sad-sack news operation, I conceded, but that could be a plus. I could return to Nashville, where I had once practiced print journalism, and later law, and where I was still well known. Channel 2's news operation had always run last in ratings and respect, so there was ample room for improvement.

I could spend the last years of my career building, making Channel 2, and perhaps even Nashville, better. My experience might even help to start a trend among network correspondents, to parallel the print reporters' tradition of returning to the local scene. It would be an inspiration, rather like the one I had felt, years before, when my colleague at the *New York Times,* James Reston, purchased an obscure weekly newspaper in Martha's Vineyard, Massachusetts. The young reporters had watched with envy as Reston had built it up, toward a day when he could preside over it in his semiretirement.

I was generating a full head of idealistic steam when Peterson punctured my balloon.

"Local television," he said, "is not the *Martha's Vineyard Gazette.*"

He went on. By its nature, he said, local TV news tends to be superficial. House fires and car wrecks play better to TV audiences than thoughtful analysis. Station owners are often remote, avaricious, and likely to forget promises. News directors are hired and fired like football coaches. Each new hire can upset everything that went before. Ratings are everything, and often the anchor's best efforts won't improve them. An anchor can fail because a competing station offers "Wheel of Fortune" at the same time that he is delivering the news, or because another channel hires a twenty-three-year-old former cheerleader as a competing anchor.

Peterson was compassionate enough to pull his punches on the subject of anchor maturity. He had just begun to wear glasses on the air and his ratings had survived, but he had been around long enough for his bifocals to project an air of reassurance. He implied that my efforts to build an audience would probably not rely heavily on sex appeal.

I protested that a legend of local anchordom, Ralph Renick, was still holding forth in Miami in his midsixties, and that white-haired Jerry Dunphy had been king of the ratings in Los Angeles for years.

Peterson informed me that Renick had retired and that in his last few years he had not done well. (Translation: his ratings had slipped. Blessedly, neither of us knew the grisly details—that after thirty-five years at the peak of the ratings with the local CBS station, Renick slipped one Nielsen point behind the competition and he was immediately gone.) Dunphy, Peterson added, had earned his audience before his hair turned white. Neither of us could think of a person who *became* a local anchor on the downside of fifty.

Peterson eventually saw that logic would not prevail that night. Sensing that I was headed for Nashville, he managed to put a good face on local anchoring: the pay was good, everybody knew you, there was no heavy lifting.

I appreciated his courtesy, but I was leaning toward home for other reasons.

In the previous five years, CBS News had become increasingly obsessed with ratings and entertainment-style news. Many of us who had built our careers on straight reporting had not fared well. Older correspondents who no longer photographed favorably had been laid off or sidetracked into humiliating menial positions. I had escaped for a while, but my legal specialty had not lent itself to the glitzier new CBS style, and there had been signals that the depressing eclipse of my older colleagues would soon be in store for me.

Throughout my life, my view of myself had been of success. I felt proud and secure in it, and I was always happy to work to make it prove true. It had meant academic honors and scholarships at Yale and Vanderbilt, a law degree from Oxford on a Fulbright scholarship, a tour of duty with the Marines, a good law practice, high-level government service, the authorship of two books, and award-winning performances as a journalist. To me it was unfair and unacceptable, after all this, to be at the crest of my profession, contemplating failure.

The answer seemed obvious. I would go on to another success. I would take the risk of becoming a middle-aged local anchorman, and I would make it work.

My barber-chair reverie was mercifully cut short by the whirring of the hair dryer that signaled the end of my new hair styling.

One look into the mirror told me that my accommodation to new circumstances had gone too far. The hair stylist had given the new anchor her concept of the local anchor look. It could best be described as soap opera afro—the fluffed out, shaggy look made popular by younger brother Bobby Ewing of "Dallas" fame.

It was obvious that, to the hip hair stylist, real anchors don't part their hair.

But on me the result was a curly mass of white hair that looked vaguely like an overage Wolf Man. All I lacked was the fangs.

I realized that I had been treading the border between you're-only-as-old-as-you-feel and there's-no-fool-like-an-old-fool. I had backpeddled over the line. It was time to retrench, establish my own identity in my new role, and succeed or fail with that.

I borrowed the stylist's comb and replaced the anchorman's afro with a no-nonsense middle-aged part. Then I returned to the studio with my jaw tucked out, determined to make it, if at all, on my own terms.

That resolve was tested, soon enough, as the Can Man continued to gyrate that evening before the camera and my rehearsal time slipped away.

It was questionable whose situation was more tenuous: his, mine, or—in an odd way—the public's.

Earlier that week, the Roper poll had published a new survey. It showed that for the first time, a majority of the American people received *all* of their news from TV. Traditionally, that had meant the networks. But network news was in decline. The best hope appeared to be local TV—that it could improve, and mature, and meet its promise. Otherwise, the public would simply be less well informed than it used to be.

As the Can Man struggled and I gazed out from the floodlighted anchor desk, a bizarre kind of logic seemed to settle upon the scene.

The chain of events that had brought me to WKRN

had also given me a unique perspective on the passage that American communications was going through. I had been involved during crucial periods with key institutions of journalism, but always as a quasi-outsider— with the perceptiveness that a stranger to the culture can have. I had been a lawyer in the role of a journalist for the *New York Times,* then a former print reporter at CBS during its golden years and its decline, and finally, a network correspondent new to the world of local TV. If local news was poised to assume a larger role in informing the American people, I was probably as well prepared as anyone to observe and take part.

But for the moment it had become obvious that I would not practice that night. By the time the Can Man got it right, the real anchors would be ready to take over the anchor desk and prepare to deliver the late news. I gathered my practice scripts, climbed down out of the anchor desk, and with all the dignity I could muster, slumped off into the hot Tennessee night.

The wide studio doors were left open on such nights, and for a long distance I could look back and see the bright studio floor. The Can Man was still in trouble. I was in trouble. But everybody else was in trouble, too.

2

Barefoot in Television

A man came running into the CBS newsroom, shouting. I was impressed not so much by the shouting but that nobody noticed it. To me, it was something you would notice. This was November 20, 1972, my first day at CBS after seven years as the Supreme Court correspondent for the *New York Times*. Nobody had ever run shouting into the newsroom at the *New York Times*.

"Lesley, Lesley, you smiled!" the man shouted. "Goddamit, you smiled!"

He was yelling at a sassy-looking young blonde who was standing with me at the other end of the CBS News newsroom in Washington. Lesley Stahl was also just starting with CBS, having graduated from a local TV station in Boston. She had been out with a camera crew that morning shooting her first standup (wherein you stand up, look at the camera, and emote) and had obviously committed some indiscretion.

As the man rushed the length of the newsroom toward us, I was struck by how similar to a newspaper the scene appeared outwardly, yet how very different it was in operation. Television news had been created by defectors from newspapers, journalists who had brought along at least the forms of the world of print. The newsroom had as its centerpiece the usual news "desk"—a series of desks that, at a newspaper, would house the city editor, assignment editors, copy editors, and rewrite men. At a newspaper, the rest of the room would be reporters, cheek-by-jowl at their typewriters (this was before computers).

CBS had the same news desk, but it filled the entire room, and the people at the news desk were, mostly, not editors but dispatchers. In place of copy pencils, they were working their phones and radios, shuttling around Washington the army of camera crews, reporters, equipment vans, and couriers necessary to collect video and put it on the air. The difference was this: television is dominated by logistics. At the *Times,* the essence of journalism had been finding out what had happened—usually by telephone—before the deadline. In television, being there *when* it happened, with a camera, was everything.

Around the edges of the CBS newsroom, the newspaper influence faded away. Things were organized in a way that reflected the real world of TV.

A bank of film-editing cubicles dominated one side wall. (This was also before Videotape.) Along the opposite wall were radio broadcasting booths, with broad windows where famous people could be seen, broadcasting news. Across the rear of the room the big-name reporters were on display. Since these luminaries were also media stars, they were lined up to be seen in open-front cubicles, arranged according to a subtle combination of seniority and stardom.

That meant that George Herman was in the first cubicle, alongside Roger Mudd, Marvin Kalb, Daniel Schorr, and Dan Rather. My room was tucked away in the back, along with such lesser-knowns as Bob Schieffer, Bruce Morton, Robert Schakne, Bernard Kalb, Robert Pierpoint, and Nelson Benton. These were not mere reporters, but "correspondents," which meant that they were highly paid, deep-voiced and predominantly male.

CBS also had "reporters," who did odd jobs, stakeouts, and radio spots. These lesser lights had little desks in the corridor, a network's version of the ghetto, featuring three women and the sole black, Bernard Shaw. Shaw did not stay long. He soon figured out that his best bet was the Cable News Network, where he became a big fish in a small puddle that got bigger. Later, when Bernie Shaw became the lead anchor of CNN and lined up with Rather, Brokaw and Jennings to interview heads of state, I wondered how often he thought of his little desk in the back hall at CBS.

Most CBS "reporters" back then were women, due to a corporate strategy to head off sex discrimination suits. That thinking had brought in Lesley Stahl and the even less-experienced Connie Chung, who otherwise might not have been considered ripe for the network.

Connie has always looked years younger than her age, and when she arrived dewy-eyed at CBS just three years out of college, there were those who did not take her seriously. Connie responded with pure hustle. She was a tiny bundle of energy who always seemed to be charging forward. It often worked wonders, but not always.

One day her assignment was to get a comment from George Meany, the burly, grumpy chief of the AFL-CIO. Connie ambushed him in the lobby of a Washington office building and scrambled along at his heels, camera rolling and microphone jutting up at his cigar, as she yammered away with her questions. Meany strode stonily across the foyer and into an elevator that was being held open for him. As the doors slid together, Connie charged in after him, still thrusting the microphone. The microphone, unfortunately, was attached by wires to the camera, and the camera was being held by the astonished cameraman back in the lobby.

The elevator began to move. The horrified camera crew reeled out cable. Fortunately, the elevator traveled only one floor—down to the garage, where Meany huffed into his limousine, leaving Connie, microphone in hand, wide-eyed and speechless.

In those days, Connie Chung was alleged to be the only non-black female at CBS who was not a blonde. That was a slight exaggeration, but only slight.

Somewhere in the antiquity of TV journalism, the founding males had concluded that the ideal woman to present the news should be young, pert, and blonde. By the time I reached the network, the stereotype had become deeply ingrained. I had a sense those first few weeks of moving into a culture in which the women had all been recruited from the cheerleading squad at UCLA. Until you got used to it, it was difficult to tell them apart. President Nixon tended to deal with the problem by calling them all "Judy," on the apparent assumption that he might be addressing NBC's Judy Woodruff. This was not a solution that pleased Lesley Stahl.

But on that first day for both of us at CBS, Lesley had other concerns. The man who had yelled across the room at her continued to rant at the same pitch as he approached us. He was a dark, intense young fellow named John Armstrong (now an intense middle-aged top banana at ABC News) who obviously knew that his spade beard gave him a wicked look and who just as obviously relished the scene he was creating in the newsroom.

I was soon to learn that television people enjoy such scenes. They are constantly shouting, whooping, and jiving in their newsrooms. It is as if in recognition that television glories in covering chaos; and that when it is not present, a bit of it should be created, as if to stay in practice.

"Lesley," he bawled, "this is not Eyewitless News. Go do it again, but leave out the smile."

It was the only time I was ever to see Lesley Stahl cowed. She had committed an unnetworkly act—reverting, on her first day, to the coquettish style that had served her so well in local news. Lesley slunk off to do her standup again, this time with proper CBS solemnity.

I was impressed, in a way that would eventually work to my disadvantage. I could not foresee that CBS's penchant for gravity would not last. Soon enough, the network would be encouraging its correspondents to deliver the news with all the toothsome pizzazz they could muster. But in the meantime, years would pass before I could face a camera without looking as if I had just eaten a pickle.

Another event that first day at CBS drove home the reality that I had entered a more theatrical journalistic world. I learned that I might soon have to go out on strike against my new employers, for reasons that would have blown fuses throughout the Columbia School of Journalism. As a television correspondent I was required to join a union dominated by entertainers, actors, and bit players who worked in TV commercials, and the actors and bit players were unhappy with their pay.

This unlikely alliance grew out of the fact that broadcasting started out as purely a medium of entertainment. In the 1930s, when radio stations began to broadcast a bit of news, it was read by the same announcers who recited the commercials and presided over the variety shows. This view of the broadcast journalist-as-reader persisted, even after newspapermen were brought in to do the work.

That heritage was still strong at "The House of Murrow" when I signed on in 1972. My contract with CBS referred to me throughout as "Artist," and the oldtimers at CBS News frequently spoke of me and the others as "the talent." As a print reporter, I had belonged to the Newspaper Guild, a nuts-and-bolts union of working journalists and other newspaper employees. At CBS, our union was the American Federation of Television and Radio Artists—AFTRA—considered a nuts-and-dolts organization by many of the journalists who were required to belong.

All this became apparent that first night, when I met with my fellow toilers at CBS to plan strategy for the walkout.

The meeting, held in a dimly lit room over a singles'

bar near the CBS news bureau, was unlike any union gathering I had ever imagined. There was the "working class," convened at a long table, with Roger Mudd anchored at one end and Eric Sevareid presiding over the other. Between them sat two rows of wage earners wearing expensive suits and the tense expressions of men whose every day off the job would cost enough salary to buy one of those suits. I sensed that zeal for the strike did not run high.

Eric Sevareid sat silver-haired beneath a single light fixture, scowling out over the proceedings, while the others railed against the walkout called for the next day. Everybody agreed the situation was insane. We were all being paid more than we had ever earned before, and we had no quarrel with CBS. But that had also been true five years before, when AFTRA had hit the bricks for thirteen days and Walter Cronkite had been replaced at the anchor desk by a terrified CBS paperpusher named Arnold Zenker.

Some of television news' biggest names had balked at that strike—Chet Huntley had crossed the line and anchored for NBC—for the same reasons that generated the grumbling among the CBS correspondents that night. They resented being teamed professionally with entertainers, and they felt that they were being used by the nonjournalists who dominated the AFTRA union. The walkout would not even be a journalists' strike—it was a sympathy action to prop up the entertainers' future negotiations. There was little said in favor of it above the singles' bar that night.

Finally, Sevareid spoke—or rather, he whispered. Off camera, Eric always made you lean forward. But to have Sevareid hold forth in the flesh was always an attention-getter. The room became instantly quiet.

"This is what to expect," he hissed, "when you belong to a union composed of actors, jugglers, and tap dancers." Sevareid curled his lips with special contempt when he said "actors, jugglers and tap dancers," and it seemed to strike his fancy. He said it several times during his speech.

His point was that we were trapped by a history that lumped us with performers with whom we had little common ground. At some point in time, he said, the journalists might depart AFTRA as a matter of principle and reason, but it would be a shambles to do it in the face of a strike. As the meeting broke up, I found myself joining in the grumbling over journalistic careers so heavily influenced by mere performers.

It turned out that I was able to go to work my second day at CBS, after all. A judge reinforced our belief that a walkout by AFTRA would be stupid by ruling that it would also be illegal.

But if I had known then what I have learned since, I would have noticed the legendary little cloud begin to take shape on the horizon of my life. I was no longer just a journalist—I was a television journalist. And though I had made a private promise to keep show business in its proper place, entertainment had become a significant factor in my profession, whether I liked it or not.

———

At its prickly best, journalism is constitutionally protected insurgency—and every good reporter is, to some extent, a rebel. If you scratch the most civilized of them deeply enough, there will be signs of the influences that encourage them to go against the grain.

During the Depression, my father preached for a living in such centers of Arkansas culture as Malvern, Forest City, and Texarkana. He happened to be a Presbyterian, but the experience gave me some appreciation of why the Roman Catholic church forbids its clergy to marry and have families.

If it is true that no man can be a hero to his valet, the problem is compounded in a preacher's family, in which the offspring are not only exposed, up close, to the human frailties of the Cloth, but are also expected to share in the presumed pieties of the father. This gets complicated, because some denominations expect more piety than others, and some clergymen are smarter than others about cushioning their children from the expectations of the faithful.

I have always thought that sociologists have missed a bet in failing to recognize, along with the Type As, workaholics, and other classes of driven people, a special subcategory known to my generation as "PKs." The term refers to preachers' kids, who comprised a vigorous and sometimes subversive minority in the churchy South of my day.

It was an article of faith when I was growing up that PKs all fell into one of two categories—goody-goodies or hell-raisers. The theory was that preachers' kids either bought the religious family line or rebelled against it, resulting in conduct that was either obnoxiously pious or aggressively rebellious.

As a PK who resolved early in life to lean toward the latter course, I knew that the psychology of preachers' kids was more complicated than that.

It was important that my father was ordained in the Presbyterian church, a denomination that catered to the upper middle class of the smalltown South. Presbyteri-

ans considered themselves above the hellfire-and-dam-
nation extremism of the more fundamentalistic
churches, as well as the puritanical life-style that went
with it. So my father was not under heavy pressure from
his flock to make a holier-than-thou example of his children, and he wisely avoided doing so.

One of my friends was the son of an ostentatiously
pious Methodist preacher who forbade dancing, card-
playing, moviegoing, and other sinful pleasures. When
the preacher hit the evangelism circuit each summer, his
son always made the parsonage the site of the drunkest
teen-age party in town. Every adolescent in town looked
forward to the preacher's vacation, but even at that age
most of us knew there was something unhealthy in the
way the pastor's bedroom was set aside for serious sex.
My friend eventually fulfilled the classic profile of the
"bad" PK: trouble with school, marriage, and career.

My father was sensible enough not to give me such an
inviting ogre to rebel against, but he could not change
the fact that some people expected the preachers' kids to
be abnormally virtuous.

Little old ladies, for some reason, all seemed to feel
that the only way to relate to the minister's family was to
cluck me under the chin and say, "What a good little boy
you must be!" My style was to smile sweetly and say to
myself: "You old biddy, I'll show you someday!"

The result was to nourish a low-key PK rebellion that
was not likely to produce a felon—but that might, along
with other adverse influences, someday turn out a journalist.

———

Some of the oddities about the television correspondents who populated my new world were, on close ex-

amination, superficial. At CBS, correspondents frequently did routine things while talking out loud to themselves in theatrically deep, resonant tones. They were rehearsing their standups. Nobody thought it strange.

That first day at CBS I was wandering down a quiet hallway, approaching a cross-corridor, when I heard a voice approaching from the left, speaking with a deep and stirring urgency about a new American setback in the Vietnam War. I stood back, expecting someone to come hurtling past with a bulletin for the network. Instead, a young man who had been introduced to me as Pentagon correspondent Bob Schieffer sauntered by, speaking about the latest hostilities. Schieffer nodded pleasantly, continuing his recitation as he headed for the water fountain.

I recalled that Schieffer had spoken with a normal voice when I had met him only hours earlier. Now, rehearsing in his broadcast voice, he was recognizably the same person, but speaking with a throaty resonance and force that he did not use in conversation. Inwardly, I drew myself upright, promising that I would not put on a phony voice in order to practice my profession on the air.

It was one of a series of reservations that were to dissolve quickly in light of the realities of TV.

Nobody, I learned, spoke with a "normal voice" when broadcasting, because everyday conversation sounds unconcerned and lackadaisical on the air. The trick is to add just enough punch and energy to come across as normal in the unreal process of talking to someone out of an electronic box.

Developing a natural-sounding broadcast voice takes skill and practice—especially because network correspondents alternate between radio and television during a typical day, and radio requires a little more punch than TV, where the picture helps carry the illusion of naturalness. But to all of my new colleagues, different on-camera and off-camera voices had long since become second nature. I had expected to enter a world surrounded by people making small talk in resonant, rich voices. A few of them had the pipes to carry it off—Bill Plante, Marvin Kalb, and Roger Mudd lived up to my expectations. But for the most part, the conversations around the network newsroom were carried out in voices as unremarkable as my own.

Another superficial distinction of network journalists was that the men sometimes wore makeup, especially late in the afternoon before going on-camera. This was necessary to blunt the reflection from bright studio lights and merciful to those developing bags under the eyes, but it often struck outsiders as showy and vain.

Once, when Dan Rather was stuffing his trenchcoat into the luggage bin over an airline seat, his compact fell out of a pocket and rolled down the aisle. A stewardess pounced on it and, with a high flourish for all to see, called for the identity of its owner.

Rather was so shamefaced he refused to claim it and had to scrounge for makeup at his next stop.

————

One of the duties of the preacher during the Depression was to deal with the streams of people who had nothing but miseries and needs.

They would straggle into the Presbyterian minister's

manse in Texarkana, where my father presided over the church's fund of five dollars per week for the needy. The money always gave out early in the week, but still the unemployed fathers would come, sit in the living room with my father, and search for some basis of hope. Flimsy French doors separated that room and the bedroom behind, and it became an irresistible attraction for me to sit on the floor behind the drawn shades and listen to adults admit being desperate and afraid.

One evening a man's voice drifted through the door with an unforgettable urgency.

"Preacher," I heard him say, "I can't find a job. My money is all gone. My children are hungry, and I don't know what to do." The man did not ask for money, and that day my father did not have any to give. But the two of them seemed unable to end the conversation, which drifted painfully on.

I ran to my drawer, where I had a penny, saved for a visit to the downtown candy counter. Then I crouched on the floor behind the drawn shade, squeezing my penny in my hand and trying to raise the courage to go through the door and give it to the man whose children needed it so much. I sat there in frozen misery, unable to move as the conversation dwindled away and the man left. My father later tried to console me that the man would be all right without my offering—that he could come back early in the next week, when there would be money again from the church.

I never saw the man again, but I have remembered my regret hundreds of times over the years. It always seemed that a bit of that regret was present as I made the decisions that steered my life toward activities that I believed had some element of giving. It may seem corny now, but those instincts led me to become a lawyer and a journalist—trying, I think, somehow to give at least a penny.

———

It seemed to me that, beyond the surface show-biz distinctions, my new colleagues in television were cut from a different mold than print journalists. The television correspondents seemed more driven, and insular.

Each network correspondent in Washington had won an intense professional competition to be there. First, each had beaten out hundreds of local TV reporters who had aspired to be chosen by a network; then each had won out among all of the network correspondents who wanted to make it to Washington. CBS, ABC, and NBC, together, employed only about 50 correspondents in Washington, at a time when the Congressional Directory listed 1,173 print journalists working in the nation's capital. The struggle to get there produced a don't-tread-on-me detachment among the TV correspondents that was strikingly unlike the collegial clubbiness of the *New York Times*.

Part of this was because the newspaper reporters tended to cluster around the newsroom, working the phones, while the television correspondents had to be out with the camera crews. This produced a convivial life style among print people that was not all to the good. Lunchtime at the *Times* often became a multi-martini affair that wound down at midafternoon, with the reporters wobbling back to their desks to get themselves straightened out in time for the evening deadline.

Television correspondents, for all of their dashing

TV image, were much more disciplined and sober. Their glamorous aura encouraged stories of booze, drugs, and the fast lane, but their jobs required a sharp focus and a crisp tongue. One of my colleagues at the *Times* died of a pickled liver in his early thirties, but I never saw a CBS correspondent during working hours under the influence of anything more insidious than one hundred-proof ambition.

On the downside, collegiality was not the fashion in network TV. The correspondents' vivid personal styles got in the way.

At lunch with Mike Wallace, you were likely to be cross-examined. Bruce Morton, whose TV scripts were so lean and sparse, was famous for his long, silent lapses. Bill Moyers was so occupied with the somber matters of the world that it almost seemed an impiety to engage him with small talk. Walter Cronkite sometimes found it awkward among younger colleagues to be anything less than the featured anchorman and occasionally monopolized gatherings with war stories.

Years after I joined CBS, I ran into Marvin Kalb at a party. As we fell into the kind of superficial small talk that strangers exchange, I realized that after working alongside Marvin for a decade, it was the first time he and I had ever tried to hold a social conversation.

Sometimes this insularity among the correspondents produced competition that would have been unthinkable among newspaper colleagues.

Once I tracked down a renegade FBI agent who claimed to have evidence of corruption in the higher reaches of the Bureau, and who agreed to an on-camera interview for the "CBS Evening News." The catch was that he was lying low in Los Angeles and I would have to fly to L.A. from Washington to make the connection. Within hours I was holed up with a camera crew in the Beverly Wilshire Hotel, waiting for my G-man.

At the time appointed for our meeting, the telephone rang. It was his lawyer, informing me that Mike Wallace had offered to let the FBI man tell his story on "60 Minutes"—but only if he would keep the information fresh by canceling his interview with me. While I had been flying to California, the FBI agent had been on a plane to New York to meet with Mike.

I was back in Washington the next night, still fuming, when Wallace phoned to give me the last laugh. By then it was late Saturday night, Mike had spent a long day with the FBI man, and his allegations did not hold up. The interview was worthless, and Mike had called to let me say "gotcha."

It was legend at CBS that Walter Cronkite had once been a victim of a Mike Wallace exposé. In the course of a "60 Minutes" piece on journalist-junketing at corporate America's expense, Mike had taken pains to point out that Cronkite was an occasional traveler on the freebie circuit. Walter was known to nurse dark feelings about that, so when I spotted an item in a newspaper one day disclosing that "60 Minutes" had been conned out of $10,000 by a sharpie who claimed to know the location of Jimmy Hoffa's body, I knew it was a story made for the "CBS Evening News." I phoned New York to volunteer for the assignment but was told that so many correspondents had stepped forward that the story would be told by the substitute anchor, Morton Dean.

Almost every CBS correspondent nursed some

bruised feelings toward "60 Minutes." At one time or another, most of us had fumed over "60 Minutes" trying to take over one of our stories, or of tracking down a promising story, only to discover that "60 Minutes" was already onto it but hadn't bothered to tell anyone else at CBS.

It was embarrassing to sleuth around on a story only to be aced out by another reporter from CBS News. "Why don't you people work together?" outsiders would ask after they had been badgered by telephone calls from a "60 Minutes" producer and then me. The answer was obvious—"60 Minutes" was a top-rated television program that earned millions of dollars for CBS and played by its own rules. They never shared information with the rest of us, never cooperated on stories, never bothered with a courtesy call when they invaded our turf. For the rest of us at CBS it was like having a rich, spoiled cousin in the family; outsiders were impressed, but it could be a pain to everybody else.

Among the correspondents at CBS, the hands-down personification of in-house competitiveness was Daniel Schorr. Schorr represented, in one rumpled, crafty old package, both the best and least-admirable aspects of network hustle. He somehow defied the middle-age slowdown that bedevils most graying correspondents, but his ambition and drive to get on the air led to periodic turf squabbles with other CBS correspondents.

Over the years, my dealings with Schorr usually left me with an urge to count my change. In even casual conversations, he seemed to go away with more information than he gave, and in the smallest matters he always managed to come out on top. I came to view our dealings with a sort of amused inevitability, reminiscent of the comic strip scene in which Lucy holds a football and invites Charlie Brown to kick it. Always, at the last second she pulls it away, leaving Charlie Brown to kick the air and land flat on his back.

On the climactic day of the Watergate story, August 8, 1974, when President Nixon announced he was leaving office, each network's news division put on a TV news extravaganza. All red-blooded Washington correspondents were clawing to get on the air. To have Daniel Schorr approach me in that atmosphere should have flashed "tilt" throughout my caution systems, but I was lusting for a bit of airtime myself, and Schorr had concocted a proposal that seemed to benefit us both. Since I had been covering the legal side of Watergate and he the investigative, he suggested that we propose a joint appearance: I would expound on future legal moves, and Schorr would talk about the likely future course of the Watergate investigation.

The producers bought it. We would structure it as a minisegment on the future of the Watergate investigation, with Walter Cronkite interviewing Schorr and me. I typed out a question for Cronkite to ask me about Nixon's potential immunity from prosecution, and Schorr prepared one about the investigation.

For a while it appeared that the program would run out of time before Schorr and I could have our moment of glory. But in the last few minutes, our turn finally came. The camera turned toward us, the red light went on, and Walter Cronkite asked my question about Nixon's immunity.

Schorr answered it.

Before I could open my mouth, he was off and running with a well-composed, articulate response. Then Schorr tossed the well-chewed carcass of the subject over to me. I blathered. Schorr smoothly shifted the subject to the future of the investigation. His exposition was well composed and impressive. With time running out I tried to elbow into the discussion, and managed to look simultaneously stumbling and pushy.

The camera then moved on, leaving me mentally flat on my back. The football had been pulled out from in front of me again.

Most CBS correspondents were not driven to cutthroat extremes in their pursuit of TV success, but almost all were driven. They were high-voltage people whose special ambition had been to make it to the television pinnacle—which, at that time, was the networks. On a superficial level I was different, a one-time Southern lawyer who had been hired by CBS News to cover Watergate.

But even in those first few days at the television network I felt instinctively at home. I could tell that most of my new high-speed colleagues would become my friends for life, and I felt comfortable on the glitzier track that my journalistic course had taken.

For while I was not a true child of television, I was probably the closest next thing—a descendant of Southern preachers, plying the 1970s version of the family trade in a world gone high-tech.

In hindsight, it seems logical that the gently backsliding offspring of a Southern preacher would bottom out in a television newsroom. Growing up as a preacher's son in the Texarkana of the Depression was an invigorating mix of hardscrabble and—strangely enough—privilege.

In those days, Texarkana didn't offer much beyond a civic split personality. It had been built (nobody knows why) on a swampy, mosquito-infested stretch of flatland, undistinguished by anything except that the main street straddled the state line between Arkansas and Texas. When you undertook to show somebody the town sights, you took them down and pointed out the painted stripe down the middle of State Line Avenue. This landmark divided the states and also ran through the middle of the Post Office, which had been built squarely in the center of the street in a Solomonlike compromise between the U.S. senators from the two states. Beyond that, there wasn't much in Texarkana in the 1930s but hard times.

Fortunately for me, my father had a job, as pastor of the Arkansas-side Presbyterian church, and an ambivalent niche in what passed for the privileged side of life.

The Presbyterians were relatively well off, but for those who couldn't afford to put money in the collection plate, it was customary to donate to the preacher's family in kind. This form of charity had its down side.

It meant that I grew up in hand-me-down clothes from my playmates, during the era when little boys wore Bobby Jones-style knickers that were designed to be gathered above the calf by an elastic band. The blight of my young life was that I had extremely skinny calfs and never inherited my playmates' knickers until the elastic had long since lost it grip. Thus I grew almost into manhood sporting a unique style of trouser that drooped baggily to within a few inches of my shoe-tops.

My two brothers and sister and I were also the recipients of numerous free piano lessons, for which all but my sister had no talent. This was a less-than-perfect solution also for those teachers who were forced by lean circumstances into this form of giving.

Once, after my bother Otis had been taking piano for almost a year, the teacher bustled out into the schoolyard and grabbed my brother Hugh, who looked like his older brother but had never taken a piano lesson in his young life. The teacher delivered an entire lesson with the dumbstruck younger brother at the keyboard and never figured out that it wasn't the untalented older brother, Otis.

But the in-kind tithing system made up for all its shortcomings by permitting us to attend a marvelous little private school that was run out of a frame house by one of the ladies of our church. Mrs. Pete Patterson was straightlaced and tough the way a woman could be who had been born in Kentucky just six years after the end of the Civil War, abandoned by a no-good husband, and made her own way in the Southwest while part of it still belonged to the Indians. She was a stern believer in classic education and personal communication who taught school the old-fashioned way—by rapping your knuckles. We were taught no-nonsense three Rs, and also public speaking, Greek and Roman mythology, the great operas, and the Bible.

Her school was named Patty Hill School for an educator who had been progressive in her day, and it used the "open classroom" concept—years before its time—out of necessity. All six grades were taught in two rooms, so the classes were separated only by the fact that they sat at different round tables. That meant that while the teacher was instructing the sixth graders, a younger child waiting his turn at the second-grade table might just get interested in what the big kids were learning and learn it himself.

The end result was a houseful of motley-looking little children of the Depression, unsuspectingly becoming achievers. I have a photograph of the entire student body—forty-five of us—when I was in the second grade. You can recognize, among the young faces, a speaker of the Arkansas House of Representatives, one of the southwest's hotshot oil drillers, a Texas women's tennis champion, and H. Ross Perot, the only one who made a billion dollars.

In the school photograph, there is a skinny little boy in the middle, with his cheek in his palm, mugging the camera.

That's me.

3

Breaking In

When I went on the air in December of 1972, it created quite a stir among the viewers of CBS. People seemed angriest in Brooklyn.

"Where did you get that country boy you put on the TV?" wrote a man from Brooklyn. He filled a page with specifics about how funny I talked and ended with a blast at CBS for putting on the air a person who "is hard to understand and is prejudiced."

I was impressed that the man from Brooklyn probably had no idea how grating his speech would be to most other Americans and that, as late as 1972, people would assume that anyone with a Southern accent was a redneck who beat his slaves.

There were, indeed, some ashen faces at CBS over the fact that their new legal correspondent sounded like a reject from "Hee Haw," but they were in no position to complain about it to me.

CBS had no procedure for breaking in a print journalist to the mysteries of the tube. An outsider might imagine that a media giant would approach the task of body-snatching a journalist off the *New York Times* with sophistication and stealth. Indeed, the preliminaries were predictable: a lunch with Sevareid at the Metropolitan Club, conversations with the chief of the Washington bureau of CBS News. But when matters moved on to the stage that did not even exist in my newspaperman's vocabulary—"the audition"—the Columbia Broadcasting System acted with disarming unconcern. I was instructed simply to leave the *Times'* Washington bureau at lunchtime, walk around the corner to the CBS studio, and sit down in front of a camera.

"When the red light goes on," I was told, "read into the camera."

I couldn't believe it. There I was, braced to resist network pressure to visit a voice coach, get a nose job, and have my teeth capped, and they considered me broken in when they told me about the red light.

I had been advised to type out a dummy story, but nobody thought to have it transferred to large teleprompter type. I was also not clued in to a basic rule of television—speak as if communicating with one person, not the multitude.

So when the red light went on, my performance landed somewhere between Southern Preacher and Cornpone Politician. Even I knew it was awful, so I proposed a different tack. I would go out with a camera crew, prepare a filmed report patterned after the ones I hoped to do for the evening news, and submit that as my audition to CBS headquarters in New York.

This gave me the benefit of an artifice that television

puts over on the public every day. Because the story was being recorded in segments and pieced together, the bad takes were thrown away. I was able to repeat my stand-ups and narration until I could put together one complete run that was not jarring to the non-Southern ear. This was shipped off to New York, and I was on my way, sensing that CBS's surprising nonchalance about my looks and voice was a promising omen.

There was still the chance that my nonnetwork demeanor might trip me up when I confronted the CBS brass in person in New York. But an off-the-wall incident involving Roger Mudd grabbed everyone's attention and turned that into a breeze.

Four of us met for lunch in an imposing conference room at CBS News headquarters on West 57th Street. My plan had been to conceal my ignorance of television—and my mushmouth accent—by pretending to be the silent type. I sat down and began to smile a lot, but it quickly developed that the three men from CBS were not the exotic video creatures that I had expected. Richard Salant, the president of CBS News, was a former lawyer; Gordon Manning, in charge of hard news operations, had come over from *Newsweek;* Bill Small, the chief of the Washington news bureau, was a no-nonsense journalist. We were just getting acquainted over soup and still on our good behavior when an attendant approached Salant and whispered something about an important incoming call. Visions of a major disaster or corporate emergency flashed before me as Salant excused himself and took the call a discreet distance away across the room.

Salant murmured into the phone for a few moments and then shouted "Yes—dammit, tell him yes."

Salant was still upset enough when he pulled back up to the table to let us in on the important call. "That was Roger Mudd in New Orleans," he fumed. "He claims tourist is booked and he wants to fly home first class."

This, it turned out, was vintage Roger Mudd. He was irked at a new company directive that forbade first-class travel except in emergencies approved by a top executive of the company. The assumption was that nobody would actually request permission. They reckoned without Roger. It has been alleged that Roger "hates up," but his disdain for his corporate masters was more principled than that. Roger tended to look down on anyone who did not actually report the news. Over the years, this earned him a reputation for needling network executives, and in the case of the anti-first-class manifesto, Roger apparently saw an opportunity to needle and subvert at the same time. His tactic was to take the rule literally and go to the very top for permission whenever he wanted to fly in style.

In any event, it broke the ice for me. After a casual and noneventful luncheon, I went away a correspondent for CBS News.

For the next few months I was Huck Finn in TV-land, struggling to adapt the rustic ways of a pen-and-paper journalist to the glitz of TV.

The Southern accent proved to be the easiest part. After about a week of escalating phone calls to CBS from all around the country (except from the Bubba Belt, where it sounded perfectly natural), Bill Small drew me aside.

Small had spent much of his early career in Louisville, Kentucky, and my voice sounded just fine to him.

But the Grown Ups (as the executives in New York were called when they imposed their wisdom on ours) had persuaded him that my diction needed some polishing up.

He gave me a small voice recorder and one instruction: "Take your scripts home each night, read them into the recorder just the way you broadcast them on the air—and listen."

It was a humbling experience. When people chat with each other they tune out odd pronunciations, inflections, and cadences and just listen to the message. But when a voice comes oozing out of an electronic box like warm grits, a listener can gag on every mushy sound. Radio has this effect more than TV, where at least there is the distraction of pictures, and as I subjected myself to my voice each night I understood why some of the network's radio audience had taken it so hard.

The theory that anyone forced to listen to that voice each night would change it worked.

I learned to filter out some of the nasal twang and to pronounce the endings of words that ended with "ing." CBS had hired a professor at Barnard College as its speech consultant, and he became my pen pal. Professor Richard Norman was his name. One of his jobs was to write memos to me.

The professor was tolerant, in principle, of provincial speech on network air. It was the specifics that gave him distress. He would cheerily start a memo with, "It's good to hear a Southern voice on the network," and then sandbag me with the admonition that, "although some listeners will regard such pronunciations as "bein' " and "sayin' " (for *being* and *saying*) as substandard."

But there was never any pressure from Professor Norman, or from anyone else at CBS, to clear my voice of its Southern flavor. I would have resisted that as phony, and it eventually became an asset to have a voice unlike any other in network journalism.

There had been a few previous Southern voices in news broadcasting, notably Douglas Kiker on NBC and Bill Moyers at PBS. But for some reason I was usually cast as the Jackie Robinson of broadcast good ol' boys. It made me a hot item on the ham-and-turnip-greens lecture circuit, but Southerners sometimes overplayed its significance.

For instance, the 1976 Democratic National Convention was packed with honeysuckle-and-magnolia types who had come to Madison Square Garden to nominate Jimmy Carter—and some of them seemed to assume that I was on their team. Once, as I was interviewing a Carter delegate on some arcane point of convention rules, she suddenly turned the tables on me by volunteering sweetly, "We just want to say how much we appreciate all you've done for Jimmy Caah-tuh." I knew she meant that I had made many outlanders more accustomed to the sound of Southern speech, but I wasn't sure that all the viewers would appreciate that. I stammered something about being out of time and made a fast toss back to Uncle Walter.

I have always felt that classic Southern mothers are pushier than Jewish mothers, who have undeservedly been given the edge because of the subtlety of Southern ambition. While the legendary Jewish mother constantly badgered her sons to "be somebody," the Southern mother told them from their earliest years that they "are somebody." By plying them with an alleged magnolia-scented heritage of vanished plantations and outgunned Confederate brigadiers, the Southern mother could generate more guilt over the prospect of failure than could be developed by any lecture about wasting the sweat of an immigrant grandfather's efforts.

At least, in our family it worked that way.

My mother immersed my two brothers and me (girls were not included) in a folklore of Southern gentility brutally truncated by The War and pointed to a parade of kin who had left Arkansas hamlets to lead big-city law firms, preside over Yankee universities, and head college history departments.

The message was that much was expected of us and that anything less than dazzling success would be abject failure. This dovetailed with a clerical influence that channeled my ambition into journalism.

It is no accident that American journalism is afflicted with numerous offsprings of Southern preachers. I have compared notes on this with ABC's News's Jim Wooten, whose father preached in Presbyterian churches in Maryland. Neither of us can identify a preacher's offspring among our kin who has ever built a bridge, started a company, or manufactured a product. Instead, there is a consistent pattern of people who have made their way by manipulating words and ideas.

In my case, the signs surfaced at the age of five. I was in the kindergarten of Patty Hill School, where the high point of the day came in midmorning, when the children spread little rugs the floor, sat in a circle, and had milk and cookies. The exceptions were my sister Jenny and I, who sat in the circle but passed on the milk and cookies, for the lack of the nickel that my father would have had to pay each day for the refreshments.

One day the teacher was absent, and the substitute, in her innocence, asked, "Who wants milk?"

I had desperately wanted milk—chocolate milk— each morning for what seemed to me a long and deprived life. I responded truthfully, looking the substitute teacher squarely in the eye and holding up my hand.

I remember it as the most satisfying milk I had ever tasted. I also recall vividly the reckoning, when my parents were notified that I had opted into the milk program during the substitute teacher's tenure and that the bill would have to be paid.

As I recall it, my father was stern but understanding as I explained how precisely I had responded to the substitute teacher's wording. He probably suspected then that he had brought forth not a cleric but a lawyer—or perhaps worse, a journalist.

Another aspect of print journalism that didn't translate well on the air was the scholarly sounding byline. The *New York Times* had excelled at this. Its journalists were presumed to be distinguished, and they tended to affix their names at the top of their articles in a style appropriate for doctoral dissertations in classical studies. There were such impressive bylines as Vartanig G. Vartan, Harrison E. Salisbury, W. Felix Belair, Murray J. Rossant, H. Erich Heinemann, and John Noble Wilford. Middle initials were expected. Tom Wicker had been granted a special dispensation to affix his name without one, but when I joined the *Times* I felt the need for all the dignity I could muster. So as a *Times* reporter I had always used the byline "Fred P. Graham," for my middle name, "Patterson."

But on television a distinguished sign-off sounds affected and stuffy, and nobody had attempted it since Howard K. Smith and Irving R. Levine. I tried to have it both ways by signing off my broadcasts as "Fred Graham" but instructing the writers in New York to have Cronkite introduce me with the "P" in the middle.

Cronkite went along with it for the first few days and then confronted me with a choice: if I would call myself Fred P. Graham on the air, then so would he, but if it was too much for me, count him out.

I have been Fred Graham ever since.

There was also a problem with my job title. When I was hired by CBS, the company issued a press release announcing that I would serve as its legal correspondent. A flaw in this description was soon detected by Salant, president of the News Division. Salant was my kind of journalist, a lawyer untainted by any tenure in a school of journalism. Whether it was in spite of this gap in his education or because of it, Salant was a tower of journalistic principle as leader of CBS News. He was a stickler for high journalistic standards, which gave the people in the News Division a comfortable sense of direction that was in sharp contrast to the rudderless meandering that crept in later, when CBS undertook to mix journalism with entertainment.

But as a Harvard-trained lawyer there was always something of the frustrated jurist about Salant. He persisted in attempting to reduce journalistic concepts to written dicta, issuing a stream of rules and guidelines that would have done credit to Oliver Wendell Holmes.

Shortly after I joined CBS, Salant turned his keen legal mind to my job title and found it wanting. Salant issued a directive to the staff, noting that "if Graham is the legal correspondent, then by implication, all the other correspondents are illegal correspondents." He decreed that I should be the "law correspondent," and the job has had that title ever since.

I learned early that people took their television news with much more emotion than what they read in print. They also tended to direct their feelings personally at the TV correspondents.

There was never much mail at the *New York Times,* and the little that came tended to be from such right- (or left-) thinking citizens as law professors, civil libertarians, and members of the League of Women Voters. The mail that streamed into CBS was blue collar, hard-hat fare that pulled no punches.

One letter to me written in huge block letters said in its entirety, "YOU MISERABLE BASTARDS." Another accused me of being "one of those smart-alec, egocentric, Dan Rather type of reporters." One lady raked me up and down for my journalistic misdeeds and then, in a P.S., asked me to send an autographed picture.

Shortly after I made the switch to CBS I was strolling down a Washington sidewalk with my schoolboy son Grier when a car screeched to a halt, stacking up traffic behind it. The driver rolled down his window, leaned out, shook his fist at me and shouted, "Goddam you, Fred Graham."

Satisfied, the man rolled up his window and drove away.

Grier looked up at me with a quizzical glance that said, "This never happened when you were with the *New York Times.*" I was sorting through ways to explain it when he took my hand and continued with me down the street, apparently assuming that such scenes were the normal fare of a life in television.

———

My opportunity to write for the *New York Times* came because my father moved to the city—not New York, where it would have been almost unthinkable to aspire to a job with the lofty *Times,* but Nashville, Tennessee, which was soon to become a remarkable breeding ground for *New York Times* bylines.

Preachers get promotions by moving to bigger churches, and my father snared one in Nashville just as I was growing into my teens. With my background in the small Texarkana schoolhouse as my secret weapon, I showed my heels to my classmates in the Nashville public schools. When the time came to graduate, I wrote to Yale, Harvard, and Princeton and volunteered to attend, should appropriate scholarship aid be forthcoming. Apparently stunned, all three said yes, and I chose to accept Yale.

After graduation and a sabbatical in the Marines, I returned to Nashville and Vanderbilt Law School. To pay the bills, I turned instinctively to words—and blundered into a job as a cub reporter on a newspaper that was on the brink of a legendary feat of journalistic chutzpah. The ambitious, young staff of the *Nashville Tennessean* was about to invade the newsroom of the *New York Times.*

There had always been a strong bourbon-and-magnolia strain in the staff of the *Times*. At that time, the late 1950s, the two top editors were Turner Catledge, out of Mississippi, and Clifton Daniel, a courtly North Carolin- ian. Even then, the *Times* was sometimes tweaked as a newspaper "in a city of Catholics, owned by Jews and run by Southerners." But there had never been a mass infiltration of the *Times* staff from one obscure news- room in Dixie such as the *Nashville Tennessean* was about to pull off.

It happened because the big story in those days was the civil rights turmoil in the South. The *Tennessean* was small enough to let young reporters cover the story and liberal enough to print the results with no holds barred. Young hotshots gravitated to the *Tennessean* to make their marks.

The first to move on the *New York Times* was a North Carolinian with a poetic writing touch and a nagging social conscience, Tom Wicker. Once Wicker got his foot in the door of the *Times* he engineered an invasion of the jewel of Yankee journalism from the ranks of Nashville's reporters. Next went my roommate, David Halberstam. Then Bill Kovach, Wendell Rawls, John Hemphill, He- drick Smith (who worked for UPI in Nashville and tagged along), and, after a few years practicing law, me.

To be with the *New York Times* in the mid-1960s had a quality of elitism to it that does not exist in American journalism today. The *Times* was the undisputed pinna- cle of the profession. An oft-told story, though borrowed from the *Times* of London, caught the essence of the *New York Times'* position. It was said that at the White House one day, as reporters were being ushered into the Oval Office, the attendant announced, "Mister President, the people of the press, and the gentleman from the *Times.*"

When I was hired by Managing Editor Clifton Daniel, he left me with this parting thought: "Always remember," Daniel said; "The *New York Times* does not need you. You need the *New York Times.*"

It was true, but it bred a smugness about the *Times* that did not always serve the paper well.

Shortly after I joined the *Times,* the only other newspaper that it considered a competitor, the *New York Herald-Tribune,* expired. That left the *Times* with a sense that there was no competition, that all the news that was fit to print was, indeed, in its pages. This cultivated a gentlemanly complacency that left the newspaper vulnerable as stories developed in areas that the *Times* had not traditionally considered newsworthy.

I was as guilty of this as any of my colleagues, in my own field of legal news. My predecessor in the job, Anthony Lewis, had won a Pulitzer Prize covering the legal beat, and I shaped my coverage as if he had patented the mold. I concentrated on the stories that had customarily interested the *Times*—the Supreme Court, civil rights, organized crime, reapportionment, church and state, and congressional legislation. I prowled the troubled South in the wake of Martin Luther King, Jr., anticipated the problems of Justice Abe Fortas, forecast the backlash against the liberal Warren Court, monitored the rise of electronic invasions of privacy, and noted the early signs of wrongdoing by J. Edger Hoover's FBI.

These were aspects of broad issues and trends that had always concerned the *New York Times.* Where it—and I—tended to get caught flat-footed were the oddball and swarmy incidents seeping from the Nixon administration that at first did not seem properly fit to print but proved to be threads that unraveled major stories.

This happened to me with the Dita Beard-ITT scandal, which began in June of 1971 as an allegation by columnist Jack Anderson that the ITT Corporation had agreed to underwrite part of the cost of the 1972 Republican National Convention in exchange for receiving an antitrust ruling from the Justice Department. That was the mundane part of the story. The juicy sidelights included a memo written by ITT's whisky-voiced lobbyist, Dita Beard, claiming that Attorney General John Mitchell "is definitely helping us . . . but cannot let it be known," a meeting between lobbyist Beard and Attorney General Mitchell at a Kentucky Derby cocktail party, and the mysterious backstage presence of ITT's swashbuckling president, Harold Geneen.

All this was too gamy for the *New York Times,* which was not in the habit of pursuing leads surfaced by Jack Anderson. Anderson's allegation, which proved to be the first revealing public exposure of corruption in the Nixon administration, simmered for six months before we picked it up in the *Times.*

To a lesser extent, the same thing happened with the reports about the madcap exploits of Martha Mitchell, the attorney general's wife. Most of her escapades seemed too undignified to be recounted in the *Times,* but eventually her split with her husband exposed the thuggish instincts that guided some of the actions of the Nixon Justice Department.

There was a gentility about the *Times* that sometimes got in the way of take-no-prisoners journalism. This happened when the men around J. Edgar Hoover tried to snooker me into running a story about Dr. Martin Luther King, Jr.'s alleged sexual escapades.

This happened shortly before Dr. King's death, at a time when the FBI had made no effort to conceal its hostility toward King and, incidentally, me. I had tried to report evenhandedly about the FBI, which had landed me on Hoover's "Do Not Contact" list—a roster of journalists who were not to be notified when a good story was being leaked. Hoover's underlings took his instructions seriously. Once, when the *New York Times'* food writer, Craig Claiborne, was writing a story about famous people's favorite dishes, he asked me to find out what J. Edgar Hoover liked for dessert. I submitted his question to the official FBI spokesman, who said he didn't know, and dashed off a proud memo that I later found in my FBI file: "I did not tell Graham that the Director always has rice pudding." (Hoover also always ate at Harvey's restaurant, so I took lunch there that day and learned about the rice pudding from a waiter.)

When two of Hoover's top aides began to ply me with stories of Dr. King's private life, it was clear to me they were not out to help me win a Pulitzer Prize. It drove Hoover up the wall that King's relations with white women went considerably beyond the missionary position, and Hoover's aides would deplore the situation in such lurid detail that it was obvious they had bugged King's bedroom. They encouraged me to write a story about King's depravity but warned that they would deny it if I attributed my information to them.

I wasn't about to play that game, but it seemed to me that there might be a story in Hoover's rumor-mongering campaign against Dr. King. A news peg surfaced when a Southern congressman published a speech in the Congressional Record quoting Hoover as having criticized King's morals in secret testimony. That finally put Hoover on the record as being the source for the rumors that were circulating about Dr. King. All I had to do was get King's reaction and I would be off and running.

Dr. King handled this one with diplomatic finesse. He dispatched Andrew Young, then a fresh-faced preacher still in his twenties, to meet with the *Times'* Washington bureau chief, Scotty Reston, and me. Reverend Young stonewalled us.

"If President Kennedy had taken time to respond to all the rumors about his personal life, he would not have had time to run the country," Young said. "Dr. King is in the same position. He will have no comment on this."

This meant that if we were going to run the story of the FBI's devastating charges against Dr. King, we would have to do it solely on the unsubstantiated word of men who would deny they said it. Hoover would accomplish his purpose by getting the charges out, and we would get the blame for trafficking in gossip.

With no more attribution than we had, the story was deemed not quite fit to print. I didn't fight the decision because I had little stomach for smearing a civil rights hero for the satisfaction of the FBI. But I have since regretted that we did not go with this important story, for what it would have told about J. Edgar Hoover's FBI.

The *Times'* elitist chickens came home to roost after the Watergate break-in. The burglars were arrested late on a Friday night/Saturday morning, and the first mention in the *Times* was in as unsigned report in the back pages of the Sunday edition. It had the look of a local police story, a type the nation's leading newspaper did not normally pursue.

There was a sleepwalking sense about the *Times'* Washington bureau that weekend that seems incredible in the light of what Watergate became. Everyone I saw was going about his or her normal assignment, with only an idle remark or two about the break-in and with no visible effort being made to get the paper on top of the story.

Several days passed before the *Times* began to catch on. By then, Bob Woodward and Carl Bernstein of the *Washington Post* were off and running, and the *Times* has not been alone on the pinnacle ever since.

4

Medium Rare

Television journalists become uncomfortable when they are called TV personalities, but like it or not, to a certain extent the description fits. Nobody in my previous life was ever called a *New York Times* personality. Yet as a television journalist, I discovered that some people reacted with a certain awe—or contempt—on encountering someone whom they had previously seen only on TV. It was almost a reversal of the illusion that persuades a viewer that an image on the screen is a real person; to see that image in person seemed almost unreal.

One blustery winter night in 1978 I was pursuing a story about a country judge who had illegally ordered the sterilization of a pretty young girl. I tracked her mother to a farmhouse outside Auburn, Indiana. As I hammered on the door, my camera crew and I huddled against the blizzard until an elderly woman shuffled up and peeked out. She took one astonished look at me, and before I could say a word she announced, "You're not Fred Graham." She kept repeating, "You're not Fred Graham," until my camera crew got into it and chimed in with, "You're right, lady," and, "He's not."

Finally a younger woman (another daughter) appeared behind her and let us in. She said her mother couldn't believe that a person on TV would be in Indiana. The mother was so taken aback she spoke on camera, even though it was she who had asked the judge to order the sterilization. (The Supreme Court eventually ruled that the girl couldn't sue the judge because judges are immune from being sued for damages, no matter how illegal their decisions are.)

Another time I was staked out in a car in a black neighborhood of Jacksonville, Florida, with my camera crew in another car down the street, waiting for an occupant of one of the small shotgun houses to come home. I fell asleep, and a passing neighbor recognized me. My colleagues were in stitches as the man went around the neighborhood, fetching people to come out and stare at the television correspondent napping in a car on their street.

I eventually came to understand that, for many people, television represents their association with the world of events beyond their immediate lives. Many of the individuals they see on the screen are the major figures of the world; yet on the same screen, and in the same size, they also see the unimportant translators of events, like me. When they encounter us they sometimes want to make a small connection, as a link to that grand world seen only on the tube.

Usually the people who approached me in restaurants, airports, and other public places were cordial and polite, and I enjoyed it because they were nice and it made me feel important. But it was sometimes a problem for some of my more prominent colleagues.

People who approached Eric Sevareid always said the same thing—that they admired his commentaries on TV. As often as Eric heard this, he never came up with a comfortable response to it. His attempts at a smile would usually come out as a pained grimace, and as he struggled to make small talk, the stricken television fans would sidle awkwardly away.

With Dan Rather the problem was different, because his presence in any public place changed the scene and charged it with electricity. Once, when a group of us were on a fishing outing, Jack Nelson of the *Los Angeles Times* stood too close to his wife's back-cast, and she threw a fish hook through his earlobe. Rather volunteered to drive Nelson to the hospital emergency room in a nearby town. It was a nice gesture—but when they got there, Nelson was left sitting for a while in the waiting room, with a long black worm dangling down from the hook in his ear, while the nurses devoted their attention to Dan Rather.

It is a striking experience to be in a restaurant or lounge and have Dan come in to join the group. Always, the hum of conversation in the room cranks up a couple of notches. People rubberneck around, nudge each other and point, until someone can't resist the urge to come over and say a few words to Dan Rather.

Dan is a genuinely polite person, and he always responds as if a normal conversation is taking place. But since he's Dan Rather, his public encounters are never completely normal, and this sometimes casts Dan in a faintly ridiculous role. He'll often say, "I'm Dan Rather," or some other pleasantry that comes across as mildly phony, since everybody knows who he is—and most everybody already has a strong opinion of what he's like.

I suspect that this accounted for many of the public scrapes that involved Dan early in his career, such as the time a cab driver tried to take him against his will to South Chicago, and the tussles he's gotten into in public places. It was Dan trying to be your everyday polite smalltown boy, when many of the people who accosted him had already decided that he's a very different piece of work. In recent years he has felt the need to have a bodyguard or two hovering around when he goes into certain public situations, a melancholy commentary on what television can do to journalism.

For those of us at CBS who were less controversial figures but were still fairly recognizable, the minor league celebrity could have its rewarding moments.

My most memorable brush with public recognition came during the 1976 Democratic Convention in New York. The social highlight of that event was an exclusive party thrown by *Rolling Stone* magazine for Jimmy Carter. Invitations were highly prized, because the party was to be an assemblage of the most prominent and glittering figures from the worlds of politics and the media.

Somehow my invitation did not arrive.

I had planned to spend the evening with Bob Schieffer, who was quick to whip out his invitation and assure me that, since I was with him, the party would also be open to me.

The party-givers had taken over a handsome East Side brownstone house for the occasion, and when Schieffer and I arrived, it was the closest thing I had ever seen to a celebrity riot.

Some unscrupulous people who had not been invited had crashed the gate, packing the house to the point that the fire marshal had closed the front door. The blare of a lively party could be heard from within, but a police officer had been posted to keep out all comers, except to take the place of someone who had left. The result was a surly crowd of celebrities packed around the front door, clutching their invitations in disbelief, as actor Paul Newman heckled them from an upstairs window.

Suddenly a taxi pulled up and Walter Cronkite stepped out. He strode forward, the mob parted like the Red Sea, and Cronkite walked through the door and into the party.

At that, Schieffer decided to act. "Come on," he said. "I've got an invitation, too. We're going in."

He began to push his way toward the front of the crowd, with me hunkered sheepishly behind him, unconvinced that this was going to work. When Schieffer reached the police officer, he presented his invitation to the young woman from the *Rolling Stone* staff who had been designated to rule on matters of entry. Obviously well into the spirit of the party, she took one unfocused look at Schieffer and shook her head.

Then she gazed over his shoulder at me, and a knowing smile of recognition swept across her face. I knew in a flash that this would be a marvelous coup—that my distinctive white hair had made an impression, that she had recognized me and not Schieffer, and that I would never let him forget it.

"Officer," she said, "let that man in. That's Howard K. Smith!"

A subdued Howard K. Smith took his friend Bob Schieffer into the party, and a good time was had by all.

———

To many journalists, to abandon a job at the *New York Times* for the glitter of television was so unthinkable as to be almost depraved.

Only one *Times* reporter had committed such an act in recent years—Bernard Kalb, who had been persuaded by his brother, Marvin, that a recognizable form of journalism could be practiced at CBS. Bernie Kalb had then distinguished himself in his first TV interview by thrusting a microphone at a senator, asking a question, and then tucking the mike under his arm to scribble down the answer in his pad.

But there were growing indications that the upper heights of American journalism were taking a new shape, with television elbowing in at the top. Polls kept showing that a rising number of people got their news from TV, and television journalists became increasingly prominent in the profession.

To me it was self-evident—any form of journalism that included Eric Sevareid could not be inherently superficial. I also knew and admired Mike Wallace, and from time to time I discussed with them the possibility that I might join their TV ranks. The discussions were brought to a head by Watergate. CBS officials realized that this would be a legal as well as a political story, and they approached me about switching to the network as its legal specialist.

My belief had always been that every now and then in life it's good to roll the dice. My legal associates had been aghast when I took a chance and left law practice for the *New York Times*. After eight years there, even though it struck most print journalists as a little tacky, I was ready to switch to TV.

One of my colleagues at the *Times*, attempting to be supportive about my television plans, assured me that I would find success. "You've got the suits," he soothed.

But a young man who rushed up to me at a Senate hearing was more candid. Almost in anguish, he asked, "Why did you sell out?"

———

My adjustment from print journalism to television was essentially easy because I was covering the Watergate story, which got me on the air almost daily and gave me a crash course in on-the-job training.

The most fundamental change was in the writing. It turned out that writing for the *New York Times* was not the best training for the brief, punchy style required by broadcasting.

The longest ongoing infringement of the Truth in Labeling Act was the reputation held by the *Times*, when I joined it in the mid-1960s, as a tightly edited newspaper. This impression had been created by a prim style that persisted in referring to any villain short of an ax murderer as "Mr." and in tediously defining terms that everybody already understood. All the while, its reporters were free to run amok with length and dullness.

The general rule was to write as much copy as required to tell the story. On the Supreme Court beat, with its reams of opinions on decision days, that often meant writing as fast as you could until the 6:30 P.M. deadline— and then a bit beyond, when you could beg a few more minutes. The result was long, often rambling pieces with a low priority on style and punch.

Radio and television required almost the opposite: short sentences that unfolded the facts in a sequence that a listener could easily follow.

I was surprised to discover that the time limitations of broadcasting were not as frustrating as a print reporter might think. First of all, in terms of pure communication, broadcasting won in a walk. The *New York Times* gave me the luxury of telling its 750,000 daily readers perhaps more than they wanted to know, but on a big night, my two minutes on television would reach 20 million people. Also, many newspaper readers don't go beyond the first few paragraphs, while the broadcaster knows that the listener will hear his entire report.

The secret for the broadcaster was to decide which information, at a bare minimum, must be reported in order to tell the story and then rate the other facts according to their importance, to be tacked on if time allowed. That meant sacrificing some information to make the central point. But because we were reaching as many people as we were, and with the additional visual impact that television could deliver, there was very little frustration in the brevity of our reports.

The hazard was that, in selecting the crucial points to be made and those to be sacrificed, the broadcast journalist would sometimes miss the important point and not get around to reporting that at all. That happened to all of us from time to time, but for the most part we had a sense that our few minutes on the air were enough to inform the public adequately about the stories we were reporting.

A more delicate challenge for the rookie television correspondent was learning to "write to pictures." The problem is that the pictures seen on television make a sharper impression on the viewer than the words he hears. So if the pictures convey one message and the words another, the viewer is likely either to get only the visual message or to confuse the two.

The obvious answer is to write words that send the same message as the pictures. The obvious problem is that sometimes you don't have the right pictures. This was often true of legal reporters, who usually could not take their cameras into court. It explains why a multitude of TV legal reports have begun with the classic uninformative line, "The defendant arrived at the courthouse . . ."

Even with helpful pictures, often in the crunch of getting on the air in time the reporter couldn't get the words and pictures to match. This was often the case in the hurly-burly days of the Watergate story, which took place in that primitive era when cameras used film instead of videotape. CBS had a big, stinking film-developing tank in a corner of the Washington bureau, and it always took twenty-five minutes, no matter what.

That meant that on a tight deadline the writing had to be completed while the film was still in the soup. Then the developed film would be rushed to an editor, who had perhaps five minutes to match the pictures to what the correspondent had written. High-tech in those days meant that the editor would strip off lengths of film, measured from his outstretched hand to his nose, allowing five seconds for each strip.

Having thus timed the run of pictures to match the length of time the correspondent was expected to talk, the editor would hand the roll of film to the swiftest news clerk around, who would bolt down the stairs to the film projectors in the studio below. Nearby, the correspondent would be poised behind a microphone, ready to read. A few moments later, Cronkite in New York would introduce the piece and the correspondent's words were expected to match the pictures.

In my case, they often didn't. Having just left the *New York Times,* it took me a while to master brevity, and on more than one occasion I would still be droning on in impressive Timespeak well after the pictures had run out and the screen had gone black.

I finally got the message one evening as I sat clutching my script and narrating a piece on the "Evening News." The hand of chief producer Ed Fouhy slid in under my armpit and crossed out the last two paragraphs. I read down to the deletion and signed off, abashed that the story had made about as much sense as it did in its original form. It was obvious that brevity was preferable to on-the-air editing, and after that I usually managed to write my stories short enough the first time.

One benefit of my newspaper background was a feeling that television reporting could benefit from more coherence and sense of perspective. It struck me that television was afflicted with a compulsion toward scoop-ism that sometimes got in the way of informing the public. Competition was fierce between the three major networks, especially on the Watergate story, and our superiors tended to gauge our success in terms of which network had scooped the other each day.

The problem was that a scoop was defined as some fact that had not been previously disclosed, without too much concern for how illuminating that fact might be about the overall Watergate story. As a result, some of our pieces featured the previously unknown but inconsequential fact, which might not tell the public much and might actually create confusion about the meaning of Watergate.

The tip-off to this kind of thinking was the three TV monitors that were a standard fixture of every television newsroom. They displayed the three networks side by side, and there would be agony if a scoop popped up on one of their screens before it did on ours. I always wondered at the validity of this as the basic measure of how well we were performing, since few viewers watched all three networks at once, and the winner of the daily scoop contest might not necessarily be doing the best job of informing the public.

I got as much satisfaction as anyone from the scoops that I managed to dig up. But I also made it a point to try to step back from the daily story once each week and present a piece that gave an overview of what we had learned and what it seemed to mean. It proved to be a useful device, especially during the period when the news was dominated by the complicated constitutional issues surrounding the Nixon tapes and the impeachment proceedings.

It also paid off in recognition, as these were the reports that were cited when I was given the George Foster Peabody Award, one of the most prestigious prizes in broadcasting, for my coverage of the legal issues of Watergate.

My early efforts to adjust from print to television generally worked well, but there were some bumps along the way.

One special problem was learning to finesse the efforts of politicians to manage the news by taking advantage of television's inflexible deadlines.

My lesson came one evening in the winter of 1973. White House press secretary Ron Ziegler attempted to defuse the scandal over ITT's alleged use of improper influence to obtain a favorable antitrust ruling by releasing a complicated justification just before air time. It came in the form of a voluminous "white paper" that purported to prove that President Nixon had no fault in the matter. Because the late release gave me only a few minutes to digest the document and get it on the air, I was confronted with laying the official denials before the public, with little opportunity to balance them with any critical perspective.

It was a news manager's obvious way of playing "gotcha."

In the taxi ride from the White House to the CBS bureau there was only time to scribble a few notes, and I made the mistake of trying to say too much. I did not have it well in mind as I rushed into the studio, sat down before the camera, and heard Cronkite announce that I was ready with the story from Washington.

Then, just before my turn came, the makeup lady made an ill-advised last-second effort to do her job. She darted forward and plopped a compact into my hand.

Thus, just as the red light went on, I looked down and discovered that I had been appearing on television each night wearing a face powder called "Gay Whisper."

What came next was not, as President Nixon might have put it, "perfectly clear." I delivered a rambling summary of the White House's explanation, determined that next time I would attempt to say less and say it right.

One reason why life on a morning newspaper is more civilized than reporting for TV and radio is that after midnight there is no rational excuse for a newspaper editor to wake you up. The next deadline does not come until the following evening, no matter what. That being the case, a call late at night to a *New York Times* reporter meant that an unusually important story was in the works.

"Fred, this is Neil Sheehan. I'm in a hotel in New York, and I've got a problem."

I had a problem, too—I was only half-awake; Sheehan's was that he had obtained the top secret Pentagon Papers for the *New York Times,* and he was afraid that Attorney General John Mitchell was going to try to take them back.

Neil explained that he and several other *Times* reporters and editors were holed up in the New York Hilton, preparing a series of articles that would blow the lid off how the United States had blundered into the Vietnam War. It was Wednesday night, June 9, 1971, and the first installment was to burst into print on Sunday morning. Sheehan was concerned that Mitchell might stage a series of FBI raids in an effort to get the Pentagon Papers back. Neil had made two copies—the one at the hotel, and one hidden away at his home in Washington.

What if the FBI managed to find them both? Sheehan wanted me to put his Washington copy of the Pentagon Papers on ice.

I took him literally. Later that night I drove to his home, where his wife Susan helped me pack the twenty-three thick folders of secret documents into the trunk of my car. Then, in the early hours of the morning, I put them where I was sure the FBI would never think to look—in the deep freezer in my garage.

It happened that my house sat close to the curb on a busy Washington street. The built-in garage opened so that the freezer was in full view for any motorist to see. For the rest of that week, Sheehan's lawyer, Mitchell Rogovin, cringed each day as he drove to work past my house. Three young Graham children could be seen riding their tricycles in and out of the garage near a large white freezer containing twenty-three frozen packages of the Pentagon Papers.

Finally, on Sunday, June 13, the Pentagon Papers story flashed across the front page of the *New York Times*. It seemed to be, by any definition, a sensational news story, and I watched with fascination that morning as the secretary of defense, Melvin Laird, made his previously planned appearance on "Face the Nation." He would be questioned by George Herman, Bob Schieffer, and John Finney of the *New York Times*, savvy journalists all. I assumed they would wring him dry on the Nixon administration's reaction to this major security breach. From his response, I hoped to discover if there were plans for the feared FBI raids that we had foiled by putting the papers in deep freeze.

Nobody asked Laird about the Pentagon Papers.

It was a spectacular demonstration of how journalists can differ on what is a story. The panelists plodded through a forgettable half-hour on the dreary minutiae of the Vietnam War. Nobody thought to ask Laird about what was to become one of the top news topics of the decade.

Thus President Nixon's defense secretary did not disclose that the administration intended to respond in court—and not by sending G-men out in search of Pentagon Papers on ice.

———

For a former newspaper reporter accustomed to presenting his copy in the dignified columns of the *New York Times,* mastering the standup was a special agony.

The daily work of a TV correspondent requires that, on short notice, he stand somewhere, look into the camera, and deliver a coherent statement into the lens. The entire run of the standup must be flawless because the camera is focused on the correspondent's face and there is no artful way that flubs and gaffes can be edited out. Standups are also typically done ten minutes before air time, facing a gaggle of tourists from Alabama spellbound at the spectacle of the TV reporter fumbling such simple lines.

A few correspondents managed it on pure memory. Marvin Kalb seemed to be able to read his script one time and then reel it off flawlessly into the lens. I became convinced that Kalb had a photographic memory that worked like a teleprompter. The tipoff was that he always blinked his eyes at the end of a standup, just before he signed off. My theory was that he could mentally reel the words off behind his eyeballs, read them into the camera, and then "click!" blink to switch off his teleprompter as he signed off. Bruce Morton and Dan Rather had such a natural sense of the spoken word that they could almost make it up as they went along. But for the neophyte TV correspondent with a flabby memory, mastering the standup could be a nightmare.

When I was having a rocky time in my early stages, one of our White House correspondents, Bob Pierpoint, came to my rescue. He explained that several of the reporters at the White House had developed a one-take system for handling the frequent, hurried standups that the White House beat requires.

Pierpoint's technique was this: Write the script and read it into a tape recorder as it is to be delivered. Plug an earpiece into the recorder, run the wire up your sleeve, up the back of your neck, and into your ear. Hold the recorder behind your hip, and when the cameraman gives you the signal, push the button. Then, as the standup is piped into your ear, repeat the words into the camera.

Once a reporter masters the trick of saying each word an instant after it comes dribbling into his ear, the system works wonders; it has since been adopted by many of the correspondents for CNN, where the work requires many standups and the hip young reporters have enough bushy hair around the ears to hide the wires.

But the technique does cultivate a certain glassiness of eye, as the reporter gazes into the camera, listening to the words trickling in one ear and repeating them before the next word makes him forget. I always suspected that President Nixon had been misled by that when he complained about "the leers and sneers of the correspondents"—it was not leers and sneers, just Pierpoint and his colleagues, glassily focusing on repeating the words pouring into their ears as they told the nation the story of Watergate.

I mastered the trick of repeating the words, but not the art of making them sound sincere. It seemed phony to be playing Charlie McCarthy to my own Edgar Bergen, and I remained uneasy about using the Pierpoint technique until I came a cropper with it one day and gratefully gave it up.

It happened during the early hectic days of Special Prosecutor Archibald Cox's investigation of the Watergate coverup. There was a major break in the story late one afternoon, just before the "Evening News" went on the air. I had just enough time to get to the Special Prosecutor's Office in downtown Washington, get the information, and film one standup.

At the time, the earplug seemed my salvation. I scribbled down the story, read it into my recorder, stuck the plug in my ear, rushed out onto the busy sidewalk, faced the camera, and let the recording roll. Unfortunately, just at that moment a line of buses at the curb began to gun their motors into my unplugged ear. The result was that I could clearly hear the words coming into my ear, but not the ones I was saying into my microphone.

The film was rushed back to the studio, into the soup, and onto the air—with extraordinary results.

It was like an imitation of an announcement made by a computer. There I was, speaking in my normal voice, but with the flat cadence and level inflection of a well-programmed robot. I sounded faintly like one of those ersatz earthlings that pop up in science fiction movies, speaking English learned in outer space.

Everyone at CBS agreed that it was a remarkable performance—and encouraged my decision never to use the earplug technique again.

The intricacies of high tech also conspired against me when I upgraded my newspaper wardrobe for television. My prized purchase was a handsome tweed suit, with tiny flecks of white and dark blue that blended together into a sophisticated soft gray. I did not know about a feature of television called the moiré effect, because I did not understand how television worked.

My new suit taught me a lot about both.

It turns out that TV works by projecting electrons from one end of a television tube against the screen at the other end. On the inside of the screen are 525 lines of tiny phosphorous dots of different colors that fill the screen so tightly they appear, to the eye, to be a solid sheet. When the TV camera takes a picture, it receives an intricate message as to which of the colored dots to illuminate by shooting them with electrons. The camera transmits this message to the television tube, which creates, magically, a color picture.

Things get complicated, though, when the colors of the object being photographed are mixed together in tiny patterns—such as in an expensive tweed suit.

That means that when the camera attempts to decide which of those little dots to illuminate, it is confronted with not just one color but a mixture of two, such as in a white and blue tweed. This confuses the camera, which tries to resolve the matter by projecting first the color white, and then the color blue, with perhaps a bit of purple in between.

The result is the swimming effect sometimes seen on television, when the colors of a finely textured fabric change constantly in distracting waves. I had seen this happen to scarves, ties, and other tightly woven accessories, but it was not until my new gray tweed appeared on camera that anyone had seen it happen to a correspondent's entire suit.

After one luminous appearance on CBS, producer Ed Fouhy banished my new suit from the airwaves, and I had learned another lesson about electronic journalism.

Not surprisingly, my crash course in television reporting gave me an exaggerated sense of the importance of pictures. The visual side of broadcast journalism was the part that always tripped me up, and thus attracted much of my attention. I made the mistake of concluding that the visuals were the most important part. So in the early days of my switch to television, I developed an exaggerated sense of the show business side of my new career. This resulted in two memorable appearances by me on the network.

The first came shortly after I joined CBS, when the Supreme Court handed down a decision upholding a public high school teacher's use of a tennis shoe to paddle a student. I was instructed to prepare a brief story to read on the air during the noontime news program that the network broadcast in those days.

From the network's viewpoint, this was a minor element in a little-watched broadcast. But for me, facing my first live appearance on CBS, it was the launching of a television career.

Determined to live up to the occasion, I stopped by a gym down the street from CBS, and borrowed a tennis shoe. Thus, when I reached the dramatic highpoint of my forty-five-second report, I reached under the anchor desk, whipped out the tennis shoe, and slapped it down on the desk.

My colleagues were either too stunned, or too polite, to comment on this, which I took to be confirmation that such antics were par for the course on TV.

I was on a roll, and the next day I had an inspiration that led to my first appearance on the "CBS Evening News." I sold the Evening News staff on an innovative way to present the predictable report by the FBI that crime was still rising. The basic reason for the upswing in crime was demographic; the baby boom that had followed World War II had matured into a horde of young men who were just at the age when people are most likely to do bad things.

I proposed that we illustrate this by taking pictures in a maternity ward, to show how babies now can mean rising crime later. Unfortunately, my producer for the story was the imaginative John Armstrong of the satanic beard, who had the inspiration that I should do my standup in among the babies. This seemed reasonable, until the hospital required that I protect the infants' health by wearing a surgical gown.

The resulting performance, even by television standards, was too much. There I was, Doctor Kildare on the "Evening News," discussing the crime rate among the squalling babies.

That evening bureau chief Bill Small took me aside and, in his subtle way, brought CBS News's philosophy into clear perspective.

"Forget the goddam pictures," he said. "Just report the news."

That, basically, was the gist of our marching orders from the time I joined CBS in November of 1972 until Walter Cronkite was replaced in the anchor seat by Dan Rather in March of 1981. During this period we were print-style journalists who showed pictures while we told the news. It meant that our values were essentially those that had guided journalists for centuries. We understood these values; they gave us a firm sense of what was news and how it should be covered.

It was the golden age of television news. At CBS we had the best of all possible worlds—the glamour and excitement of TV, plus the standards and prestige of the top broadcast organization in the business.

In all those early years, I never heard anyone raise the possibility that it would ever change.

5

Courtly Television

"**I** wouldn't sit on the bench if there were a television camera in the room."

"But Chief Justice Burger, in this courtroom you must support your positions with rational reasons. What are your objections?" In the recurring fantasy that tantalized me during the fifteen years that I covered the Supreme Court for television, I would be the Supreme Court justice behind the high bench, and standing below at the lawyer's lectern would be Warren Burger.

Burger's situation would be the same as any attorney before the Supreme Court—to make a logical case for his position against allowing television cameras in the Supreme Court.

He would use the exact quotes he had written or spoken in public—and I, using the questioning technique the justices employ in court, would blow him away:

"The lights hurt my eyes."

"So why ban radio coverage of the Court? Haven't you been told that the newest TV cameras can operate with the lights as they are now in this courtroom? Anyway, didn't CBS offer to have special light-deflecting eyeglasses made for you by Walter Cronkite's very own oculist?"

"Anyone who's interested in how the Court works can read about it."

"What does that say to the majority of Americans who get most of their news from television?"

"We aren't in show business. You would have nothing but a distorted conception of what goes on in the Court unless you put on the entire proceeding. If there were some way of saying that no one else could reproduce any part of that, any segment of it, without producing all the rest of it, that conceivably might open things up."

"But doesn't the New York Times *report only the tiny fraction of courtroom arguments that it considers interesting?"*

"When you get cabinet meetings on the air, call me."

"Isn't there a difference between a cabinet meeting, which is not open to the public, and a Supreme Court argument, which is?"

"One problem with having cameras is that other justices would ham it up. Some of them already do when the courtroom is crowded."

"Is there anything that would make coverage of the Supreme Court possible?"

"My funeral."

It has been said that Warren Burger had the look of a chief justice who had been sent over from central casting. With his striking white pompadour and his formidable bulk, Burger was an arresting figure in the center of the Supreme Court bench. He disliked television with a righteous zest, and his opposition was so wholehearted that everyone assumed cameras would remain outside the Supreme Court as long as he was there.

But if central casting had been selecting a person to personify the less dramatic dignity and wisdom of the ideal associate justice, it might well have chosen John Marshall Harlan.

Harlan seemed born to be a Supreme Court justice. He had been named, farsightedly, for his grandfather, Associate Justice John Marshall Harlan, who had himself been named for the country's fourth chief justice, John Marshall.

Harlan was the kind of patrician figure who, in his seventies, was still referred to in legal circles as "John Marshall Harlan, the younger." He had the bearing of a man who went home to a butler and a bottle of port. The product of a wealthy family, of Princeton, Oxford, and Wall Street, Harlan was the type of Old World gentleman who responded to the justices' obligatory private viewings of confiscated pornographic films by muttering, periodically, "By Jove, extraordinary!"

One of the first things that I learned when I came to cover the Supreme Court was that the conservative Harlan occupied a special position of reverence on the liberal Warren Court. If it were possible to say that one person was more principled than others in a group of upright men, Justice Harlan would have been the consensus choice.

Harlan was the kind of purist who observed the separation of powers by not voting in presidential elections and by not applauding at the president's State of the Union address. He believed that the Court should exercise restraint and leave decisions on sensitive social issues to the legislatures, but he also believed that the Court should follow its precedents, once established, whether the individual justices agreed with the results or not. This led Harlan, the Warren Court's "Mister Conservative," to vote for liberal positions in followup rulings to the Warren Court's landmark decisions. To many people, on the Warren Court and off, John Marshall Harlan was the conscience of the Supreme Court.

When Harlan died in 1971, it was, for the nation's television viewers, a nonevent. For seventeen years Harlan had been one of the most powerful decision-makers in the government. Yet there were no moving pictures of him, because television cameras were not allowed in the Supreme Court. So the television networks were left with lifeless black-and-white head shots of Harlan cropped from Supreme Court portraits and peering over the anchors' shoulders as they told briefly of his demise.

The black-and-white pictures made Harlan look so old-fashioned that he could have been taken for John Marshall Harlan, "the older"—the photographs reflected the same state of the art as those taken when Harlan's grandfather was on the Court. With no lifelike pictures, the networks could not effectively tell Harlan's story, so they did little more than mention his passing and move on to speculation about his successor.

That incident did much to nudge me toward a career in television journalism. I was fascinated that television had recently shown astronauts walking on the moon but had never managed to show a justice sitting in the Supreme Court. It made no sense that an influential justice could affect millions of Americans' lives and yet be a nonperson to the majority who got their news from television.

The Harlan obituary persuaded me that television had to learn to do better in covering the Supreme Court. I found myself puzzling over how I would cover various stories if I were doing it for a network. Within a year I had discussed my ideas with Eric Sevareid and Mike Wallace. Ready or not, CBS was about to take on a Southern-speaking transplant from the nation's stuffiest newspaper as its first law correspondent.

When I joined CBS in 1972, no television organization made a serious effort to cover the Supreme Court. NBC had hired a first-rate lawyer-reporter to do it, Carl Stern, but then had lost its nerve and stuck him mostly on the radio. CBS's philosophy of covering the Supreme Court could best be described as "rip and run." If a wire service machine burped up a report that said the justices had done something big, the first available reporter (if possible, George Herman, who was a fast study) would try to catch up by "Evening News" time. ABC seemed to follow the assumption that the Supreme Court was so dull that if the network ignored most of what the Court did, nobody would notice.

It was understandable why television downplayed the Supreme Court. In a world in which everybody else *wanted* to be on television, only the justices and the Mafia avoided it. The Mafia at least had a defensible reason, in that it had much to hide. But the Supreme Court's aversion to television seemed to grow out of an imperious

resistance to change that took the form of judicial elec-
trophobia.

Habits change slowly, when at all, at the Supreme
Court. Knickers were worn by the all-male pages there
until 1963 (they disappeared then in a flash when a page,
mortified by the giggles of teenie bopers in the audience,
took his case to a sympathetic Chief Justice Earl Warren). Only two years before, the Court abandoned its
nineteenth-century noontime gavel in favor a 10 A.M.
starting time. In arguments before the Court, the federal
government's attorneys still wear a style of formal morning attire that is otherwise seen only at presidential
inaugurations and fancy weddings. And it has been only
in the last decade, long after the days when a justice
would be expected to sit with a chaw of Red Man in his
jaw, that the Court removed brass spittoons from the
side of each Justice.

This attachment to the past is best symbolized by the
crossed quill pens that are placed on the table at the disposal of every attorney who comes to argue before the
Court. Not for a century has anyone picked one up and
tried to write with it, and the Court long ago stopped
providing ink. But the goose quills were there when
Daniel Webster argued before the Court, and to this day
hundreds of European geese lay down their lives each
year so that the tradition can go on.

This quill-pen mentality has produced a fear of electrons at the Supreme Court—a suspicion of electronic
communications so deep that irrational barriers stand
against the flow of electricity.

Electricity is allowed within the chamber, to light the
premises and even to amplify and record the voices of the

justices. But a firm line has been drawn against permitting electrons to *leave* the courtroom, bearing sound or images.

This electron barrier was tested at the time of the arguments in the Nixon tapes case, when twice as many reporters signed up to sit in the press section as could be accommodated in its seventy-five seats. Several reporters joined me in asking that a wire be run from the courtroom into an adjacent conference room, where the excluded journalists could hear the arguments on an amplifier. This petition was rejected without a hearing, and the unlucky reporters had to file their stories based on secondhand quotes from those who managed to swing a seat inside.

As of this writing, no radio or television transmission has ever been permitted to convey events from inside the courtroom out. To keep this electron barrier secure, reporters and visitors to the courtroom have never been allowed to make sound recordings of the arguments, for fear that the public outside might be permitted to hear them.

Before I learned better, I used to believe that the justices' aversion to electronic communications was merely thoughtless repetition of nineteenth-century behavior. I felt that if the justices could just see how painless modern communications could be, sweet reason would prevail. Then, in my fantasy, the Court would realize how beneficial it would be to let the public in on its deliberations, and the electron barrier around the courtroom would melt away.

So I conspired to penetrate the Supreme Court's anti-electron perimeter and to broadcast the recorded voices of the justices during Court arguments.

In recent decades the Court had made sound recordings of its arguments, so that the justices could go back
and check what had been said. These recordings were
squirreled away on an ears-only basis for the justices. By
1969, the Court realized that the growing stacks of old
recordings were of no further use in deciding cases and
were beginning to cause a clutter. They were too valuable to throw away, but if they were simply given to an
institution that would let the public listen to them, people might begin to ask why they shouldn't be permitted
to hear the Court's proceedings as they were happening.
It was a question of maintaining the electron barrier, so
that people wouldn't question why it existed.

So the Court concocted a lawyerlike agreement with
the National Archives, which permitted the justices to
unload the old recordings on the archivist, while making
certain that they could not be heard by ordinary citizens.
The deal permitted the Archives to play the tapes only
for government officials and others engaged in "serious
scholarly and legal research."

I made it a special project to obtain a bootleg copy of
one of those tapes so that I could broadcast, for the first
time on radio and television, the actual voices of an argument in the Supreme Court. My target became the arguments in the famous Pentagon Papers case, in which the
Justice Department had tried unsuccessfully to stop the
New York Times and the *Washington Post* from publishing
the government's top secret analysis of how the United
States became enmeshed in the ruinous Vietnam War.
The tenth anniversary of that landmark First Amendment decision was coming up, and I could see a certain

irony in using it to pierce the silly electron barrier maintained by the justices.

It took some cloak-and-dagger work, but by June 30, 1981, the anniversary of the decision, I had obtained a leaked copy of the recording and was ready to go.

It was the first time (and as of now, the only time) that the actual voices of the justices and counsel in oral arguments had been broadcast over the air. CBS broadcast a special fifteen-minute report on the CBS Radio Network, plus a long television piece on the "CBS Evening News." The TV report was limited by the basic handicap that comes with the absence of cameras in the courtroom; the only pictures were motionless color-pencil sketches, on a screen capable of presenting life. But the drama of the event poured from the screen, and especially from the radio, as the justices and the attorneys were heard to wrestle with the dilemma of maintaining a free press when the nation's security might be at stake.

For palm-sweating impact, the broadcast was not exactly in a class with "Miami Vice" or "Wheel of Fortune," but all of us at CBS were pleased. I had demonstrated that electronic coverage of the Court could be interesting and tasteful, and I assumed that the Court would get the point.

In making that assumption, it turned out that self-satisfaction had clouded my judgment.

The chief justice went into orbit. Burger blamed the National Archives for the leak; nothing so wicked had happened so long as the recordings had been kept within the Court. After an unsuccessful hunt for the leaker, Burger decreed that no more recordings would go to the Archives—and for the next five years, none went.

Others didn't take it quite so hard, and I was nominated for an American Bar Association Gavel Award. A few months later a acquaintance who was a member of the Gavel Award selection committee gave me a call.

"Did you know your friend Burger is after you again?" he asked. I said I didn't know it, but I wasn't surprised. "We voted to give you the Gavel Award," he explained, "but Burger has complained to the Board of Governors, and they've come up with a new rule that will prevent you from getting it."

The American Bar Association, which had a well-worn track record of toadying to Chief Justice Burger, had indeed produced a creative reinterpretation of its rules, which the ABA said precluded me from receiving its award. The ABA had an old rule, designed to discourage surreptitious taping of court proceedings, which said that Gavel Awards could be given only for courtroom recordings that had been "authorized by a judge"—and since the *broadcasting* of this one had not been authorized by the chief justice, the ABA decreed that the CBS entry was illegal.

Bill Leonard, the president of CBS News, fired off a letter to the ABA, protesting that it had changed the rules after the fact. "It is not for you, or anyone else," he said, "to suggest that we should obtain the permission of public officials before we broadcast information about them."

The ABA reconsidered and honored me with its Gavel Award.

Because of the circumstances, that award took on a depressing symbolism as the years went on.

I had demonstrated that television and radio coverage

of the Supreme Court could be interesting and instructive, and the legal profession had certified that fact with its highest award. But the resistance from the chief justice made it clear that broadcast news could expect little cooperation from the Court for the foreseeable future.

The odd thing about Burger's hostility toward TV journalism was that he made some important changes at the Supreme Court that helped the print journalists do a better job. In fact, Warren Burger, the grinch of the electronic media, earned a reputation as a reformer of the Court's antiquated procedures for dealing with the press, which had been neglected by his idealistic predecessor, Earl Warren.

Chief Justice Earl Warren was by nature an open, gregarious man, whose instincts were to operate with a common touch. He lived in my neighborhood in Washington and was a familiar burly figure, prowling the shops and walking to work each morning. Warren was easy to spot because he always wore a sky-blue double-breasted suit (his clerks claimed that he had winter and summer versions, all identical). The contrast of Earl Warren ambling alone along the sidewalk and Warren Burger in his limousine with its armed driver suggests that Chief Justice Warren would be far more open to the press. It was almost the opposite; Earl Warren had a reason—or at least, a justification—for being distant.

As the figurehead and moving force behind a Court that was upsetting applecarts throughout the country, Earl Warren made a point of being oblivious to the outcry that it created. He was the Rhett Butler of judicial public relations; frankly, he didn't give a damn. It was his way of demonstrating that the Court was acting on principles unaffected by the public's reaction, but sometimes the posture was a little hard to believe.

One day in 1967 I mentioned to him that on my last trip South I had seen a new series of huge billboards declaring "IMPEACH EARL WARREN." His only response was, "Oh, are they still doing that?" as if he had not cared enough to follow the news.

In fact, Earl Warren and his Court's liberal decisions had generated a law-and-order backlash of enormous political importance, which made it short-sighted for him to be cavalier about the public impact of what the Court was doing. Warren was a shrewd public man who probably watched the election returns as carefully as Supreme Court justices are alleged to do, but his public-relations-be-damned blind spot created problems that could have been avoided.

The most egregious was a blundering opinion Warren wrote in a follow-up ruling to his landmark *Miranda* v. *Arizona* decision, which held that police must advise suspects of their rights prior to interrogating them about crimes. Warren intended to cushion the impact of the *Miranda* case by holding that it would not apply to confessions obtained by the police before the Court created the new rule. But Warren carelessly wrote the opinion (in a case called *Johnson* v. *New Jersey*) so that he did, inadvertently, throw out a number of confessions that were already on paper.

Defense lawyers across the country pounced on Warren's gaffe, and a parade of self-confessed criminals walked free—giving Earl Warren's old political enemy from California, Richard Nixon, a law-and-order issue to flog all the way to the White House.

The jurist who profited most from that was Warren Burger, and as chief justice he took pains to facilitate the news coverage of the Court—as long as it was the kind of press coverage he wanted.

Burger never conceded that there was a legitimate public interest in such matters as the justices' health, their finances, their reasons for disqualifying themselves from cases, their votes on deadlocked appeals, and their off-the-bench activities. To him, news media's role was to convey to the public the official actions of the justices, no more. Thus Burger became an enthusiastic reformer of the *mechanics* of covering the Supreme Court, perhaps in hopes that by facilitating our efforts to cover the formalities we would be less likely to fritter away our energies on personalities and gossip.

It was amazing how enlightened Burger could appear, simply by changing some of the musty old procedures that his predecessors hadn't bothered to question.

One was the hoary custom of distributing the Court's opinions to the press in the courtroom as the justices announced the decisions. This quaint tradition dated back to the time when only a half-dozen reporters regularly covered the Court and each had his own little-red-schoolhouse armrest chair stationed in front of the long judicial bench, with a pneumatic tube that ran down into the floor. Whenever a Justice began to read an opinion, a page would bring each of us two copies—one to read, and the other to drop down the tube. There was a row of closetlike cubicles below, and the justices apparently assumed that any reporter worth his porkpie hat would have a colleague waiting breathlessly, poised to send the decision out on a news ticker.

Regrettably, I never had a collaborator on the Court beat, and some years earlier the pneumatic tubes had been sawed off beneath the floor and didn't lead anywhere. Burger switched to the practical system of handing the opinions out in the press room.

One leisurely Supreme Court custom was the practice of not issuing the official thumbnail summaries of the justices' opinions until the decisions were published in law books, months after they had been announced in court. Burger had the summaries printed along with the opinions that were handed out on decision days, to the immense relief of harried reporters confronted with reams of judicial legalese on a busy day.

But Burger's crowning reform concerned a venerable Supreme Court tradition that caused the year's most important decisions to be hoarded and issued in large batches on the last three or four Mondays of the term. Nobody recalls why Mondays had been singled out for this purpose, but the result was a confusing torrent of decisions that were easily misunderstood and misreported by the overwhelmed Supreme Court press. Burger simply had the Court meet several days a week toward the end of the term. With the decisions spread throughout the week, the hysteria in the press room declined and the quality of Supreme Court reportage improved.

Despite the clout that Burger swung on housekeeping issues, he could not have kept the TV networks at bay singlehandedly. Most of the other justices were on his side and seemed to enjoy the fray.

Byron White once stated his objection to me this way: "I can't see why the Court should do anything to make

CBS richer." White said he might consider permitting cameras if only the Public Broadcasting System was involved. When I tried to argue that newspapers had made money for years off their coverage of the Court, all I got was a stony stare.

The other justices have kept their reasons mostly to themselves. On the one public vote the Court has taken on the question (when radio broadcasters petitioned in 1986 to cover the arguments over the constitutionality of the Gramm-Rudman deficit reduction law), three justices said they favored allowing electronic coverage: William J. Brennan, Jr., Thurgood Marshall, and John Paul Stevens. The others said no, but didn't say why.

One argument that I never heard a justice make against permitting cameras in the courtroom is that Supreme Court proceedings are so dull that it is a public service to keep them off the tube. On this the justices missed a bet. Many of the court's cases involve narrow embellishments of obscure rulings, and the debate in such cases rocks along at the excitement level of watching cement set.

On slow days in Court, I perfected the art of dozing sitting up, marred only by the fear that I might topple forward with a crash and waken others in the chamber. One day, as I was wavering close to a coma, a page tapped my shoulder and handed me a note from Chief Justice Burger.

It read alarmingly like the admonitions that had come from classroom teachers across the years.

"Please join me in my chambers during the noon break," the chief justice had scribbled.

When I appeared, Burger used his advantage craftily.

Without mentioning my drowsy presence in the courtroom, he took exception to a report I had done the previous week about his alleged reluctance to attend an upcoming American Bar Association meeting in Las Vegas. Burger had been a victim of his own bad timing. According to a source of mine within the ABA, Burger had chosen the occasion of a bar association meeting in New Orleans to inform the ruling fathers of the bar that he might skip their next meeting in Las Vegas because of his skittishness about the casino city's racy public image. The irony of Burger going to New Orleans to object to visiting Las Vegas had been great; I had not been able to resist filming my report on Bourbon Street, against a background of hooting Mardi Gras celebrants and girlie houses.

In his chambers, Burger conceded that he was undecided about going to Las Vegas, but he claimed the uncertainty was all due to the fuss that my story had generated. Las Vegas, he insisted, is a pleasant place, and he had nothing against it.

Relieved that the chief had let me off the hook without needling me about dozing in court, I did a follow-up piece pointing out that he might still attend the Las Vegas meeting. Burger eventually went and gave every impression of having a good time.

Sometimes the pace at the Supreme Court is so lackluster that even the justices get bored to distraction. My first taste of this came early in 1965, shortly after I began to cover the Court for the *New York Times*. Justice Arthur Goldberg sent a page over to my seat in the press section of the courtroom, with a note inviting me to join him in his chambers after the gavel.

Goldberg and I had an unusual, if not unique, relationship: during the previous two years, while I was employed as assistant to Secretary of Labor W. Willard Wirtz, I had also served as the justice's ghostwriter.

This was complicated, but with Goldberg, things tended to get that way.

Before becoming a justice, Goldberg had been one of the most energetic—some said meddlesome—secretaries of labor in living memory. He was forever intervening in labor disputes around the country, sometimes with spectacular success, but other times to the confusion and consternation of the two sides in the dispute.

Despite the mixed results, Goldberg considered himself a world-class negotiator—and after President Kennedy appointed him to the Court in 1962, Goldberg retained a sort of dual hangover from his labor secretary days. One element of this was a feeling that his negotiating skills should not be wasted but should be focused internationally in the cause of world peace. The other was a notion that he still exercised some residual powers at the Labor Department, where I had taken a job in 1963. This latter sentiment on Justice Goldberg's part provided some moments of discomfort for the new secretary of labor, W. Willard Wirtz, the least of which was to share the ghostwriter of his speeches—me—with Mr. Justice Goldberg.

During the mid-1960s, when Goldberg was planning a major speech, I would periodically be summoned from my office in the Labor Department to Goldberg's Supreme Court chambers to prepare a draft of his address. There was obviously some delicacy to this arrangement, and Goldberg later became convinced that I had been his speechwriter when he was secretary of labor—not when he was a Supreme Court justice.

Over the years he persisted in introducing me to strangers as "my speechwriter when I was secretary of labor." I corrected him quietly a couple of times, but it never took. Finally, when he was very much the center of attention at the National Press Club one day in 1979, he trotted out that old line again. I couldn't resist replying: "No, that was when you were on the Supreme Court." But Goldberg, not a world-class listener, never caught on.

On the day when Justice Goldberg sent me the note in the courtroom, he was suffering from an acute attack of his off-the-bench itch. Sometimes he soothed this condition by dialing up Lyndon Johnson at the White House to offer advice, but the word around the Court was that the president usually proved unavailable for a chat.

This time, Goldberg was planning an indirect approach.

The chief justice of India was planning a visit to Washington, and Goldberg saw it as an opportunity to get in the swim of high-level international diplomacy. He explained to me that relations between India and the United States were strained because of differing views on the U.S. escalation of the Vietnam War, plus bad personal vibes between President Johnson and Indian Prime Minister Bahadur Shastri.

Goldberg wanted to broker a sit-down, patch-it-up meeting between the two leaders, using the Indian chief justice as cupid. He had laid on a reception for the visiting jurist, and he proposed that I get the word to the

White House that Justice Goldberg stood ready to pass the word through the Indian chief justice that the United States was prepared to deal.

The idea struck me as more worthy of Rube Goldberg than Arthur, and—worse—Justice Goldberg seemed almost pathetically bored with the bench and eager to ingratiate himself with Lyndon Johnson and touch events outside the Court. I told him that I could pass his suggestion to the White House through a friend of mine on Johnson's staff, and I did—but I felt that Goldberg was demonstrating a weakness for extrajudicial shenanigans that could only lead to trouble.

Lyndon Johnson was not one to overlook a flaw in someone else that could be manipulated to his own advantage. Within six months, in July of 1965, LBJ maneuvered Goldberg off the Court and into the showy but toothless job of ambassador to the United Nations.

Despite the sometimes somnolent quality of the Supreme Court hearings, I knew that there would be a place for them on television if the justices would permit it. Any television-viewing public that will watch bowling and the House of Representatives will provide an audience for the Supreme Court. Only a few masochists would watch entire arguments, but even the Supreme Court has its glittering moments, and the tapes of those would make the Court acceptable on the "Evening News." By incorporating them into condensed reports about issues before the Justices, the networks could substantially expand their coverage of the Supreme Court.

The thing that always puzzled me was why the justices didn't *want* to televise their hearings. Forty of the state supreme courts permit TV coverage with no adverse effects, and the U.S. high court has far more compelling reasons to let the public in on what it is doing.

Its decisions are more controversial and more often misunderstood than the state supreme courts', so there is every reason to publicize what is under consideration. It is unsettling enough in a democratic society to have unpopular edicts come thundering down from an unelected priesthood, but to have them burst upon the scene with little advance warning and inadequate explanation compounds the damage.

Yet that happens regularly at the Supreme Court, because the large segment of the public that gets its information from television and radio has been denied a full view of the preliminaries. Stories about Court arguments can't compete for television time because TV executives hate to leaden their screens with color-pencil sketches and secondhand recitations of what happened inside. The result is that there has been inadequate coverage of the Supreme Court, because television reporters have been restricted to the video equivalent of communicating with a quill pen.

Early in my tenure at CBS I decided to make the best of the situation by developing a technique for covering Supreme Court cases without going inside the Supreme Court. My approach was to go to the community where each dispute arose, take pictures of the scene, interview the people involved, and present the legal question through the stories of the people who raised it. This seems obvious now, as it is the way all the networks do it. We pioneered it at CBS, and while it was TV legal journalism at its best, as long as we were excluded from the courtroom it was not good enough.

I eventually concluded that the justices' ban on cameras in the courtroom told less about television than about the psychology of being a justice.

Surprisingly, no psychology professor has devoted his career to studying the mentality of Supreme Court justices. They are, after all, a unique class—the only nine Americans who have a lifetime constitutional mandate to put on black robes and issue orders to everyone else.

Whenever lawyers assemble and drink, the conversation inevitably turns to the tyrannical conduct of certain U.S. district judges. These jurists are widely believed to suffer a special form of brain damage, brought about by the effects of a guaranteed lifetime job in black robes and accompanied by arrogance, impatience, and shortness of temper.

The same psychology would presumably apply to a pronounced degree to Supreme Court justices, because they do not even face the hazard of having their decisions reversed.

That being the case, it is surprising that their conduct is not more deviant from the norm than it actually is. In the Supreme Court there is almost none of the bullying that goes on in some federal trial courts; the justices' style is to be relentlessly patient and polite with the attorneys.

An occasional exception during my tenure was Thurgood Marshall, who would sometimes direct cutting ridicule at lawyers who opposed the civil rights positions that he usually favored. This was unfair, and seemingly out of character for Marshall, an easygoing man who, off the bench, appeared to give considerable attention to pacing himself. He kept banker's hours, let his law clerks do much of his work, and generally seemed content to outlast Ronald Reagan. One justice told me, with some awe, that he hadn't seen Marshall climb a stair in years. Marshall had once devoted substantial energy to the bottle (he claimed he inherited this from his father, who, he said, belonged to "Alcoholics Unanimous"), but the justice geared back on the grape as he mellowed into his seventies.

Even though the usual decorum in the Supreme Court would do credit to any court, the justices, whenever possible, always arranged things so that those instances of bad form that did occur were not communicated to the public. They even went so far as to protect themselves from the written record of what they had said. In an effort to make it difficult to pin an embarrassing quote on the justice who said it, official court reporters were forbidden to identify the members of the Court in their transcripts, other than as "Justice."

Back when the Supreme Court reporters sat at individual desks (the ones with the mysterious pneumatic tubes) strung out along the front of the bench, we could often eavesdrop on the justices' private conversations. Once, when a particularly stuffy lawyer made an unusually pompous point, Justice Brennan leaned over to Justice White and commented, "Bullshit." The reporter who was seated nearby heard it and passed it around, and not long afterward Chief Justice Burger had the bench sawed into three pieces, with the ends swung forward. He said the purpose was to let the justices see each other better, but the effect was also to displace all of the reporters' seats into a side alcove, well out of earshot.

Even with the justices willing to go to such lengths to

preserve decorum, I witnessed a few deviations from normal procedure.

One day an attorney walked up to the podium, took one look at the justices, and fainted. On another, as a Texas lawyer explained why his client should not go to jail for drug peddling, Chief Justice Burger, neglecting to turn off his microphone, leaned over to Justice Brennan and boomed out over the Court's public address system: "This thing is as phony as I've ever seen." One afternoon a lightbulb fell from a ceiling fixture with a grenadelike boom that had Justices and attorneys ducking for cover. On another day a female Justice Department lawyer, taking literally Burger's edict that women attorneys would not be permitted to argue cases in pants suits, appeared in a feminine version of the traditional morning suit—complete with cutaway jacket and pin-stripe skirt.

But the most memorable breach of decorum was inflicted by Larry Flynt, the outrageous publisher of *Hustler* magazine. Flynt was in court appealing one of the many libel judgments against his magazine, and when it became manifest that his side was not faring well, he shouted:

"Nine assholes and a cunt!"

It was later disputed whether Flynt had been off on his count, but the result was clearcut. Flynt spent the next seven months in a prison mental institution. He also lost the case.

But for the most part, the justices' control of their environment served well to protect their dignity, and they realized they would lose some of that protection if they allowed gavel-to-gavel TV coverage. They would be seen when they were unprepared, missed the point, committed an embarrassing gaffe, or reached an age when it was time for them to retire. At the end of my fifteen years at CBS most of the rest of official Washington had opened up to television coverage, but the Supreme Court, and those who reported on it, had been left behind.

This meant that as the networks moved toward a jazzier, more colorful news style, legal news would be increasingly pushed into the background by more visual competition. It wasn't particularly healthy for the legal system, and it certainly wasn't good for the prospects of a correspondent who hoped to made a career broadcasting legal news on TV.

6

The Supremest Court in the World

The most vivid example I ever saw of how poorly the public understands the Supreme Court was the day Newton Estes tried to punch out Justice Byron White.

It happened one July morning in 1982 in Salt Lake City, where Justice White and I had gone to address the Utah Bar Association. White was scheduled to speak before I was, and while he was being introduced and was still seated, a large man rushed up from the audience, ran around behind the justice, and began to pummel him on the head with his fists.

My instinct was to take notes. I had never seen a justice punched before, and I was impressed with the dignity with which Byron White carried it off.

"Whizzer" White was a tough cookie, a former all-pro halfback with a neck like a tree trunk and a head like a rock. He just sat there with a long-suffering scowl, giving every impression that he could have risen up and flattened the man if it had been appropriate. Meanwhile, his assailant stood behind him and pounded away at the top of White's head, driving home each punch by shouting such words as "Filth!" "Pornography!" or "Dirty pictures!"

It then occurred to me that I was not there as a reporter but as a normal person—and that I was free to act like one.

So I jumped up and helped wrestle the big man away from White and off the podium, where several of us kept the arm-weary attacker cornered, waiting for the police to arrive. The local television corps had come out in force for Justice White's speech, and as the photographers came scrambling over with their cameras rolling, I saw an opportunity to question the assailant on camera before the police took him away. That done, I would need only an on-camera standup and a recorded narration to throw together a quick report for that night's CBS Evening News. I knew I could borrow the local CBS cameraman briefly to get that done.

So I grabbed a mike and began to put White's attacker through my best network-style third degree.

"He's causing four-letter words to come into my living room through the TV set," the man replied. "The only way I know how to stop it is to go to the source!" The TV cameramen zoomed in.

The man said that his name was Newton Estes and that he had become increasingly disturbed by the Supreme Court's decisions favorable to pornography and court-ordered busing. Earlier in the week Estes had been startled to hear a four-letter word blare out from his television set, and he decided he must do something, "to keep our civilization from going down the tube." The newspaper had reported that a Supreme Court justice was coming to speak, so Newton Estes decided to lodge a direct protest against recent goings-on at the Court.

At that point in Estes' interrogation the police arrived and I was freed to prepare my television report. I handed the mike back to the cameraman who owned it, and, with the crisp self-assurance of a network correspondent in the provinces, I ordered; "Let's find a good spot to do a standup."

"I can't," the cameraman replied.

"Why not?"

"I'm with NBC."

It turned out that the overexcited CBS cameraman had pushed the wrong button and jammed his camera. My exertions on behalf of Justice White were televised that night only on the rival network.

I returned to the lecture hall, where Byron White got off a good line about being "hit harder than that when I came to Utah to play football" and then droned through a lecture that was not in the same class with the pre-speech fisticuffs. I tuned him out by daydreaming about how little the average American knew about the real people beneath the robes of the Supreme Court and how typical it was that Newton Estes had slugged the wrong justice.

The Supreme Court had, indeed, often ruled to protect the rights of pornographers, but Byron White had frequently voted to lock them up. He was a flinty, hard-nosed, law-and-order type who was often mistakenly taken for a liberal because he had been appointed to the Court by President John F. Kennedy. (A friend of mine who knew both White and Kennedy well claimed that sex had more to do with White's appointment than ideology. He said the two men had met when White was a dashing Rhodes Scholar at Oxford and a mean hand with the English ladies and that young Jack Kennedy had been so impressed he decided then and there that White was meant for greatness.)

In any event, the symbolism was all wrong in punching Byron White as a protest against the Supreme Court's permissiveness toward pornography. But the mistake was understandable; the Court has traditionally been so withdrawn from public view that even though its nine members are among the most powerful figures in the nation, most citizens don't know much about them. (Newton Estes, it turned out, wasn't quite what he seemed to be either. A decade after the incident, Estes pleaded guilty to a child pornography offense, so in some ironic way he might have punched the right justice after all.)

One benefit of the Supreme Court's isolation from the public is that so few acts of violence have been directed at the justices. No branch of the government has agitated the citizenry more, yet the justices are such remote figures that the crazies of the world don't tend to focus their violence on them.

When I first went on the law beat, the Warren Court was infuriating large blocs of the American public with regularity. Yet security was nearly nonexistent; only a couple of bored-looking bailiffs were on guard in the courtroom at any given time.

I used to marvel that someone didn't walk in some day, as the Puerto Rican nationalists had done across the street at the House of Representatives, and mow the

Court down like blackbirds off a fence. Chief Justice Warren Burger, ever the skeptic of human conduct, reinforced the bench with bulletproof armor plate, so the justices would at least have a place to duck. He also added metal detectors and more guards. But still, there was always a sense of detachment at the Court from the furies that the justices occasionally stirred up.

If any member of the Court seemed a likely target of some aggrieved citizen's ire, it was Justice Harry Blackmun. He had written the Court's abortion rights decision, *Roe* v. *Wade*, which had agitated some zealots to the point of dynamiting abortion clinics. But in those days the justices kept themselves so cloistered that nobody knew what Harry Blackmun looked like.

One day, when Blackmun was strolling about Capitol Hill on his usual noontime walk, I saw him amble up to a raucous anti-abortion demonstration and stand around for a while, watching. Nobody recognized him.

But in time Blackmun did become the target of batches of hate mail from anti-abortion extremists, plus the subject of a few death threats—and, eventually, the object of one of the weirdest incidents ever to involve a justice of the Supreme Court.

One evening in March of 1985, as he and his wife Dottie were relaxing in their high-rise apartment across the Potomac from Washington, a bullet crashed through the window and plowed into the arm of a couch. There had been a recent rash of bombings of abortion clinics by a group calling itself the Army of God, and it was natural to assume that a right-to-life hothead had taken a shot at Justice Blackmun.

But I had been in Blackmun's apartment. It struck

me as physically impossible that anybody out to get Blackmun could have fired that shot. I talked with the FBI men who were investigating the incident, walked over the ground that a gunman would have had to confront, and concluded that Justice Blackmun had been the victim of a coincidence so unlikely as to defy explanation.

Blackmun's apartment was in a building that loomed high above the Potomac river banks. If a person had stood anywhere between the building and the river and fired a shot up through Blackmun's window, it would have hit the ceiling, not the couch. The only way a shot could have slanted down, through the window and into the couch, was if it had been fired in an arc from across the river, in Georgetown. The shore there was about a mile away—so far that Blackmun's apartment building looked like a distant blob. The slug that crashed through Blackmun's window was a caliber normally fired from a pistol, which would be hardly accurate enough to hit Blackmun's building, much less his window, at that distance.

Georgetown is a rowdy night scene, and the only logical explanation was that a reveller stood on the bank with a pistol and fired a high-spirited shot into the air—which happened to come crashing down through the window of the Supreme Court's most controversial justice.

It is not an explanation that satisfied Justice Blackmun. So, in the files of the FBI, the case is still classified as officially "under investigation."

Because the justices took such pains to remain remote from the public, people often asked me what relations, if any, the justices had with the journalists who covered the Court. The answer was that I had close friendships with several of the justices, others kept me at arm's length, and there were several fuzzy relationships in between.

Justice Potter Stewart was around my house enough while my children were growing up that, when I took my six-year-old son David to court for the first time, he brought the house down by pointing at the bench and shouting excitedly:

"Hey, Dad, Potter Stewart's on this court!"

I also counted Harry Blackmun and Lewis Powell among my friends. William Rehnquist would join me for lunch, but kept his guard too high for a close friendship. Chief Justice Burger and I somehow maintained a friendship, which rose above many mutual provocations to the contrary.

One relationship that did not survive was a friendship with Abe Fortas that grew out of the fact that both of us hailed from Tennessee. I became disenchanted when I learned that Fortas had given hawkish advice to President Lyndon Johnson about the Vietnam War, at a time when Fortas was ruling against conscientious objectors from the Supreme Court bench. In May of 1969 Fortas resigned from the Court under fire for his off-the-bench activities, and on the following Sunday morning my disenchantment poured forth in a long article I wrote for the *New York Times*.

That morning Fortas woke me up with a telephone call and ended our relationship with this:

"Mr. Graham, what you wrote this morning in the *New York Times* is enough to drive a man to kill."

Fortas let it go at that, and we managed never to converse again.

I was too awed by Hugo Black to get close to him personally, and I let a decade-long misunderstanding complicate my relationship with William Brennan. John Paul Stevens and Sandra Day O'Connor were pleasant but noncommittal. My relationship with Byron White warmed up—from frigid to cool—after the Newton Estes affair. But in general, White, William O. Douglas, and Thurgood Marshall appeared to act on the assumption that where cordial relations with the press were concerned, there was nothing in it for them.

None of the justices were news "sources" in the usual sense. There was an understanding in my dealings with them that all conversations were off the record, and confidential Court business was usually not discussed. Several of the justices would help when a story needed to be confirmed or knocked down, but none played the spin-control game that is routine everywhere else in Washington. None of them tried to manage the news by putting their views, or themselves, in a favorable light.

This reticence was enough to generate culture shock among reporters who also covered the politicians of Washington and was the only aspect of the priestlike insularity of the Supreme Court that I considered to be in the public good.

Covering the Supreme Court was like being assigned to report on the Pope. Both the justices and the Pope issue infallible statements, draw their authority from a mystical higher source, conceal their humanity in flowing robes, and—because they seek to present a saintly face to the world—are inherently boring. They also both have life tenure, which implies a license to thumb their noses at the news media. Unfortunately, the lion's share of the nose-thumbing by the justices was directed at the television and radio media, in the form of the ban on cameras in the courtroom. But even aside from that, the justices were so withdrawn that covering the Court for any news medium was in a journalistic class by itself.

It was always galling to me that the Supreme Court, which had the duty of preserving a free press from threats by everybody else, was, where coverage of its own affairs were concerned, the least sensitive to First Amendment rights of any branch of the government that I covered.

The reasons were simple. Everybody in the government would like to stifle press coverage of embarrassing matters involving their own turf. But they usually can't get away with it, because there will be an election one day and the public will take out its suspicions on those who appear to be covering up—and because the Supreme Court (or some lesser court enforcing one of its rulings) will probably make them come clean.

But neither of those reasons apply to coverage of the Supreme Court itself. The justices do not have to get elected, and they don't apply the First Amendment's rationale of governmental openness to themselves.

Instead, they hide the Court's warts behind ritual and secrecy. This tended to produce dull journalism—and while the justices might feel that dull is beautiful, our job was to find out and make public as much as we could.

The result was that those of us who covered the Supremest Court in the World also contended with the strangest news beat in the nation's capital.

It was April of 1971. The Supreme Court term was grinding to a close, and Thurgood Marshall was acting strange.

The justice dispatched one of his clerks to the Supreme Court's press room one Friday afternoon to post a small notice. It explained why he had disqualified himself from voting in the case of Cassius Clay, as heavyweight boxing champion Muhammad Ali used to be called.

It was strange that a Supreme Court Justice would consider it desirable to tell the public the reason why the justice was prevented from doing his job. To my knowledge, no justice had ever been so forthcoming before, and coming in the case of Muhammad Ali, it got my attention.

When Justice Marshall had issued a brief notice, several months before, saying he would not take part in Ali's draft evasion case but giving no reason, it was widely assumed that Marshall's reason was that he had some conflict growing out of his previous tenure as a lawyer for the NAACP. Suddenly, when it was time for the case to be decided, Marshall disclosed that the reason for his disqualification was quite different—that he had taken an action on the case (he didn't say what action) when he was solicitor general in the Justice Department.

Immediately I realized what had prompted this outburst of public accountability. Muhammad Ali was going to prison because Thurgood Marshall was not available to cast the deciding vote on his behalf. With Marshall disqualified, the remaining justices had split, four to four. In the Supreme Court, a tie vote upholds the lower court—and since Ali's conviction on draft evasion charges had been upheld by the court below, Marshall's absence would result in Ali's conviction being sustained. Thurgood Marshall, the Supreme Court's first black justice, wanted the world to know that his earlier work for civil rights had not disqualified him from the case and thus ironically resulted in the imprisonment of Muhammad Ali.

On Saturday I confirmed the story with one call. Like most reporters at the Supreme Court, I had tried to seduce the justices' young law clerks to render public service by leaking information to me. At the beginning of their year at the Court, most were like fraternity pledges, so awed by the secrecy and mumbo-jumbo that they would tremble to disclose a secret symbol or mystic rite. But their willingness to gossip always warmed up toward the end of the term, and in this case, the first clerk I called was eager to tell all.

It was true. The Court had deadlocked over Ali's case, and his conviction would be upheld on Monday.

Here was a magnificent scoop. The *New York Times* would tell the story to the world on Monday morning, and later that day the Supreme Court would ratify the tale of Muhammad Ali's downfall.

Every Supreme Court reporter picks up tidbits, rumors, and gossip, but I had never had a leak firm enough to predict a decision in advance. This time I had Marshall's written hint, plus the word of the clerk, who had always given me sound information before. But there was a problem. The Supreme Court has a custom that any justice may switch sides on any case, up to the moment that they step through the velvet drapes to sit behind the bench. Another law clerk once told me how

Justice Tom Clark had done this moments before the Court was to uphold the fraud conviction of Texas wheeler-dealer Billie Sol Estes. The vote had been five to four, with Justice Clark one of the five. A few weeks later, with Clark casting the deciding vote and writing the opinion, the Court overturned Estes' conviction on the grounds that television cameras had been permitted in the courtroom.

What if the Court were to pull a similar switch with Muhammad Ali? That question gnawed at me through the weekend, until my journalistic zeal was overcome by a combination of prudence and fear. I killed the story.

On Monday morning, the Supreme Court was silent on Muhammad Ali. Several weeks later, the Court overturned Ali's conviction, eight to zero, on grounds not even raised by his defense lawyers. My friendly law clerk told me that at the last minute Justice John Marshall Harlan had changed his mind about voting for conviction, and the other Justices had thought it best to make the decision unanimous.

I was cured of attempting to scoop the Supreme Court on its decisions. You could never be sure a decision would stay put, and even if it did, the early disclosure would not be a major contribution to the public's understanding of events.

Tim O'Brien, ABC's correspondent on the law beat, was made of sterner stuff. He predicted several decisions—mostly about forthcoming actions to clobber the news media, which got a big play in the press—and he got them mostly right, except for some pesky details. (Justice Potter Stewart disclosed, after his retirement, that O'Brien had been wrong when he predicted that the

Court was going to close pretrial hearings to the press, but a last-minute switch on the Court made it turn out O'Brien's way.)

O'Brien's scoops caused a sensation. Chief Justice Burger banished a printer suspected of leaking Court papers. O'Brien took on an agent, who hustled speaking engagements for the "young guy who's got to be about the hottest thing in Washington." Carl Stern of NBC defunked O'Brien's reports as "Hey, Mom, look at me!" journalism, which Stern said was "valueless and degrading."

I thought O'Brien's scoops were a good stunt and made an interesting point. They validated the Supreme Court as the only news beat in town that could create a sensation when a reporter got a scoop.

One result of the Supreme Court's hide-and-seek relationship with the news media was that the public knew almost nothing about what some of the most powerful figures in Washington were really like. I never ceased to be intrigued by the scrambled public images of the Court's ideological bookends, William O. Douglas and William Rehnquist.

They were personal and ideological mirror-images: Douglas, the idealistic humanitarian, was cold and impersonal; Rehnquist, the authoritarian statist, was outgoing and friendly. Douglas believed that the government should be compassionate, protective, and evenhanded, and Rehnquist demonstrated those qualities in his relations with the people around him. Unfortunately, Douglas often neglected those values in his personal dealings, and Rehnquist did not think it appropriate to require them of the government.

If ever there was a man who was a living contradiction of his public image, it was "Wild Bill" Douglas, the most forceful advocate of civil rights, civil liberties, and the rights of the downtrodden who has ever sat on the Supreme Court.

People who admired Douglas's idealistic writings, and assumed that he must be a warm, engaging human being were often crushed to be told that he was not. Douglas operated on the theory that a great humanitarian didn't have to like people, and he spent much of his life proving it. Douglas was a champion of civil rights, yet he was high-handed and rude to the blacks who worked at the Court and fired his black messenger after he refused to serve at a private party at the justice's home. He was the first justice to view sex discrimination as a violation of the Constitution, yet he had a reputation for treating women clerks as intellectually inferior. Douglas always supported the rights of young people, but he was so cold and arrogant to his young law clerks that there was a private joke about giving him a microwave oven for Christmas (Douglas had a pacemaker implanted in his heart, and microwaves have been known to jam their circuits).

Douglas was an equal opportunity curmudgeon; he was inconsiderate to his fellow justices, too. The Supreme Court had two cars for the justices, a limousine for the chief justice and a second car for the other eight. Douglas kept the second car, full time. He also left the Court each summer two weeks or so before the end of the

Court term and holed up in his cabin in Goose Prairie, Washington. The cabin had no phone, which tied the Court in knots over last-minute actions that required his vote.

Douglas was one of history's most resolute advocates of the news media's First Amendment rights, yet his relations with the Supreme Court press were distant. I spoke with him less than a half-dozen times over a period of almost two decades, and I felt that I knew him less than any justice who was there during those years. Douglas did not even reveal himself during the give-and-take from the bench; he seemed to ignore the arguments, scribbling away at his own work and rarely speaking out.

My final encounter with Douglas was typically ambiguous, leaving me wondering whether he had acted on principle, or arrogance.

It happened in 1975, after Douglas had suffered a devastating stroke. He returned to court in a wheelchair looking awful, with haunted, hollow eyes and a weak, slurred voice. When that raised questions about his capacity to carry on, he invited the handful of us who regularly covered the Court into his chambers to demonstrate, up close, that he could still do the job. There was an air of self-delusion about Douglas that day that only made matters worse; he insisted that retirement "never entered my mind," shrugged off his paralysis with the quip that "walking has very little to do with the work of the Court," and invited us to come back in a month to "join me for a fifteen-mile hike."

The situation created a journalistic dilemma. I could not tell whether Douglas' slurred speech reflected a clouded mind—but if indeed he was clinging to the bench despite a mental impairment, that was a story that should be reported.

It was the kind of delicate situation that I had dealt with several times over the years by turning to my friend, Potter Stewart. Justice Stewart was a political junkie who had once been a city councilman in Cincinnati and who suffered the frustrations of one who had reached a station in life where people were reluctant to talk politics with him anymore. I had no such inhibitions, and he and I used to huddle periodically at a popular lobbyists' watering hole on Capitol Hill, where I would lay on the most scandalous gossip I could dredge up from the Justice Department and Capitol Hill and he would respond with uninformative and unconvincingly upbeat declarations about relations inside the Court.

At one of these sessions several months after Douglas's stroke, I was surprised at how forthcoming Stewart was.

He told me that this was one of those situations that had confronted the Supreme Court on a few occasions over the years, when a justice has become mentally incompetent but refused to step down. It is always a delicate matter, because justices are appointed for life, and there is no procedure for forcing them out if they overstay their competence. Justice Stewart had been through it before, with Felix Frankfurter, who had stayed on after a stroke had undermined his judgment. Stewart said it had taken a gentle nudge from President John F. Kennedy to persuade Frankfurter finally it was time to retire.

This time, the other justices delegated Byron White

to check with Douglas's doctor. White reported back that the doctor confirmed the other justices' impression that Douglas' mind came and went and that he was not always mentally competent to perform as a Supreme Court justice.

But he was dug in on the question of staying on, which presented the Court with an agonizing problem. As Stewart put it, the difficulty was that litigants might say later that they lost because of the vote of a justice known by the others to be incompetent; the result could be a cloud on the integrity of the Court, or could even result in demands for reconsideration by the losers.

So the other justices carried out an informal judicial coup, a tacit agreement that Justice Douglas would not be assigned majority opinions to write and that his vote would not be counted when it would provide the margin in five to four cases. In those situations, either one of the dissenting justices would switch to make it six to three, or the case would be held over for reargument the next term of Court.

When a justice has been as candid as Stewart was about a matter that sensitive, something unusual is going on. I took it as a signal that the justices were disposed to have Douglas's condition go public. I cast about for some way to flush Douglas out without violating Stewart's confidence and saw my chance when Douglas's office put out the word that he would undertake a special rehabilitation program at New York University's Rusk Institute.

I telephoned Douglas's home, got him on the line, and gave him my First Amendment pitch: rumors were going around that he was no longer up to the job; public confidence in the Court would erode until the questions were laid to rest; he should face my camera, state his case for remaining on the Court, and let the people see for themselves.

Douglas replied in a weak, slurred voice, but he did not hesitate. I never knew whether it was principle or arrogance—whether he felt that a champion of the First Amendment owed it to his ideals to face the public, or he believed he could carry it off. But he agreed to let me know when his treatment at the Rusk Institute was over, so that I could be there with my camera when it was time for him to go home.

After three months of grueling therapy, he lived up to his promise. The result, for him, was devastating. He had his driver stop as his car left the hospital grounds, and as he leaned out the window, it was a shrunken, diminished version of the rugged Douglas that the nation had known. The camera rolled, and I asked my questions as gently as I could:

GRAHAM: "Mr. Justice, you've been on the Court now longer than any other man. You've made your mark in history. Why not retire?"

DOUGLAS: "Well, I don't see there's any particular point, in that I'm—I have the, I have the physical capacity to go ahead and do the work. It's interesting."

GRAHAM: "Do you think it's in the public interest for people to stay in public life when they get well into years and are in failing health?"

DOUGLAS: "I think it all depends on the individual. With some, it would be a mistake; with others, it's not a mistake. With Holmes—he was with us on the bench until he was ninety-two years old, and it'd have been a mistake for him to get off it any time prior to that."

GRAHAM: "How long do you think you'll stay on, sir?"

DOUGLAS: "I have no idea. Holmes wrote some of his best opinions after he was eighty-five."

The words were coherent, but the way he looked when he said them on the "CBS Evening News" that night made it obvious that Justice Douglas should no longer sit on the highest court in the land. He tried it for several weeks, but the pain was too great, and Justice Douglas finally gave up and retired.

While people tended to assume that Justice Douglas was a warm humanitarian, Chief Justice Rehnquist had the kind of image problems that might be expected of a jurist who habitually rejected constitutional equality for women, approved the execution of allegedly insane prisoners without a hearing, denied constitutional equality to aliens and bastards, asserted that the public did not have a constitutional right to attend court trials, said prisoners had no rights to practice religious freedom, and spoke warmly of the legendary Isaac ("Hanging Judge") Parker, who cheerfully ordered eighty-eight executions.

It was sometimes said of Rehnquist that he is a strong believer in the Constitution—but he doesn't care much for the amendments. He himself has implied that there is some truth in that.

When you put together the statements he has made in court opinions, in his other writings, and especially in his Senate testimony when he was up for confirmation as chief justice, it's clear that Rehnquist places the authority of the government well above individual rights in the scale of what's important in the American system.

Rehnquist believes that the glory of the American Constitution is the strong, stable democratic government it creates. He is less enthralled by the amendments that grant individuals rights against that government. The result is a slant that leans heavily in favor of majority rule and against claims of individual rights that challenge what the majority has done.

With this philosophy as a touchstone, happiness is denying the claims of litigants who invoke the Bill of Rights, and Rehnquist has pleasured himself consistently over the years by ruling on behalf of the government and against individuals.

When Rehnquist was off the bench, it sometimes seemed that he tried to take the edge off his hard-line image by casting himself as a professorial, almost bumbling klutz. In reality, Rehnquist is a natural athlete, a good poker player, and a charming companion. Yet he often presented himself publicly as a stammering, disheveled Mister Peepers, peering fuzzily out at the world through thick, 1950s-style glasses. He became famous for his out-of-date sideburns, the Hush Puppies protruding from beneath his judicial robes, and the *Mad* magazines scattered about his chambers. Sometimes it seemed that Rehnquist overdid this and came across as a sort of self-made nerd who in reality was not nearly as eccentric and ungainly as his appearance suggested.

Once a group of reporters was jawboning Rehnquist about how television cameras should be permitted into the courtroom. I made the argument that the newest cameras had become so small and unobtrusive that the Justices would hardly know they were there. One of the newspaper reporters, hoping also to score an advance for print reporting, held up a familiar book-sized Sony voice recorder that journalists use to verify quotes and added that it wouldn't even be noticed in the courtroom.

Rehnquist pointed to it and asked, "Is that one of those new cameras?" The reporter, dumbfounded that anybody could mistake a voice recorder for a TV camera, could only mumble, "It's just a Sony."

Nobody but a chief justice could have gotten by with such an off-target stab at naiveté—but in this case, there was only a brief, stunned silence, and the conversation turned to other things.

I had first known Rehnquist as a good, if partisan, news source when he was a top official in the Nixon Justice Department. When his children graduated from an excellent public high school near his home outside Washington and mine were just at the age to enter the drug-plagued high schools in the District of Columbia, Rehnquist and I discussed swapping houses but never did anything about it.

Then when Rehnquist's son Jim reached the age when sons take pleasure in tormenting their fathers, he told Rehnquist he had decided to become a reporter. Rehnquist swallowed hard and consulted with me about how to help his son get started. Jim Rehnquist was planning to spend a year abroad, and I arranged for him to write as a freelance "stringer" for a California newspaper.

Soon after, I received a cordial thankyou note from the younger Rehnquist, neatly hand-lettered; I had neglected to ask whether the hopeful young journalist could type. He returned from Europe, studied law at Boston University, and dutifully became a respectable Boston lawyer.

Every now and then Rehnquist would drop his guard and reveal a jaundiced view of the Fourth Estate. This tended to surface over the touchy subject of Rehnquist's health. He had a chronic bad back, which gave him so much trouble in the fall of 1981 that he got strung out on pain medication. It reached the point that it was affecting Rehnquist's speech from the bench, and when his doctor reduced his dose it hit him so hard he had to be hospitalized. Through it all, he insisted that it was none of the public's business.

Shortly after Rehnquist became chief justice, a reporter asked him if he would make a commitment to keep the media informed of developments affecting his health. Rehnquist glared, curled back his lip, and let some of his feelings spill out. "My experience," he said, "has been that where that subject is concerned, you can be a bunch of vultures."

One of the humbling experiences of reporting on people who have had long careers in public life is to learn how many of them have been embittered by their treatment at the hands of the press.

I caught my first glimpse of this in 1969 after the Nixon administration first proposed "preventive detention" as a way to deal with the crime problem and I wrote a column in the *New York Times* criticizing the idea.

Not long after, I received a graceful note from a casual acquaintance who was a judge on the U.S. Court of

Appeals for the District of Columbia. The judge called my piece "highly constructive," and added: "There is too much haste on 'preventive detention' as a cure-all. It isn't. It is very dubious on several counts."

I was intrigued, because the note came from Warren Burger, a hard-nosed, law-and-order judge who, based on my impression, would have disapproved of preventive detention only because it merely threw the suspects in the jail instead of under it. Burger and I had recently become fellow faculty members of an annual summer seminar for appeals court judges at New York University, and I made a point of trying to figure out why he had gone out of his way to stroke a member of the press. We eventually developed a friendship that reflected all of the ambiguities and contradictions of his relations with the news media as a whole.

Burger had a grudge against the news media, with the angry edge of a suitor scorned. He had courted the press when he was an obscure lower court judge, with cold results. Later, he seemed occasionally eager to get even.

He told me of his frustrations as a lonely right-wing voice on the D.C. appeals court, which had staked out a more-liberal-than-thou posture to the left of even the Warren Court. This judicial feat caught the attention of the press, and the appeals court in D.C. became the darling of the *Washington Post*. Burger used to call the *Post's* courthouse reporter into his chambers and give him copies of his law-and-order dissents. But when the decisions hit the front pages, Burger's views were either buried or left out.

But Burger was also sending copies of his dissents to

Richard Nixon, and after that persuaded Nixon to make Burger chief justice, Burger had numerous opportunities to even the score. One of them pleased him so much he told me about it twice. He said he was seated next to Katharine Graham, the publisher of the *Post*, at a ritzy social function, and he announced to her—and to everyone else within earshot—that "There are only two newspapers that really cover the Supreme Court—the *New York Times* and the *Wall Street Journal.*" If Kay Graham had a retort, Burger did not report it.

It always amused me to have Burger complain to me about journalists, as if I were something else. He did it partly, I felt, because I was a lawyer. I learned, over the years, that the true importance of my law degree was not that it helped me write knowledgeably about the cases but that it removed the stigma of being a "nonlawyer." The fact that nobody has ever been called a "nondentist" or a "nonplumber" suggests that lawyers and judges tend to view the uninitiated with more skepticism than other professions do, and the shingle on my wall made them more likely to talk freely with me.

For twenty years, Warren Burger and I maintained a cordial friendship, while he carried on a guerilla campaign against the news media's efforts to report on him. He refused to let TV cameras cover his speeches, scuffled with a CBS camera crew that tried to take his picture, prohibited his law clerks from talking with reporters, called the television networks "sleazy operations" and their reporters "pipsqueaks," and presided over a system of Supreme Court secrecy that would have made the Pentagon jealous.

In October of 1972 Burger got so bent out of shape by

a story I wrote for the *New York Times* that he bellied up to his typewriter, banged out his version of a follow-up article, and sent it to me with the demand that it be printed under my byline, "as your own or not at all." Burger's concept of a reasonable second-day article was a succession of abject *mea culpas*. His first five paragraphs began as follows: "In last Friday's edition the *Times* carried an account, based on a syndicated column in another paper . . . ," "Somewhat ambiguously the *Times* account stated . . . ," "The *Times* failed to take into account that . . . ," "When the *Times* received the syndicated column . . . ," and "The *Times* was in error in . . ." I explained to Burger that if this ran under my byline it would be one of the more extraordinary pieces ever to grace the pages of the *New York Times* and that the true identity of the ghostwriter would soon surface. Burger refused to let me print the story under his byline, so I framed it on my wall as a memento of the chief justice's understanding of my craft.

The secret of our friendship was that Burger never seemed to take such tiffs personally, and I learned to ignore them, just as he did. Among those who knew Burger well, he had a reputation for doing kind, considerate things at times when people needed them most. It was not until the end of our relationship that I caught a glimpse of this firsthand.

It happened when my career at CBS was in trouble and Burger had retired from the Court to serve as the chairman of the commission in charge of celebrating the Bicentennial of the Constitution. Warren Burger offered me a job. He needed someone to handle the television and public relations chores of the commission—which meant, basically, being Burger's P.R. man. I was grateful, but I thought it best to suggest some other names instead.

The justice who seemed to nurture the most smoldering grievance against the press was Byron White, who wrote—with great relish—many of the Court's opinions that ruled against the news media. White had been provoked early and often in life by those masters of journalistic aggravation, sportswriters. As a superstar all-American halfback at the University of Colorado, he had been given the nickname "Whizzer" White by the sportswriters—a name that stuck with the justice much longer than he appreciated. The sportswriters had also asked him so many inane questions and had written so many witless comments about him that by the time White became a Supreme Court justice he had the manner of a man with a lifetime of scores to settle.

My first taste of this came on May 3, 1972, the morning after J. Edgar Hoover's death, when the rumors were flying that Justice White would be named the new head of the FBI. I tracked him down in the Supreme Court lunchroom, where he was sitting with his law clerks, and asked him if he had been offered the job.

"If I had, I wouldn't tell you," he said, and he continued eating.

That set the tone of our relationship for the next decade. At first I couldn't tell whether his stony demeanor was directed especially at me for something I had done or whether it was just the way he related to reporters. It turned out to be just Byron White's way. White was a stern, tough character. One reporter compared his attitude to a remark that one of Redskins Coach

Vince Lombardi's players had made about Lombardi: "He treats us all alike—like dogs."

Some justices felt offended by their treatment by the press, yet remained strong defenders of the First Amendment. Such was the case with William Brennan, and I, unknowingly, was the prime offender.

On Monday, June 12, 1967, the Warren Court handed down enough decisions and new Court rules to fill an entire 991-page volume of the Supreme Court's official case reports. There was no way for us even to read so many pages, much less write coherent stories about them. My failure to do so began what proved to be a long and eventually hurtful estrangement between me and a gentle and kindly justice, William J. Brennan.

Brennan was very proud of an opinion he had written that was released that frantic decision-Monday. It was a case called *United States* v. *Wade*, in which the Court declared that criminal suspects have a right to counsel when they are placed in police line-ups.

One of the problems of Supreme Court reporting is that every decision is precedent-setting, although some decisions set more precedent than others. Thus it is difficult to arrive at superlatives that adequately describe the decisions' hierarchy of importance.

Generally speaking, the low-grade decisions are said to be "unusual," "significant," or, on a slow day, perhaps even "crucial." Middle-voltage rulings are "novel," "unique," or, redundantly, "precedent-setting." Only the true bell-ringers rate "historic," or the ultimate, "landmark." During the yeasty years of the Warren Court there was a regrettable inflation in the nomenclature of Supreme Court rulings, as news editors had sent green reporters who were often extravagant in their use of Court superlatives. "Landmark" had been particularly debased, and I had made it a point of pride to use it with Spartan restraint.

The stature of *United States* v. *Wade* was such that I regarded it a "near-historic" decision—but with all that the Court had wrought that day, I had placed my discussion of it well down in an article that dealt with several cases. Unfortunately, for space reasons, that story—and news of one of Justice Brennan's favorite decisions—was chopped off at the knees by the *Times*' editors in New York. My discussion of the *Wade* case ended up on a spike.

Twenty years later, my neck still sweats when I picture Justice Brennan at the breakfast table the next morning, flailing through the *New York Times*, incredulous that the *Wade* case had not rated a story. At the time he was irate enough that his feelings got quickly back to me.

It was one of those situations when I should have taken the initiative to patch things up, but I let my pride get in the way. I told myself that the omission had not been my fault and that I shouldn't have to be the one to straighten things out. It was an immature thing to do, and it soured what had been an easy relationship between Justice Brennan and me.

The fallout came two years later, in May of 1969, just a few days after Justice Abe Fortas resigned in disgrace over questionable payments he had accepted from a shady stock manipulator. The Nixon Justice Department had helped orchestrate Fortas's departure, and soon after the FBI and IRS launched investigations of

Justice Douglas's extrajudicial activities. The Supreme Court's liberals had every reason to believe that the Nixon administration would pounce on any hint of off-the-Court improprieties.

In that atmosphere, I wrote the kind of story that makes its subjects yearn to turn journalists into toast, a story about guiltless activities that are newsworthy only because of their association with other, scandalous events.

Brennan had a modest tax shelter investment, a limited partnership in a suburban Washington apartment complex with Abe Fortas, former Justice Arthur Goldberg, Senator Abe Ribicoff, two judges from the U.S. Court of Appeals, and others. There was nothing remotely unseemly about it except that the developer, who made millions off renting office space to the government, had let an influential group of public servants in on a very sweet deal, with some controversial tax advantages.

But it became news when a local university professor sued his superiors over an academic dispute, lost in the court of appeals, appealed to the Supreme Court, and demanded that Justice Brennan disqualify himself from the case. His reason: Brennan should not sit in judgment of decisions made by the two lower court judges who were his partners in the real estate deal.

Nobody took the professor's legal point seriously (including the Supreme Court, which refused to disqualify Brennan), but with Fortas's abandoned seat still warm, it was a story. I wrote it, and Brennan was livid. He also had some reason for concern; a lower court judge known to have close ties to the Justice Department was spreading the word that the FBI was quietly investigating the apartment house tax shelter and that Brennan might be "next." The rumor-spreader seemed to be in a position to know; it was Warren Burger.

At that point, Justice Brennan apparently reached the conclusion that someone might be drawing a bead on him and that he should take evasive action. Pulling into a protective shell, Brennan resigned from a board at Harvard, quit his summer teaching work at the judges' seminar at NYU, and announced that he had withdrawn from all activities outside the court, "except my family and my church." For the next decade, the genial, outgoing Brennan, who by nature had always been more the Irish politician than the remote jurist, became a self-imposed black-robed hermit.

By the time I learned of my role in triggering this, it was too late. The justice had gone to ground and would not return my calls.

Brennan did not relent until many years later, when he reemerged as a public person in connection with his eightieth birthday celebration. He gave me a gracious on-camera interview and was kind enough not to ask whether I had ever checked to find out if the professor who accused him in the appeal had any connection with the Nixon Justice Department.

7

Watergate, Spiro Agnew, and Other Crimes

T he vice president of the United States was red-faced on the Evening News. He was angry, and he was angry at me.

"Leaks!" Spiro Agnew spit out the word as if it had a sour taste.

"Leaks have sprung in unprecedented quantities, and the resultant publication of distortions and half-truths has led to a cruel form of kangaroo trial in the media, the accusatory stories maliciously supplied by anonymous sources."

That a speech by a vice president appearing before an assemblage of Republican women in Los Angeles was reported on network television was evidence enough that something heavy was coming down. That he was going to direct it at me had been revealed the previous morning, September 28, 1973, on the front page of the *New York Times.*

The headline had said, "Agnew Reaches Decision:

Intends To Fight, Not Quit," and the story explained that Agnew's fighting words were directed at me. My old friend James Reston had pulled off the first interview with Agnew since the word leaked out two months before that the Justice Department was investigating charges that the vice president was on the take.

The interview was a signal by Agnew. He was positioning himself to launch a counterattack against the federal prosecutors by beating up on his old antagonists, the news media. He would, Reston said, allege that the Justice Department was attempting to force him from office by leaking damaging information to reporters—especially me.

Agnew had zeroed in on a story I had broadcast the prior weekend reporting that the Justice Department had the goods on him and that the chief prosecutor had crowed, "We've got the evidence, we've got it cold." As he strung out the final purple passages of his speech to the Republican women, it became clear that Agnew would hold my story up as an example of journalistic excess, threatening the very foundation of the criminal justice system.

His forthcoming struggle would not be to save himself, the vice president declared, but to preserve "the fundamental judicial principles of this country." Otherwise, Agnew shouted, "the endless 'leaks' must inevitably violate not only the rights of an individual but the right of every American."

As a drowning man reviews his past, my future flashed before my eyes. I flinched.

Agnew had singled me out as his CBS whipping-boy. He would subpoena my notes. I didn't have any notes.

My story was accurate, but I couldn't explain how I got it because it came to me through a fluke that would wreck a Chicago lawyer's career if it were disclosed.

The judge would order me to reveal my sources. I would refuse. The judge would put me in jail. Because the judge lived in Baltimore, it would be the Baltimore jail. Being a Yale man, I had always assumed that if I ever went to jail it would be the kind that had tennis courts. The Baltimore jail had no tennis courts. All it had was a very bad reputation.

My assumption had always been that, if I were ever involved in a situation such as this, I would confront it with square-jawed confidence, serene in the righteousness of my cause and the protection of the First Amendment. It didn't happen exactly that way.

Throughout most of this period, I did manage the devil-may-care demeanor that seemed to be expected. I continued to devote much of my time to Watergate hearings at the U.S. district courthouse and maneuvered Agnew's lawyers into subpoenaing me on the courthouse steps. There I tossed off a well-rehearsed response for the assembled TV cameras that made all the evening news broadcasts.

"In the legal world," I said, "If you're weak on the facts, you pound on the law. If you're weak on the law, you pound on the facts. If you're weak on the law and the facts, you pound on the table."

"This is Vice President Agnew's way of pounding on the table."

I thought that was a pretty good line, until Bill Small, CBS's drill-sergeant bureau chief, came up to me after Evening News time.

All he said was, "I saw you hamming it up before the cameras today." It was said almost as a question, as if my wise-guy response had struck a false note that had set him to wondering.

Small's quizzical instinct was right. Of all the stories I had ever reported, this one would head the list of those I would not want to become the focus of a national controversy.

The story had a flaw, and Agnew had pounced on it. It purported to quote a statement made by a high Justice Department official during secret plea-bargaining with Agnew's lawyers. On its face, that disclosure seemed to pose the questions about leaks and improper media coverage that Agnew had raised.

Beneath the surface, my story was even more troubling. It reflected many of the problems inherent in the adversarial brand of journalism that had become the network style as a result of Watergate. In the reporting of the Agnew story—by me and by others—there *had* been elements of a too-cozy relationship with the Justice Department, of a bias against the Nixon-Agnew administration, of frenzied pack journalism, and of carelessness born of arrogance.

In theory, there should never have been an "Agnew Under Investigation" story. The matter was before a federal grand jury in Baltimore, and the law says that such matters should be kept secret until the suspect is charged in an indictment.

The theory didn't pan out because a bevy of the richest government contractors in Baltimore were hauled before the grand jury, where they were accused of paying kickbacks to Spiro Agnew. Then some of them were offered immunity if they would squeal on the kick-backee. They all had lawyers, wives, and business partners, some of whom couldn't resist spreading the word that the vice president was about to take a fall. Once that broke into print, the word "Watergate!" lit up like neon in the minds of all of us who earned our bread covering scandals in Washington.

Any editor or television news producer who might have held back—on the principle of presumed innocence, or that Agnew might have been falsely accused—soon vanished into another line of work, or was trampled in the stampede to get out in front of the story.

Watergate had already certified the Nixon administration as a nest of scoundrels. Agnew's attacks on the news media had persuaded most of us that he was one of the worst. I had observed Agnew at close range while covering his vice presidential campaign, and he had come across as an unfortunate example of Richard Nixon's knack for picking small-bore people for important jobs. No reporter pursuing the bribery story ever expressed any substantial doubts to me about Agnew's guilt—so the cry of the pack that set out after the story was not "Did this guy do it?" but "How do we get the goods on this guy?" As a result, there was a pell-mell quality to the scramble for the smoking gun. This did not set a tone of caution and reserve.

With the basic story out, more information began to seep from the pores of the criminal justice system. Agnew accused the prosecutors of leaking the story in an effort to restore the Justice Department's reputation in the wake of its flabby pursuit of Watergate. He was mistaken about that. Everybody in the Justice Department who was *directly* involved in the Agnew case refused to discuss it with me and, as far as I know, with any other reporter.

But in the broader criminal justice system, a lawyers' gossip mill eagerly swapped facts, theories, and rumors about the Agnew case. The loop included other personnel within the Justice Department, the staffs of oversight committees on Capitol Hill, former prosecutors who had become defense lawyers, and various other lawyerly nooks and crannies in Washington.

An outpouring of media stories ensued about the supposedly secret investigation—and in a narrow sense, Agnew was right about the reason. There *was* a feeling in the Washington legal community of pride and relief that the Justice Department, after failing to pursue the higher-ups responsible for Watergate, was finally prosecuting a Nixon administration bigshot. This encouraged an atmosphere in which normally discreet people talked.

Against this backdrop a fluke disclosure tipped me off that Agnew was plea-bargaining with the prosecutors. Phil Jones, a fellow correspondent at CBS News, had gotten a call from a Democratic staffer on Capitol Hill with an astonishing story. The staffer had just heard from a trusted friend, a Chicago lawyer who had come to Washington for a meeting at the Justice Department. While there, he had overheard a government lawyer discuss the secret inside story of the Agnew case. All this had spilled out in a cramped office where two government lawyers had their desks, one conducting business with the Chicago visitor while the other talked heatedly on the phone about the plea bargaining.

The substance of the story went public right there.

Agnew was willing to resign in exchange for a promise that he would not be prosecuted. The chief of the Criminal Division, Henry Petersen, had taken a hard line for the Justice Department. He insisted that Agnew plead guilty and face the possibility of a jail sentence, and he declared that he had the evidence to convict Agnew if the case went to trial. After the government lawyer hung up, his roommate looked at the flabbergasted eavesdropper from Chicago and made it official: "I guess you know what that's about, don't you? Agnew."

What we had was a terrific story carrying the ring of truth, but a story we could not use without verification from another, more traditional source. My job was to find that person.

I spent the next two days combing through every source I had. What I got was a perplexing blur of fact and fiction that had become a typical phenomenon of Watergate-era reporting. At the Justice Department, the story had quickly become a rumor that many had heard but nobody with firsthand knowledge would confirm. People who wanted to appear more important than they were would affirm that the story was true, but when pressed for verification they did not seem to be in a position to know. One aide confirmed that Petersen had held out for a guilty plea, telling Agnew's lawyers, "We've got the evidence; we've got it cold," but he wouldn't say how he knew that. (Petersen told me later that he had said words to that effect to some of Attorney General Elliot Richardson's assistants, who apparently spread the quote as part of the plea-bargaining gossip.) At times I even suspected that I was hearing echoes of my own questions asked of other sources; my inquiries (and other reporters') were becoming part of the feedback.

By "Evening News" time on Friday evening, the story was ricocheting around the Washington rumor mill, but I still could not assure my superiors that it was true. I chose not to do a story and went home for the weekend.

During the night a call came from the CBS News national desk in New York.

"The *Washington Post* confirmed your story," the night man said. "It's all over tomorrow's front page— 'Agnew Plea Bargaining.' "

As he filled in the details, I felt the familiar sag of every reporter who has let a great story get away and can't decide whether to be proud of his high standards of verification or ashamed of being chicken. Based on the *Post*'s information, I could tell that my story had been accurate. I agreed to record it later over the telephone for the morning radio news roundup.

A few restless hours later, still in the dumps over being beaten on the story, I rolled out of bed, sat on the floor, and—with my baby daughter Lys crawling all over me—wrote my story in longhand and read it by phone to a recorder in New York.

That is not the way they teach it in Journalism 101, and they are right. It was an unprofessionally casual way to handle an important story, and it gave Agnew's lawyers the ammunition they needed to launch their counterattack. All of my information about the plea bargaining proved correct, but when I added, "Petersen was quoted as saying, 'We've got the evidence, we've got it cold,' " that gave Agnew's lawyers an opening to claim that Petersen had been talking directly to me.

They did—and even though it was obvious from my script that Petersen hadn't said it to me, Agnew's lawyers counterattacked on the issue of a top prosecutor smearing the vice president on CBS.

Over the next few weeks, Agnew's side turned the "leak" issue into a sideshow that shoved the main event into the background.

They subpoenaed my notebook, not knowing that for the hectic days in question it contained mostly reminders to have my shoes half-soled. My lawyer denounced the subpoena as a violation of the First Amendment and a threat to freedom of the press. Agnew's lawyers called for a court hearing, at which they would grill me and eight other reporters about the sources of our Agnew stories.

This request was enthusiastically granted by the presiding federal district judge, Walter Hoffman, a grumpy old curmudgeon famous for his tyrannical inclinations and his dislike for the press. Judge Hoffman promptly lived up to his reputation by growling that "we are rapidly approaching the day when the perpetual conflict between the news media, operating as they do under freedom of speech and freedom of the press, and the judicial system, charged with protecting the rights of persons under investigation for criminal acts, must be resolved!" That said, Judge Hoffman huffed from the courthouse and, when a TV crew tried to take his picture, knocked down a cameraman with his car.

At that point, the sideshow took center stage. Judge Hoffman set an early date for the grilling of the reporters. Publishing and broadcasting executives issued ringing declarations of support. Right-wing politicians defended Agnew by accusing the media of piling on. Two reporters from New York protested that Agnew's lawyers had unfairly not subpoenaed them, because they were from out of town.

Meanwhile, Henry Petersen was taking a pounding from Agnew's attorneys for allegedly spouting off to CBS. There was an irony to their claim that Petersen had come down hard on Agnew to compensate for Petersen's powder-puff investigation of Watergate. Petersen told me later that Agnew himself had gone to the White House, complaining that the Baltimore prosecutors were being too hardnosed in their investigation of him. He asked that Petersen be placed personally in charge.

"I guess Agnew thought I'd taken it easy on Nixon in Watergate and that I'd be a soft touch." Petersen smiled. Agnew's tactic backfired. When his lawyers came to the Justice Department to cut a deal, Petersen tried to slam-dunk the vice president. So later, when my quote gave Agnew's team a club to use against Petersen, they hammered him with it.

At that point my Presbyterian heritage blindsided me with a force not covered by the First Amendment: guilt. I had gotten Petersen into this, and it seemed to me that I should get him out. I issued a statement declaring, "Mr. Petersen has never discussed the merits of the vice president's case with me." There is a theory among some journalists and their lawyers that you never disclaim anyone as having been a source, for fear of triggering a narrowing-down process that could eventually identify the true source. My superiors at CBS and my lawyer turned out to be members of this school. I caught some heat from both for handing Petersen a free pass that might give Agnew's lawyers a wedge to crack me with someday in court.

It didn't work out that way, and I was never queasy over the chance I took. Journalists sometimes forget that they ask sources to take chances almost every time they probe for sensitive information, and when a public figure is unjustly taking a drubbing for being too open, a reporter should assume the risk of taking him off the hook.

In any event, my legal position had become so fragile that I had little to lose.

One solution would have been to explain that the leak had been a fluke. The catch to that was that the Chicago lawyer would have to be persuaded to step forward and admit that he had passed along to the Democrats a conversation overheard while doing business in Richard Nixon's Justice Department.

When Phil Jones ran that suggestion past his source on Capitol Hill, I could all but hear the screams from the Senate Office Building.

"There's no way you can ever disclose that name!" said one scream. "He'd be dead as a lawyer in Washington!"

Having lost the option of telling the truth, I turned to my lawyer. He advised me to pack my toothbrush and razor for an extended stay behind bars. Justice Byron White—possibly with a vision in mind of me in the Baltimore jail—had recently written a hardnosed Supreme Court opinion wiping out any First Amendment right of a reporter to refuse to divulge a source in situations such as this.

So on the appointed day of the hearing I packed my

briefcase with a toothbrush, a razor, and a long, racy novel and prepared to do some time in the Baltimore jail.

Judge Hoffman's courtroom was astir that day. I at first attributed this to the cumulative pleasure of a roomful of spectators waiting to see nine reporters held in contempt and hauled off to the local poky. I realized that something else was afoot when the government's legal team arrived. It was led by Attorney General Richardson, whose presence did not seem necessary to dispatch a gaggle of reporters to the hoosegow.

Next, a court officer stepped over to the table where the reporters and their counsel were waiting. He whispered to John Mudd, a lawyer for *Time* magazine, who had the same impressive demeanor as his brother, Roger Mudd.

"Mr. Mudd, there's an important phone call for you on the telephone down the hall. It's from a lawyer from Richmond who says he's working with you on the Agnew case," the bailiff said.

Mudd rushed down the hall and grabbed the phone.

"John!" an excited voice said. "We've just heard that Spiro Agnew is going to cop a plea at your hearing!"

Mudd screamed something about calling him out of the courtroom to tell him what was about to happen in it and ran back down the corridor. The courtroom door had been closed, and a Secret Service agent was blocking the way.

"Nobody gets in," the man said. "Something important's happening in there."

Something historic was happening, and Mudd missed it.

Spiro Agnew entered, somber but composed. It was

obvious, from the moment he appeared, that this was the end of his vice presidency.

The lawyers and the judge went through the formalities, with Agnew saying just enough to make it clear on the record that he agreed with what was being done. Agnew had cut a deal with the Justice Department. He had resigned as vice president and had entered a plea of no contest to the government's charges. The prosecutors accused him of failing to pay taxes on kickbacks he had received and did not ask for jail time.

As the proceeding unfolded, it became painfully apparent that the patsies in this affair had been us.

Agnew's attacks on me, Henry Petersen, and the "leaks" had been a ruse to give the vice president's lawyers leverage in their plea bargaining with the prosecutors. The strategy had worked. By threatening to carry out a long and nasty leak investigation from the vice president's office, Agnew cooled the prosecutors' determination to force him into a guilty plea and a possible jail sentence. While the news media had been fuming over the leak probe, Agnew, the prosecutors, and Judge Hoffman had quietly put together a compromise. The judge found him guilty of tax evasion and gave him probation.

As Agnew was hustled from the courtroom, Judge Hoffman slipped down from the bench and vanished into his chambers. To me, Agnew had just given new meaning to the term "moot case." With his case resolved, there was no need for a search for leaks, or a refusal to testify, or a trip to the Baltimore jail.

My reaction was relief at the freedom to go back to reporting the news, rather than making it; I won an

Emmy award, along with my colleagues on the "CBS Evening News," for our coverage of the events of that day.

But a sense of unease lingered about the Agnew affair. It seemed to represent a signal, a yellow flash of caution, that the reassuring journalistic certitudes of the Watergate era were wearing thin.

For the first year, covering Watergate for CBS had been "white hat" journalism. We were the good guys pursuing the villains, as the public hissed and booed the other side. The four of us on the CBS Watergate "team"—Dan Rather, Dan Schorr, Lesley Stahl, and I— were treated by many as honorary members of the prosecution, participants in an historic cleansing of a corrupt presidency. The Agnew affair brought forward the first disturbing shades of gray: a skeptical judiciary, complicated relations with government sources, the competitive pressures of pack journalism, occasional incidents of carelessness, and a hardening of public attitudes against Watergate-style reporting.

At first, Watergate had tended to obscure these warning signals because the public had its attention glued to the chase and didn't ask many questions. But once the consensus of the Watergate era began to fade, people became more willing to pause to consider the side issues churned up by the new style of aggressive journalism. Some tensions were inevitable in a journalistic process that boiled down to making public what some people wanted to keep private. But television, with its fierce competition, early deadlines, and immediate impact, seemed to sharpen the ethical issues inherent in all journalism.

On one occasion I was even accused of acting uneth-ically by supposedly attempting, as a journalist, to per-suade a fellow lawyer to violate *his* legal ethics.

It happened soon after the existence of the White House tapes became known, when a young Washington lawyer named William Dobrovir subpoenaed one of the tapes and, surprisingly, got it. The case was a civil law-suit growing out of President Nixon's decision to in-crease federal milk price supports, and the subpoena seemed to catch the White House by surprise. One day the tape arrived at attorney Dobrovir's little walk-up of-fice over an electrical appliance shop.

I heard about it and rushed over with a CBS electron-ics technician equipped to transpose the slow-turning White House tapes into a speed that could be played on an ordinary tape recorder.

Frustrated by his inability to play his tape, Dobrovir was at first amenable to my offer of a deal: my technician would fix his tape so that he could understand it if he would let me make a copy to play on the air.

The understanding was this: I would hold my copy of the tape until the lawyer filed the original as evidence in court. I suggested four-thirty some afternoon, just before the courthouse closed. Then I could play excerpts from my tape all that evening on CBS, while our competition at NBC and ABC ate their hearts out (if any).

But while the technician was doing his work, attor-ney Dobrovir's phone rang: it was Carl Stern of NBC making his own pitch for the tape. Then about a half-dozen other reporters called with the same idea. At one point the phones became so busy that I was fielding other reporters' calls. I told them the tape wouldn't be available for several days. It began to dawn on Dobrovir that if he let me have the tape early there would be a press riot.

He reconsidered our deal and reneged. I left, tapeless.

That evening, Dobrovir played the White House tape for the entertainment of a Georgetown cocktail party. Among the audience was an employee of ABC News, which one-upped me by broadcasting an exclusive story about the playing of my tape at the party.

The trial judge was not amused. He called Dobrovir into court and raked him over the coals for his extrajudicial use of court evidence.

Elements of the conservative press added insult to my injury at being scooped by charging that I had unethically solicited the lawyer to violate his own code of ethics. The claim was that I had encouraged Dobrovir to try his case in the media in violation of the ethical rules against pretrial publicity and that I had enticed him to violate the lawyer's oath to demean himself "uprightly."

I replied that the complaints against me were in the same class as the Tennessee politician who accused his opponent of being "up there in Washington committing nepotism with his own daughter." I was up there in Washington doing what reporters do, trying to get news. It was not my job to worry about a lawyer's uprightness or to agonize about the legal code of ethics before asking an attorney for information. But the incident served as an early warning of how the emotions and tensions generated by television news tended to make ethical issues larger than life.

————

Arlene Francis, a former actress turned talk show host, taught me my first lesson about television and ethics. From her I learned how television, and the people who appear on it, inevitably use each other—and how this can be done without compromising the ethics of either side. It was a valuable lesson, and I learned it early.

During World War II, my mother admired Arlene Francis's radio program, "Blind Date," and we often listened to it together. We thought it was romantic and patriotic for the program to give the servicemen a chance to win dates with beautiful New York models and to treat the winners to evenings at the Stork Club or the Copacabana.

By 1949, when I went north for the first time to enroll at Yale, I knew nothing of television—it had not yet reached Nashville—but I had picked up a pointer or two about seizing opportunities. A brief article in the *Yale Daily News* noted that Arlene Francis had shifted "Blind Date" to television and, with the war over, had switched her attentions to college men. Her representative would appear at Yale to select some college types to go on her show.

I volunteered, laying on all the Southern charm that an eighteen year old could muster. They chose me, and within weeks after seeing TV for the first time, I went off to New York to be on television.

Prior to the show, Arlene Francis took me aside and made it clear that the qualities that had caught their attention had been my Southern accent and my position on the Yale wrestling team. She hinted pointedly that I should play up this combination for the benefit of the TV audience. I was young, but I had not been born yesterday—so when the show got under way, I came on like a cross between Andy Griffin and Hulk Hogan. The object was to be more charming than the fellow from

Princeton, who also wanted to win the girl, so at one point I swooped him up across my shoulders and swung him around in an exaggerated wrestling spin.

This created the dramatic high point of the show; the Princeton man's foot struck Arlene Francis in the eye and sent her reeling across the stage. I did not win the girl and considered my television career prematurely ended.

To my surprise, they summoned me back for a repeat performance the next week, saying I had been a big hit. I wondered about that, since I had not won the date. Asking no questions, I returned to New York.

There, all was revealed. Miss Francis had developed a shiner from my wrestling escapade of the week before. She was wearing a black eye patch with a bright "G" on it, to drive home the point that the program was sponsored by the makers of Gruen watches.

My return appearance gave her the opening for a light-hearted explanation of the eyepatch—and, of course, the "G".

I responded with a thick Southern accent and no wrestling holds.

This time, I won the girl.

It was a harmless introduction to the back-scratching relationship that always exists between the people of television and those who agree to go on the air. When television people put someone on TV, there is always an unspoken price—that the person will try to be informative, interesting, even entertaining. Everyone who wants to appear on television, either to sell an idea or a product or to flatter his own ego, implicitly agrees to pay this price.

This subtle trade-off also applies to television news,

and it is present whenever TV reporters conduct an interview or attend a news conference. The reciprocal benefits are so obvious that I have always wondered at purists who wring their hands over another version of this back-scratching phenomenon—the frequently cordial relationships between Washington journalists and the high government officials who are their sources.

The critics' implication is that the reporters are being used—that they soft-pedal their critical scrutiny to preserve their access to the high-and-mighty. The reality is that reporters and their sources use each other on an ongoing basis and that every reporter avoids burning his sources whenever possible. It is the same whether the sources are in high positions or low, and so long as the journalists do not ignore negative stories to preserve their contacts, it is just business as usual, and no harm done.

My experience in Washington was that the information to be gained from good relations with high government officials far outweighed the occasional discomfort of being too close.

I did have a bad moment with Attorney General Richard Kleindienst, who was sometimes known to blubber when in his cups. One night at a banquet we were seated together at the head table, and while the featured speaker was holding forth, I tried to pump Kleindienst about the legal troubles that eventually led to his conviction for fudging on the truth during congressional testimony. Kleindienst broke down and began to weep into my ear. I was caught between trying to appear sympathetic enough to encourage Kleindienst to be indiscreet but not so chummy that I would look bad if we were photographed by the TV cameramen recording the speech. None did, and eventually Kleindienst stopped crying and finished the evening as if nothing had happened.

The Nixon men posed little danger in the coziness department. Most preferred to keep a chilly distance from the press. Attorney General John Mitchell made an early attempt to thaw things out by having thank-God-it's-Friday sessions with reporters in his office on Friday evenings. The idea was to sip a few drinks and loosen things up, but Mitchell got drunk and abusive on a couple of occasions, and everybody was relieved when he gave it up.

My experience was that the men close to Nixon weren't very revealing anyway. But one day, after the scandals had been laid bare, I caught Bob Haldeman in what seemed to be a thoughtful and reflective mood. As White House chief of staff, Haldeman had been at the president's side during the most wrenching experiences of that historic period, and I saw an opportunity to gain a rare insight into events that the rest of us had only witnessed from a distance. I asked Haldeman what was the most important lesson that he had learned from those years.

He thought for a moment, and then in slow, thoughtful tones, said there was one lesson he had learned.

"The president," Haldeman said, "should always have his press conferences at eight o'clock in the evening—not in the morning, as we usually did. If you wait until evening, you get a much bigger TV audience, especially on the West Coast."

I gave up.

Only one of the Watergate figures seemed to grow and learn from the experience. John Ehrlichman came to the Nixon White House uptight, aloof, and arrogant and emerged from the trials of Watergate loose, friendly, and arrogant. Ehrlichman's saving grace was a sense of humor, which he managed to maintain in public most of the time, despite troubles that would have broken many men.

Ehrlichman spent much of one Thanksgiving holiday on trial in Judge John Sirica's court. During the lunch break on the Friday after Thanksgiving day, Ehrlichman and I could find only one dreary greasy spoon cafe open in deserted downtown Washington. The counterman recognized Ehrlichman, who mustered a wry joke about how, if it wasn't for the honor, he'd just as soon not be on trial over the Thanksgiving holiday.

"Oh well," chuckled the counterman, "no rest for the wicked!" Horrified, he clapped his hand over his mouth, as Ehrlichman had his only laugh of the day.

Ehrlichman got the last laugh on many of us.

His life seemed devastated after Sirica sentenced him to two and a half to eight years in prison, his marriage broke up, and he went off to serve his time. Three years later, in February of 1979, I arrived in Chicago one bitter cold night—travel-weary, disheveled, and in need of a comforting experience. A colleague and I straggled into one of the city's most expensive restaurants and presented ourselves to the dubious maitre d'.

As the captain peered first at us and his reservation book, I caught the eye of a bearded man seated with an attractive women at one of the best tables in the house. It was Ehrlichman. He had been out of prison for several months, and stories had circulated that Ehrlichman had moved to Santa Fe, launched a promising career as a writer, and become a free spirit. I thought it would be nice to pause and chat with him on the way to our table. I made a mental note to be suave about this and not permit our encounter to become awkward because he was a former jailbird.

Just as Ehrlichman spotted me, the maitre d' decreed that the restaurant was full and began to back my colleague and me toward the door. An obviously rehabilitated Ehrlichman shot me a truimphant smile and a see-you-later wave, as the captain ushered us out into the night.

The purists who say Washington reporters should keep high public officials at arm's length obviously do not understand how difficult fending off a Washington politician can be.

George Bush had a way of inviting people home whom he probably didn't really want as guests. During the political season of 1984, the story went around that Bush had run into Gary Hart, who said he was about to spend some time in Maine, where a Democratic presidential primary was coming up. Vice President Bush, whose job Hart was ultimately trying to terminate, piped up with, "Barbara and I have a place at Kennebunkport. We'd love to have you come and stay there."

I lived near the vice president's residence in Washington, and on the Sunday morning before the election, my wife and I were waiting to play on a neighborhood tennis court when Bush came jogging up. As his Secret Service agents eyed me warily, Bush chatted with us for a while. We mentioned that the court would probably be closed down, in respect to a nearby church service, before we got a chance to play.

"Say, I've got a tennis court at my house," the vice president said. "Why don't you come on over and play on our court?"

It was an intriguing invitation because Bush didn't know me well enough to justify an offer like that, yet he seemed to mean it. It occurred to me that such gestures may be freebies for people in the vice president's position—they get the satisfaction of offering, and nobody ever says yes. For a moment I was tempted to accept, just to see how it would play. But the Secret Service men looked crestfallen, and Bush's invitation seemed too well meaning to risk turning it sour. So I said no, and he and the relieved Secret Service men jogged on their way.

———

One reason why television news churned up so many ethical issues in the wake of Watergate was the perception that network news had become the King Kong of journalism. It was true that under certain conditions, TV news had considerable weight to throw around and could trample various interests in the process. As an insider, I felt that TV's clout was often exaggerated, because I had seen that television news could be ineffectual when a story did not have the ingredients of good TV.

From the outset, Watergate had the requisite heroes, villains, and suspense to be boffo TV; only pictures were lacking to make the story a television smash. They were often provided by the supposedly video-savvy minions of Richard Nixon.

They did it, for instance, on the weekend of the "Sat-

urday Night Massacre," in a clumsy effort to play down
the firing of Archibald Cox as Watergate special prosecutor. The Nixon men waited until the networks had completed their evening news broadcasts on Friday night
and then notified Cox he was being discharged—assuming that the public reaction would be cushioned by the
normal weekend news slump and that by the time the
networks returned to full-scale news coverage on Monday evening things would have cooled down.

It worked just the opposite way.

Walter Cronkite happened to be in Washington that
Friday night to receive an award at a Press Club banquet. I was there, in a tuxedo, when the word began to
filter through the hall that something heavy was coming
down on the special prosecutor. I borrowed a Sony audio
recorder and jogged a half-mile through Washington's
dark, empty streets to the Special Prosecutor's Office.

The scene there was a mixture of anger and righteous
indignation. President Nixon had ordered a stop to the
subpoenas of the White House tapes. Young men on
Cox's staff with ties askew were muttering curses, clearing out filing cabinets, slamming documents around, and
generally making every rebellious gesture short of bar-
ricading the street. Archibald Cox seemed a tall, crewcut
island of calm, but when I asked for a comment he made
a defiant statement into my recorder.

I jogged to CBS in time to appear, sweaty tux and all,
in a special report at the top of the CBS local stations'
late news broadcasts. That broadcast had an events-are-
happening immediacy that all but shouted "stay tuned."

Friday night's touch of drama grabbed the public's

attention, and it remained riveted to TV throughout the weekend. The Nixon administration complied with a series of made-for-television images that could have substituted for the coup scenes in a banana republic rebellion.

There were the FBI agents sealing off the entrances to the Justice Department, the professorial special prosecutor—bow tie, crewcut, and all—challenging the president at a press conference while his staff carried cartons of documents away to private hiding places, the little-known solicitor general, Robert Bork, taking over for the fired attorney general, and the lights burning into the late hours at the White House.

The result was a firestorm of public reaction that threw President Nixon into permanent retreat but did little to teach his handlers the hazards of incriminating pictures.

When Nixon's faithful secretary, Rose Mary Woods, later told an unlikely story of having accidentally erased eighteen and a half minutes of a White House tape, there was, at first, little the public could do but wonder. But then the White House released a glorious color picture of Miss Woods demonstrating how the "accident" allegedly happened—an innocent reach for the telephone while her foot appeared to be groping for the recorder's erasure pedal. I couldn't resist billing it on the air as the "Rose Mary Stretch," and it quickly convinced millions of television viewers that the Nixon White House must have much to hide.

But when television news lacked striking pictures, or an emotional tale to tell, it could be curiously impotent.

I learned this when I revealed on the "CBS Evening

Second grader Fred Graham mugged the camera (center, hand thoughtfully to chin) as Texarkana's Depression-era overachievers sat for their school portrait in 1938. The first to become a billionaire was (top row, second from left, white shirt and black belt) H. Ross Perot.

Law practice in Nashville involved such scenes as grilling a portly detective while gesturing toward a worldly-looking client. Graham quickly switched from litigation to reporting on the law as a journalist. (Gerald Holly/*The Nashville Tennessean*)

The "Tennessee Connection" gave Graham a link to Justice Abe Fortas and Tennessee Senator Albert Gore Sr. The friendship with Justice Fortas ended when Fortas termed one of Graham's articles "enough to drive a man to kill." (George Tames/NYT Pictures)

On June 15, 1971, after a federal judge ordered the *New York Times* to cease publication of the Pentagon Papers, editors James Greenfield, Max Frankel and Graham discussed how to report the story in the *Times*. The editors did not know Graham had hidden the Pentagon Papers "on ice." (AP/Wide World Photos)

Chief Justice Warren Burger conducted guerrilla warfare against the news media. Through it all, he and Graham remained friends.

At the *Times,* the Graham byline included a dignified middle initial.

Graham's first appearance on the "CBS Evening News" included squalling babies. (CBS News, reprinted with permission)

FRED P. GRAHAM

NEWS
THE WHITE HOUSE

As fellow members of the CBS "Watergate team," Graham and Dan Rather raked in the Emmy Awards in 1973.

On the night President Nixon announced his resignation, Graham and Daniel Schorr prepared questions for Walter Cronkite to ask. Schorr had all the answers. (CBS News, reprinted with permission)

Van Gordon Sauter and Ed Joyce were put in charge of CBS News shortly after Dan Rather became its star anchor. Sauter brought "infotainment" to CBS; Joyce brought the nickname, "the velvet shiv." (AP/Wide World Photos)

Graham's contract with CBS said he would become moderator of "Face the Nation." Joyce decreed that "Face the Nation" was no longer "Face the Nation," and gave the job to Lesley Stahl. Graham and Stahl remained friends, teamed up to grill Attorney General Ed Meese. (Reni Newsphotos, Inc. Reprinted with permission of CBS News)

On election night, Dan Rather left tell-tale evidence that his good-old-boy sayings had been ghostwritten by a Texas sports writer. (CBS News, reprinted with permission)

Graham attempted to broaden his career by anchoring such lesser CBS programs as the "CBS Morning News," (here, with Diane Sawyer) "Face the Nation" and "Nightwatch." The risk was that Dan Rather, and the New York Executives known as the Grown Ups, might feel that the "CBS Evening News with Dan Rather" was being slighted. (CBS News, reprinted with permission)

Graham's return to Nashville as Channel 2's co-anchor with
local star Anne Holt rated billboards and a new slogan. Some
people got the wrong idea. (WKRN-TV, Channel 2, Nashville,
TN)

Channel 2's Can Man was
a klutzy symbol of civic
good works. Unfortu-
nately, the Can Man
lacked vision. (WKRN-
TV, Channel 2, Nashville,
TN)

Energetic weatherman Tom
Siler dropped his routine as
the "Weather Wizard," but
still confronted the weather
map with the windmill style
of a man fighting bees.
(WKRN-TV, Channel 2,
Nashville, TN)

Graham hoped to contribute substance to the broadcasts by engaging in "meaningful happy talk" with co-anchor Anne Holt. (Tim Campbell)

News" the story behind the rift between one of Washington's most prominent politicians and FBI Director J. Edgar Hoover—and nobody noticed.

Back in 1971, when Representative Hale Boggs of Louisiana walked onto the floor of the House and called for the resignation of the director of the FBI, it grabbed the kind of attention on Capitol Hill that Pavarotti would have received strolling onto the stage of the Met singing rock.

Boggs was the kind of establishment figure who would not be expected to tangle with Hoover. He was the Democratic majority leader of the House, a prudent politician who knew that Hoover's reputation for punishing his critics was thoroughly deserved. But Boggs used harsh words in accusing Hoover's FBI of suppressing the Bill of Rights and adopting "the tactics of the Soviet Union and Hitler's Gestapo." Many people agreed that what Boggs was saying was true, but his reasons for saying it were never revealed. The following year, on October 16, Hale Boggs took off in a light plane over an Alaskan glacier and was never seen or heard from again.

Two years after Boggs' disappearance, I obtained a packet of documents found among his papers that seemed to explain the congressman's blast at Hoover. Boggs had been a member of the Warren Commission that investigated the assassination of President John F. Kennedy, and he had been concerned about questions raised by a prominent author and critic of the FBI's handling of the assassination. In an effort to discredit the author, the FBI had sent Boggs sworn affidavits from two women who described some highly imaginative kinky sex they had performed with the author. As if to prove beyond doubt that the author's criticisms were without merit, the FBI sent along a snapshot of the author being kinky. Boggs's son, well-known Washington lawyer-lobbyist Thomas Boggs, told me this use of sexual scandal by the FBI turned his father against Hoover, because Boggs believed the FBI was keeping similar files on others, including members of Congress.

On January 29, 1975, I broadcast the story on the "CBS Evening News," complete with the carefully masked photograph of the author unclothed. At present, the television signal of that broadcast is still hurtling through space, trillions of miles away—and if any living creature, human or otherwise, has ever taken note of it, the word has not filtered back to me.

There was no follow-up story in any newspaper, no pick-up by the wire services, no mention, to my knowledge, in any of the books that have been written of Hoover's misdeeds. In print, this story would have become an important footnote to Boggs's career and to Hoover's reputation. But on television it flashed past, raising little but puzzled glances on its way into the void.

In contrast, shortly before I switched to CBS in 1972 I wrote a story in the *New York Times* about two other deceased political figures—John F. and Robert Kennedy—that touched off a protest demonstration in Washington. My story disclosed that President Kennedy's brain, preserved in a jar of formalin, was missing from the autopsy items lodged in the National Archives. There was a heavy hint in my story that the brain had been discreetly disposed of by Bobby Kennedy.

A group of the paranoid types who were then spinning out various Kennedy assassination theories (including the kinky author) staged a demonstration at the Archives building—and managed to imply that the real culprit was somehow Richard Nixon.

For the journalists who were presumably less paranoid and had the job of covering the Nixon administration, President Nixon became a perpetual ethical hazard. By the spring of 1974 he had been implicated in so many seamy events that the threshold of credibility about alleged Nixon misdeeds had slipped to an all-time presidential low. On May 10, 1974, I fell afoul of the Nixon enigma.

Leaks from the Watergate Special Prosecutor's Office were few and far between, but when a junior attorney on the staff heard that Richard Nixon had called Daniel Ellsberg a "Jew boy," he was incensed enough to spread the word to me.

"Jew boy," he said, was only one of numerous anti-Semitic remarks by Nixon sprinkled through the White House tapes. No, he had not heard these remarks firsthand; the tapes were tightly secured, and few people in the office were allowed to listen. But the word had flashed through the office that the president had used those words, he said, and nobody directly in the know had denied it.

At the outset I decided not to touch this one without confirmation from someone who had listened to the tapes. I had a queasy feeling about the way some journalists applied a presumption of guilt to the presidency, and I was not about to lay on this charge unless I was certain it was true. Richard Nixon did not have a reputation for prejudice, and it seemed strangely off-key that this should turn up so late in his life. But if President Nixon was the kind of man who threw around terms like "Jew boy" in the Oval Office, that was an important story—so I turned on the full shoe-leather and phone-call treatment to learn the truth.

Only a few in the Nixon White House and among those investigating it could have heard the tapes. I talked to all I could think of, short of Nixon himself. Their silence was a stone wall. Not one would confirm or deny the story; reporters would have nibbled them to death if they had been willing to play that game.

Still, the story developed a feel of truth. Some who were close to those who knew said they had heard stories of derogatory comments by Nixon about Jews on the tapes.

Then I thought of another person who must have heard the White House tapes. Albert Jenner, a plain-spoken, no-frills Chicago trial lawyer, was the chief Republican counsel for the House of Representatives in its impeachment investigation of President Nixon. I knew him well from various American Bar Association meetings over the years, and he quickly took my call from his temporary office on Capitol Hill.

Sure, Jenner said, he had listened to some of the tapes—but he wasn't about to tell me what was said on them. But Jenner was jovial and chatty—the first person who had actually heard the tapes who was willing to talk about them—and I kept the conversation going, trying to loosen him up.

When I felt I had him warmed up enough, I tried the venerable, "Would I be in trouble . . ." ploy. I told him in detail what my other source had said, that on the tapes Nixon can be heard calling Dan Ellsberg a "Jew boy" and making other anti-Semitic remarks.

"Bert," I said, "it's important that I get this right. I just want you to tell me this: if I report that Nixon called Ellsberg a 'Jew boy' on the tapes, would I get in trouble with that?"

"No, you wouldn't get into any trouble," Jenner said.

Bingo. Jenner was a Republican, with no motive to smear President Nixon with an untruth. It was the confirmation I needed, but I felt a flicker of unease. Jenner had a way of slurring his words, and the slur had worried me as he so readily answered my question. I had wondered in the past if Jenner was a drinker, and it crossed my mind again as I hung up the phone and prepared to write my story.

At six-thirty that evening, Walter Cronkite led the news by introducing my exclusive story about the anti-Semitic remarks by President Nixon. I gave it the full treatment, quoting the "Jew boy" remark and reporting that Nixon was said to have made other slurs against Jews on the tapes.

I had barely made it back from the studio to the newsroom when Bill Small came careening out of his office.

"Al Haig has been on the phone to New York, and he's going crazy," Small said. He said that Haig, then Nixon's chief of staff, had watched my report and had gone straight to the president. Nixon denied it all.

"Haig says this is going too far," Small said. "He says the president isn't anti-Semitic, and this is just tearing him down with a story that isn't true."

"We will stand behind your story," Small said. "But

it's your call, whether we go with it on the seven o'-
clock."

The "Evening News" broadcast seen in most sections
of the country is the seven o'clock version, which is a
replay of the six-thirty tape, with any gaffes or errors
smoothed out. That gave me about twenty minutes to
decide whether to leave my report in the broadcast. I
tried to call my source in the Special Prosecutor's Office
but got no answer. But I got right through to Bert Jenner
on Capitol Hill.

"Bert, Al Haig is going bananas over my report about
Nixon calling Ellsberg a Jew boy. He says Nixon never
said that. I just want to be sure you still back me up that
Nixon said those things."

"I never said Nixon called Ellsberg a Jew boy," Jenner said. He was slurring his words—more, I thought,
than earlier in the day.

It went downhill from there—with me screaming at
Jenner that I had only gone with the story because he
had signaled that it was all right and him repeating
mushily that he didn't know anything about Nixon and
Ellsberg. There wasn't time for me to yell all the things
at Jenner that I wanted to say; only a few minutes remained before the story would be fed out again. (It
wasn't until much later, after Jenner's death, that I could
bring myself to inquire into his drinking habits. Close
associates said he rarely drank to excess; that he always
slurred his speech; and that he probably did not have
enough experience with reporters to known when he
was being asked to stand behind the crucial element of a
story.)

No CBS Correspondent that I knew about had ever

broadcast a story and then turned tail within a half-hour and pulled it off the air. I was humiliated to do it, and I still thought the story was true. But I did not hesitate to pull the plug on that story. While I have often cringed just to think about it, I have never second-guessed my decision. The story had not checked out under the proper standards of verification for a story of that importance. That was part of the necessary baggage that went along with the job of informing the public about its leaders, and I had no regrets.

When I reached my source in the Special Prosecutor's office the next day, he stuck with the "Jew boy" story. Since then, other evidence has surfaced. Former Nixon aide John Ehrlichman has said that Nixon did, indeed, sometimes rail about liberals he called "those Jews," and whom he castigated as "Jewish traitors, and the Eastern Jewish establishment—Jews at Harvard." In 1988 another former Nixon aide, Frederick V. Malek, quit his high-level job with the Bush presidential campaign when it came out that, on Nixon's orders, Malek had gathered figures on the number of Jews in the Labor Department. Nixon was said to have been convinced that a "Jewish cabal" in the Bureau of Labor Statistics was working against him.

The truth about the "Jew boy" allegation cannot be settled until after Richard Nixon's death, when his legal crusade to keep the White House tapes from the public will finally end. At least one person will still care. I will travel to the National Archives to listen to Nixon's words and tidy up a loose strand in his life, and mine.

8

──────◆──────

Telling Secrets

Lesley Stahl was threatening to sue. The defendant, unfortunately, was to be our colleague, Daniel Schorr.

"I am going to get a lawyer. I am going to sue Schorr," Lesley sputtered. "Do you know what he did?"

I sighed. I knew of several things that Schorr had done lately that I fervently wished he had not done. I wished it because I had been involved and because I had not behaved so well myself.

Two weeks earlier, during the first week of February 1976, Dan Schorr had enlisted me to help accomplish something that we both thought worthwhile—and somehow a combination of poor judgment, arrogance, and fear had transformed it into a disaster. In the process, Schorr had engaged in duplicity, and I had deserted a friend.

Lesley and I stood in the same spot in the CBS newsroom where I had been two weeks before, when Schorr first approached me about the Pike Papers. Discussing the Pike Papers was a trendy thing to do those days, because Daniel Schorr had recently made them famous.

It was a time when politicians were making reputations by investigating the past misdeeds of America's intelligence agencies, and a special House committee headed by Representative Otis Pike of New York had compiled a classified, book-length report cataloguing many of the dubious things that America's spooks had done. The report documented serious lapses in U.S. intelligence efforts, such as the failure to foresee Russia's invasion of Czechoslovakia in 1968, the 1973 war in the Middle East, the coup in Cyprus, and India's explosion of an atom bomb. There were also such spicy disclosures as the CIA station in a small country that ran up a one-year liquor bill of $41,000 and the production of a pornographic film for the CIA by Robert Maheu of the Howard Hughes organization. (The CIA's skinflick was a reenactment purporting to show Indonesian President Sukarno in a compromising situation in Moscow, to be used in a convoluted plot to persuade Sukarno that the KGB had made the film and thus incite Sukarno's wrath against the Soviets.)

The Pike Committee voted to release its report, but a funny thing happened on the way to the Government Printing Office—a copy was leaked to Dan Schorr. Schorr flooded the airwaves of CBS with a litany of past adventures and misadventures of American cloak-and-dagger agencies. Many of the incidents had been disclosed in piecemeal fashion before, but the magnitude of the leak to Schorr was so reminiscent of the disclosure of the Pentagon Papers five years before that the new report became immediately notorious as the Pike Papers. Within a couple of days, Schorr had wrung the Pike Papers so dry of juicy tidbits that the CBS producers had to ask him to desist.

By then, the public was overfed on the Pike Papers, and the incident seemed to have run its course. Legally, the full House of Representatives had to vote its approval before the Pike Committee could officially release the report, but since the significant points had been leaked already, House approval seemed a predictable formality.

Few in Washington foresaw that events would be sidetracked by the coincidence of a tragedy half a world away. On the previous Christmas Eve, the CIA station chief in Athens, Greece, had been gunned down on the doorstep of his home. He was a family man named Richard Welch, and his identity had been made public by *Counterspy*, an American publication that specialized in blowing the cover of U.S. agents overseas.

With many Americans still seething over Welch's assassination, the leak of the Pike Papers to Daniel Schorr did it for spook-bashing in the United States. Public opinion swung heavily against further disclosure of secrets, politicians ran for cover, and the House of Representatives voted overwhelmingly against making the Pike Papers public.

The catch was that Dan Schorr already had a copy.

"This has got to come out," Schorr said of the Pike report that night.

An unusual thing had been happening to Schorr; rival journalists had been swallowing their pride and asking him for information from the Pike Papers, to help them develop their own stories. He had been willing to help, but he felt that a permanent solution was needed. The full report, he thought, should be available to journalists, scholars, and the American public. Schorr's point seemed logical. Nobody made a serious case that any secrets remained that could cause any harm if the Pike Papers were published.

Schorr motioned me into his office and picked up a paperback copy of *The Pentagon Papers,* put out by the book publishing division of the *New York Times* company. "This is the way the Pike Papers should be published," he said—with one exception. He explained that the *Times* company had received the authors' royalties when it published the Pentagon Papers in paperback form, which amounted to making windfall book profits off news gathered by its newspaper reporters. Schorr felt that was wrong.

Schorr had a plan to publish the Pike Papers in book form, with an introduction written by him, and with the royalties going to support the First Amendment.

That was where I came in.

Early in the Nixon administration, John Mitchell's Justice Department had hit upon a technique for simultaneously harassing the press and the radical left. The strategy was to call before grand juries those reporters with close sources within radical groups. This would compensate for the FBI's woefully weak informer network within antiwar and black power groups, while driving a wedge of distrust between the radicals and the journalists. An early target of the strategy had been Earl Caldwell of the *New York Times*, who was subpoenaed to tell about the Black Panthers. When he refused even to enter the grand jury room, his superiors at the *Times* seemed less than eager to take on the Justice Department on such uncompromising terms.

Several of us who covered legal affairs in Washington spread the word that a meeting to consider how to protect reporters would be held on a Sunday afternoon at Georgetown University. A crowd of worried journalists squeezed into a meeting room and organized a group called The Reporters Committee for Freedom of the Press. They chose a steering committee that included Tom Wicker, Jack Nelson, Anthony Lukas, Robert Maynard, James Doyle, Eileen Shanahan, and me.

That was the reason for Schorr's approach to me: he proposed to donate all royalties from the publication of the Pike Papers to the Reporters Committee.

I polled the other members of the Reporters Committee by phone, and we agreed on two conditions—that the publication must be legal and that the committee's receipt of the royalties must be spelled out in Schorr's introduction.

To answer the legal question, I telephoned Peter Tufo, a Manhattan lawyer who was making a name as a media specialist and who had recently represented the Reporters Committee pro bono in efforts to stop the New York telephone company from secretly passing reporters' toll call records to investigative authorities. Peter was also a warm and wise counselor, my personal lawyer, and a close friend. At my request on behalf of the committee, he conducted some legal research and reported back that to publish the Pike Papers would not be a criminal act.

Schorr had already declared that his introduction to

the book would state that the royalties would go to the Reporters Committee, to be spent in defense of the First Amendment. So it appeared that the two conditions of the Reporters Committee had been satisfied.

Then Schorr raised one other matter. He said he needed the aid of a Reporters Committee's volunteer lawyer to help with the arrangements for publication. At the moment, this seemed innocent enough to me; providing pro bono legal help for reporters with First Amendment problems was something the Reporters Committee did all the time. I wrote Peter Tufo's name and telephone number on a slip of paper and handed it to Schorr.

I have often thought that if it were possible to identify one specific point in time at which the journalistic glories of the Watergate era began to turn sour, it would have been that moment. We on the Reporters Committee had moved beyond defending reporters' legal rights to assisting in a publication that was well meant but eventually came out looking like a political act. Moreover, our group stood to profit from the act; we had given in to the temptation to do well while doing good.

We had also lost control of how the events would be played out. That was in the hands of Daniel Schorr.

A few days after I gave Schorr the New York lawyer's number, Schorr came to me with a legal question: Did he or CBS own the Pike Papers? We discussed the boilerplate clause in all our contracts that required us to offer any information to CBS before publishing it elsewhere, but since Schorr had offered CBS News Pike Paper stories until his superiors implored him to stop, I couldn't tell whether CBS retained rights to the actual document.

He replied that CBS had asked him to provide a copy of the papers to its book publishing house, Holt, Rinehart & Winston, so that it could consider publishing it in paperback. But he added that Holt, Rinehart didn't seem to be interested; the publishing world had lost much of its appetite for leaked top secret reports, and this one contained long passages that read with all the zip of a plumber's manual. Peter Tufo had touched base with several top paperback publishing houses and was told that they, too, were not interested.

For the first time I began to have a queasy feeling that our venture was not as clear-cut as we had thought. How could Schorr be shopping the Pike Papers around New York if he might have a legal obligation to give them to CBS? I kept my doubts to myself. This was his affair, and it didn't seem to be going anywhere anyway.

But Peter Tufo hadn't given up that easily. He was a member of the board of directors of the company that owned *New York* magazine, and he went for advice to the magazine's publisher, Clay Felker. If ever a character could thicken a plot, it was Felker, a clever and opportunistic veteran of the New York publishing wars. Indeed, Felker had a solution: he would publish the Pike Papers, and he would donate $35,000 to the Reporters Committee.

It didn't make sense. That was far more money than book royalties could be expected to be, and the magazine was too small to publish the entire Pike Papers. Then Felker mentioned one possible alternative. The company that owned *New York* magazine also published the *Village Voice*, which might publish the Pike Papers in the form of a special supplement.

I thought Schorr would balk at that. The *Village Voice* was a shrill, left-wing publication with none of the dignity and credibility that Schorr had in mind at the outset. The *Voice* had also recently published an unflattering article about Schorr, and he had made no secret of his resentment.

But Schorr was intrigued. He said he wanted to get it over with, and the *Voice* offered an interesting angle. Schorr had dutifully sent a copy of the Pike Papers to be delivered to Holt, Rinehart & Winston, he said, but they were dragging their feet, saying nothing, but keeping him on the hook. Perhaps the best solution, he said, was for the Pike Papers to "just appear anonymously" in the *Village Voice*. His superiors at CBS would never suspect that he would leak the document to the hated *Voice*, and the deed would be done.

On Saturday morning, February 7, Schorr again approached me in the newsroom.

"It's done," he said.

Then he laughed. Schorr said that at the last minute he had grumbled to Felker about the irony of doing business with the despised *Village Voice*. Felker thought Schorr was bargaining and upped the ante from the $35,-000 he had mentioned before. He said the Reporters Committee might receive $40,000 instead. We both got a chuckle out of that—Felker thinking Schorr was bargaining, when Schorr was just having last-minute qualms as to whether this was a good idea.

It turned out that Felker would have the last laugh—because it was soon to be revealed as a disastrous idea, from which nobody benefited but Clay Felker.

The publication of the Pike Papers in the *Village Voice*

turned out to be the political equivalent of waving a red flag at a bull. The moment I saw the taunting red headline, "The CIA Report the President Doesn't Want You To Read." My stomach dropped down to my knees. There was a thoughtful introduction by one of the *Voice*'s political writers, Aaron Latham, but the context was so inappropriate and provocative that I was stunned at what we had done.

President Gerald Ford saw it the same way. He put the FBI at the disposal of the House of Representatives, to root out those responsible for the leak.

With that cold reminder that life was real and life was earnest, a series of dismal incidents unfolded.

I woke up in a New York hotel room on the morning after the *Voice*'s publication. It was clear from the newspaper stories that this was going to be a mess. Schorr was quoted as saying he didn't have anything to do with the *Village Voice* leak, but members of the Reporters Committee contradicted this, with some members carping at Schorr for the form the publication took.

Then my telephone rang. It was Schorr, furious at the members of the Reporters Committee who had blown his cover. He had a solution. The day could be saved if Peter Tufo would say he had approved the publication in the *Voice* without Schorr's knowledge or consent. At the time, I did not know that Schorr had delivered the manuscript himself, but anyway I told him that story would never wash; Schorr had told me that he had made the decision to publish in the *Voice*, and if anybody asked me (I had the FBI in mind), I would tell the truth.

Schorr wanted to try to sell Tufo on saying he had acted on his own, and he asked for the lawyer's home telephone number. I refused but agreed to call Tufo and tell him Schorr's plan. Tufo repeated—somewhat wearily by then—that he represented the Reporters Committee, not Schorr, and wanted no part of Schorr's latest maneuver. Schorr could not have been surprised when I called him back and delivered the message. The conversation ended with Dan Schorr saying something to this effect: "If he won't lie, the cover-up won't work." A chill ran through me that we had reached the point at which a remark like that would pass between reporters.

Things got worse.

Schorr issued a statement admitting that he had leaked the Pike Papers, acting through an "intermediary" furnished by the Reporters Committee. Suddenly, nobody was clamoring to step forward as Peter Tufo's guiding party. Schorr said Tufo was a lawyer for the Reporters Committee; the committee members felt that they had merely supplied his name to Schorr, who then became the client. Peter said he was representing the committee, as he had when he worked on the telephone company case.

The one person who could have made it clear that Tufo was acting in good faith as an attorney and was not to blame was me. I had only to tell a reporter that I had been the contact man, that Peter was doing pro bono work for the committee as he and many other lawyers had done, and that any confusion was due to poor communications between various persons involved.

I didn't do it. I put Peter off, saying that it would all die down; that the worst tactic was to inspire another newspaper story by making another statement. Word was circulating that William Paley, the all-powerful chairman of the board of CBS, was incensed at Schorr and that his career at CBS was hanging by a thread. The last thing I wanted to do was come forward to associate myself with Schorr's act and take part of the blame.

By saying nothing, I left my friend Peter to take the heat alone. I rationalized it as an act of prudence, but it was really an act of fear.

So as I stood in the newsroom with Lesley Stahl, it was with a weary sense of trouble that I waited for her to tell me more.

"That Schorr, he tried to blame me for leaking the Pike Papers!"

It seemed unlikely, but as she told the story, I was reminded again of my own experience with the morally distorting power of fear. Lesley had been told that on the morning when the Pike Papers burst into print, Dan Schorr had hinted to CBS Bureau Chief Sanford Socolow that perhaps Lesley could have stolen a copy of the report while it was being xeroxed in the CBS newsroom and had passed it along to her boyfriend, Aaron Latham, of the *Village Voice*. One of the producers in the newsroom added that he had lunch with Schorr on that day and that Schorr had told him much the same thing.

It was the final sour note of a consistently sorry saga. Schorr denied that he had actually tried to blame Stahl but conceded that he had let the impression stand in others' minds that perhaps that is how the Pike Papers came to the *Village Voice*. Shortly afterward, CBS suspended Daniel Schorr, and in the autumn of 1976 he resigned from CBS, leaving a lingering sense of how swiftly good times could be replaced by bad.

9

Changing Channels

nchoring television is the only branch of the performing arts in which playing in Peoria is more
complicated than being boffo on Broadway. This bit of
wisdom regrettably came to me after I left CBS for
hometown TV: anchoring at the network was simpler
and easier than at a local station and thus was not the best
training for stardom down home. It is not logical, but it
is typically television. The distinction results from a different use of pictures.

Walter Cronkite's competitors used to complain that
he had merely to sit down in front of a camera and clear
his throat to draw a 32 Nielsen share. In fact, Walter
really didn't do much more than that. Most of his copy
was written by two assistants who had been around so
long they wrote the way Walter talked—plainly.

Walter would amble into the newsroom shortly
before air time, have them roll the big teleprompter up
close (Cronkite also had middle-aged eyes), and then

would proceed to be, effortlessly, Walter. To me it was as sweet and clean as Joe Dimaggio at the plate or Larry Bird from the three-point line; a consummate professional making it look easy.

It eluded me then that what Cronkite did really *was* easy. Or at least, it was less complex and demanding than the efforts of the typical local anchor.

This is not to suggest that Walter Cronkite was anything less than the best of network anchordom. In terms of all the important personal qualities—delivery, sincerity, confidence, and authority—none have outdone him. But there is a simplicity to network anchoring that let Walter be Walter, without the distractions of co-anchors, fancy camera shots, and efforts at happy talk. This happens because network news, with the world to cover and an army of correspondents and cameramen to cover it with, always has more video of interesting events than a local station does. It gives the network evening news an anchor-friendly simplicity.

There is only one anchor, whose basic job is to introduce correspondents' prerecorded pieces and read brief "tell" stories in between. The anchor's face is not on long enough to become boring (on the contrary, Cronkite was guaranteed an on-camera ration of about six minutes' air time each night, to preserve his dominant presence on the "Evening News"), so there is no need for fancy camera angles and tricky shot changes to keep the viewers awake. It all boils down to an uncluttered network style that is actually easier for the anchor to handle than most local news programs.

Most of this had escaped me when I was at CBS, innocent of any exposure to local TV. So as I began to log experience anchoring some of CBS's news programs, I did not realize that I was a Dimaggio hitting softballs.

The delusion began with "Face the Nation," CBS's entry in the Sunday morning snooze stakes, back before David Brinkley turned church time into prime time. In those days, the real purpose of "Face the Nation" was to placate the FCC with public service broadcasting and to stroke the egos of Washington bigwigs by giving them a half-hour on television at a time when nobody was expected to watch anyway. This was reflected in the format, which had the politician sitting at a teacherlike desk, faced by the journalists in a studentlike row. Almost nobody watched, except the *New York Times,* which frequently led its Monday editions with what one of the networks' politicians had said.

I should have suspected that "Face the Nation" was not at the cutting edge of television journalism when CBS began to assign me, in the late 1970s, to be the substitute anchor when the regular anchor, George Herman, was on vacation. CBS News had an all-star team then, and plenty of the stars had a better claim on the slot than I.

I did begin to suspect one Sunday after we mistakenly put the wrong guest on the air and nobody noticed. Not even the *New York Times.*

It happened during the period after Watergate, when congressional investigators were snapping at the heels of the FBI. One Friday evening I was informed by the staff of "Face the Nation" that retiring Assistant FBI Director William Sullivan had agreed to go on our show on Sunday to discuss the Bureau's alleged misdeeds.

I was delighted. Sullivan was a devotee of the don't-get-mad-get-even school of disgruntled bureaucrats, whose ambitions to succeed J. Edgar Hoover had been thwarted by the old man and who was known to bear a grudge. Some of the most damaging news leaks about Hoover's stewardship of the FBI appeared to have come from Sullivan. He had been quoted in print earlier that week as calling the Bureau "a potential threat to American civil liberties." Sullivan had never agreed to go on camera before. I was surprised and pleased at the unaccustomed enterprise of the "Face the Nation" staff in landing him as our featured guest.

Late Saturday afternoon I discovered we had a problem.

As I began to read my research material for the next day's interview, it came to light that our William Sullivan was a former assistant director *of* the FBI, of which there were many, and not the William Sullivan who had just retired as assistant *to* the director of the FBI. Our man, William *A.* Sullivan, had spent an obscure career in the FBI, much of it in Los Angeles. The William *C.* Sullivan who had been a Machiavellian figure at FBI headquarters was not scheduled to appear on our program. William Sullivan, it seemed, was not an uncommon name for an FBI official, and "Face the Nation" had booked the wrong one.

I considered our options at that late hour, all of which were humiliating. Then I said nothing.

The next day, "Face the Nation" featured for a half-hour on national television an ernest former middle-level FBI bureaucrat who rejected every heretical idea that the eminent William Sullivan had ever expressed. The guys over at FBI headquarters must have been in stitches, but nobody else seemed to notice we had the wrong man.

There were other indications—which I might have noticed if I had suspected the matter would some day affect me personally—that CBS was not the ideal grooming ground for future local anchor stars.

Beginning in 1983, one of my regular assignments was to be substitute anchor of CBS's middle-of-the-night interview program, "Nightwatch." Until Ted Turner went on the air with his round-the-clock Cable News Network, all three of the old networks had usually gone off the air at 2 or 3 A.M. and started again at 6 or 7. Anyone weird enough to switch on his set in between got black. "Nightwatch" was designed to take the place of the black. It gave CBS an alternative to CNN in the wee hours, but it was not a major commitment for CBS News.

In fact, the high quality of "Nightwatch" became one of the best-kept secrets of American life. There was a cultlike loyalty among the few viewers who sat alone at night and watched, and among those of us who put it on the air.

We tried hard to make it good—not in the usual scramble to shave some ratings points off the rival networks (they had the good sense to be asleep)—but because it offered a rare opportunity to present information in a thoughtful way on network TV. "Nightwatch's" mission was to fill a large block of air time at the least possible cost. Thus we were spared the usual pressure to squeeze events into a fast-paced, if not quite comprehensible, few minutes. We had the luxury of time.

We interviewed politicians, writers, actors, rock stars, zealots, crackpots, and a wide variety of others who might have something to say about the viewers' world. The people we interviewed had time to express what was really on their minds. There was no reason for us to badger them for an incriminating admission or push for some nugget that might make a news "lead," because other journalists weren't watching. Nobody, anywhere, seemed to mind (if they knew) that we interviewed our subjects during the day, on tape, and then went home to bed while the network faked it as a nighttime program.

Television experts say daytime viewers often don't pay much attention; the set becomes background noise as they go about their day. We learned that those tuned to "Nightwatch" were different. They appreciated our presence because they were up for some reason and the night would have been empty without us. It fascinated me that an elaborately produced report to the 18 million viewers of the "CBS Evening News" would bring comment from nobody but my wife, but each morning brought a stack of letters from the ranks of the 900,000 Nightwatchers (we lied and claimed 2 million viewers on the rationale that we taped the show and ran it twice).

I did "Nightwatch" whenever the regular anchor was on vacation or temporarily burned out. State-of-the-art television it was not. It was a low-budget operation, and the last thing we wanted to do was jar anyone awake. We used low-key, simple camera techniques, which suited our insomniac audience but did not constitute a training ground for future television anchoring.

It did, however, put me in line as substitute anchor on the "CBS Morning News," and that anchor assignment verged on the real thing. It meant co-anchoring with Diane Sawyer on a couple of occasions when Bill Kurtis was away. To share the tube with Diane was to encourage delusions of grandeur; Diane could have made Kurt Waldheim seem warm and sensitive in the next seat.

The "CBS Morning News" was the closest thing the network had to the happy talk format I was to encounter later in local TV—and "Newsbreak" was the most distant. The brief "Newsbreaks" between entertainment programs were the ultimate expression of network news—newscasts so squeezed for time that they were controlled by a computer.

On a typical evening when I was to anchor a "Newsbreak" from Washington, a computer in New York would calculate the lengths of the upcoming entertainment programs and commercials to determine when my broadcast would be and how much time I would have. When the moment came, the computer would create a brief "window" in time—say, fifty-seven seconds—in which the CBS network would be broadcasting from my anchor desk in Washington. All I had to do was deliver the news of the evening, plus a commercial, in exactly fifty-seven seconds, at which point the computer would slam the window on me and resume broadcasting from New York.

It was stimulating to try to say something informative, faced with either (a) talking overtime and having the computer pull the plug in mid-word, or (b) rushing through my script and having to look sheepishly into the camera until the allotted time expired. I eventually mastered the art of the fifty-seven-second newscast, but it was not an education that would apply anywhere other than at a network. That seemed unimportant. I volunteered to anchor as often as I could at CBS—assuming that I would not need to use the experience anywhere else.

One hazard of ghostwriting is to concentrate on the words and pay too little attention to the deeper meanings of what is being written. This happened to me in 1964, when I ghosted a book for Lyndon Johnson's secretary of labor, W. Willard Wirtz.

In my spare time as Wirtz's assistant, I stitched a book together from speeches Wirtz had delivered about the labor problems of the future. Wirtz was a dour German with a gloomy view of the coming impact of technological change. His message was one of alarm over space-age machines destined to displace American workers who lacked the education and flexibility to learn necessary new skills.

As a young lawyer with considerable skills and even more arrogance, I edited the book without a thought that there might be a message there for me. My idea of a threatening machine had been formed during my boyhood in Texarkana, when the picture show on Saturday afternoon always seemed to include a scene of a clanking robot chasing Jackie Cooper. It seemed to me that Wirtz was warning of a day when similar robots, made in Japan, would be menacing assembly-line workers in Detroit. I was an Oxford-educated professional; Wirtz was talking blue collar peril.

Later, when I made the move to TV news, television was reassuringly high-tech. It was cutting-edge technology, freewheeling expansion, and uninhibited change. The surroundings were warm blinking lights, soft shifting colors, and mellow voices. There were no smokestacks, no assembly lines or robots reminiscent of W. Willard Wirtz. Those of us who flourished in it in those days had no cause to see that there was a look-ma-no-hands quality to television's growth—that the same space-age velocity that gave television its zip could also, eventually, make it more vulnerable to change than Detroit.

Years passed in blissful arrogance before I first saw a television set attached to a cable, offering thirty-six channels. Then the light began to dawn that Wirtz might also have tolled a bell for me.

At the time I joined CBS, in 1972, television meant "the networks"—that is, ABC, CBS, and NBC. When I went on assignment I could check into a hotel, flip on the set, and expect that there would be pictures on four channels—the three major networks and perhaps a public broadcasting station. In those days, at any given time, some 93 percent of the people watching prime-time television were tuned in to ABC, CBS, or NBC. Meanwhile, the TV audience was growing, as more people bought sets and caught the habit of watching them longer.

It was the golden age of network television. Each year the networks would increase the cost of their commercials and then raise our pay. Mine stairstepped up from $36,000 my first year to $100,000 in 1981. We came to accept this as a state of nature, a way of life that would never change.

By the end of the 1970s, television technology was on a fast track. Developments in UHF transmission, satellite availability, home videotape recorders, cable television, and backyard dishes meant that people had more choices when they switched on their sets. In addition to the three networks, television offered independent stations, religious channels, superstations, Home Box Office, sports networks, adult movies, PBS, twenty-four-hour weather, and even the Congress of the United States.

With this growing menu of choices, it should not have been surprising that the networks' share of the viewing audience began to slip. By the late 1980s their 93 percent share would dwindle to 65 percent, and some projections were that it would shrink down into the high 50s within a decade.

That is close to sliding from nearly all to nearly half. Simple mathematics would dictate that the revenues of the networks were in for a long-term decline and that network news would have to shrink with it. That prospect was ominous enough. But other aspects of TV technology were beginning to cast in question not only the continued dominance of the networks in the delivery of TV news but the very existence of the jewel of network coverage, the national evening news.

The concept of an evening news had been the brain-child of the former newspaper journalists who had invented television news in the early days. It was natural for them to present the news at a given time each day, like a newspaper. But the essence of television is that it is there to be turned on at the viewer's whim, and once cable made it possible for Ted Turner to offer continuous television news, doubts began to grow as to whether the networks could continue to summon millions of Americans to their sets to watch news each evening at dinnertime.

By an unhappy coincidence, another invention, was permitting local TV stations to nibble away at network primacy. Television waves do not, like radio, bend across the earth's horizon. They are limited to line-of-sight transmission, and thus television was created as a checkerboard of local stations, broadcasting only as far as the tip of their towers could see. Cross-country transmission was possible only over telephone lines, and that is basically what the networks did—lease lines from Ma Bell and pump out programming at certain times each day, to be transmitted to the people by the local affiliates. But telephone time was expensive, and deep pockets were required to rent a lot of it. So the networks held a practical monopoly over the miraculous power to project images beyond the horizon.

Communications satellites shattered that monopoly. Line-of-sight transmission suddenly meant straight up to a satellite and from there to almost anywhere else in the world. Compact transmitters were developed that could send signals to the satellites. Any local television station could send its own portable "TV studio" to the scene of an event anywhere in the country and transmit the story back, using its own reporters. Suddenly Dan Rather's correspondents were less in demand to tell local TV viewers about such events as political conventions, airline disasters, hurricanes, and election results.

All this structural dislocation was bad enough, but it was basically only a video-age version of Willard Wirtz's assembly-line robots. It was technological dominoes—scientific advances creating better ways of doing things and outdating the old ways.

That turned out to be—relatively speaking—the good news. Mechanical innovations had a predictable logic. Their dislocations could be anticipated. The bad news was that television had also unleashed psychological forces that were to prove unpredictable, and even more disruptive.

It is only during current lifetimes that human beings have developed the capacity to see the world beyond their actual vision, moving and sounding in a lifelike way. Over the millions of years of human evolution prior to that, people were able to perceive other persons and objects only in their presence. Then artists learned to portray people and scenes in pictures or sculpture. This was a change so stunning to human perception that art became a central pursuit of civilized culture.

So it should have been expected that when science developed the capacity to replicate realistic, moving life for people to see this would have a profound impact on the way we think and live. Television created the ability to see and hear remote objects and events in a staggering variety of ways—bigger than life or smaller, in realistic images or in deliberate distortions, at the same moment that the events happen or repeated at will.

People reacted to this in ways that constantly altered television itself. Viewers became accustomed to movement, sound, and dash on TV. Expectations were raised. Attention spans shrank. Inevitably, the couch potato's channel-switcher appeared. People began to change channels to compensate for movement they found lacking on the screen. Old habits of television watching faded in the swirling mists of change.

Taken together, new technology and new attitudes were signaling the end of the networks' golden age—but for a prize-winning law correspondent in the afterglow of Watergate, it was easy to overlook. I did have a vague premonition that, as the networks jazzed up their product to meet the competition, sedate legal reports could be the first to feel the squeeze. Some warning lights also flashed when a puzzled law professor sent me a study showing that in the last five years of the 1970s, every year each of the networks ran fewer stories about the Supreme Court than they had run the year before.

But I was a habitual optimist, and CBS in the early 1980s was an unlikely place to imagine a wolf at the door. There was still plenty of money around. I had created a tradition of first-rate legal coverage at CBS which, it seemed to me, the network would hardly dare to abandon. It was easy not to see that the potential for trouble was there, should the network's riches ever begin to dry up.

10

Infotainment

Eric Sevareid put on a long face. It had been said that Sevareid looked like God would if he wore a necktie, and indeed, when he was in a bleak Nordic mood, nobody could put on a longer face than Sevareid.

"The trouble started," Sevareid intoned, "when CBS News began to make a profit."

Sevareid was only half-kidding. The two of us had sat down in the spring of 1983 to a ritual that had been dubbed a "worry lunch" among some of the veteran correspondents at CBS. The subject was always the same: Why was CBS News drifting away from the journalistic standards that had made it the best broadcast news operation in the business?

"People forget," Sevareid said, "that television news started out as a loss leader. It was expected to lose money."

Then he launched into that day's theory regarding the decline of CBS News—a theory Sevareid conceded he had borrowed from Richard Salant, who had contributed his share to the worry sessions since he had been ushered into retirement in 1979.

From its creation, Sevareid explained, the basic business of broadcasting had been to make money selling soap. This was accomplished through the use of wildly profitable broadcasting licenses that the government gave to the broadcast companies, free. To salve everyone's consciences—and to distract the public's attention from the giveaway—Congress wrote into the Communications Act that each license holder must devote some air time to public service broadcasting. That was how news became a loss leader. As a public service, it was supposed to lose money.

Everyone, said Sevareid, benefited.

Network moguls could appear before congressional committees and gloss over the fat profits being made from the free use of the public's airwaves by pointing to the expensive exertions being made to broadcast news. Politicians could glory in their good works, serene in the realization that expanded news coverage could only mean increased publicity for incumbents. Journalists could nurture the warm feeling that their soap-salesmen masters were unlikely to make them do anything too unseemly, since the whole purpose of network news was to maintain a dignified operation to parade before Congress.

This tidy arrangement began to collapse, Sevareid lamented, when "60 Minutes" demonstrated that the news division could make money. Once CBS News became an engine of profits and each rating point came to be worth several million dollars a year in ad revenues (Dan

Rather's $2 million-plus salary was justified on the ground that each point on the "Evening News" was worth $5 million), then the goal was no longer quality but ratings.

Television news had become a victim of its own success.

Sevareid's theory that day was a maneuver to ease the conversation into the inevitable discussion of CBS's problems without ruining our lunch. But it made an important point. Later, it would remind us how thoroughly demoralized the troops were at CBS News, even before most of us realized that the future would bring severe financial cutbacks and large-scale layoffs.

Money played no part in the familiar concerns we rehashed that day. We lamented, instead, that CBS News was emphasizing entertainment over news; that older and less photogenic correspondents were being shoved aside; that Dan Rather appeared to be increasingly ill at ease and acting out the news; and that much of this had been brought on by the new men in charge of CBS News.

Later, publicity over the layoffs at CBS News would give the impression that the core of its problems had been financial. Those of us who were there, those most affected, knew that to be untrue.

At the heart of it lay a fundamental change in values at CBS News: under the new men in charge, Van Gordon Sauter and Ed Joyce, ratings had replaced journalistic principles as the guiding force of the News Division. Other institutions, including other networks, had managed to pass through lean times with their standards intact. But that didn't happen at CBS News, because even before the money crunch arrived, ratings had become everything.

By tradition (Salant, the lawyer, was an exception) the president of CBS News had come from within the News Division, someone who shared the same journalistic culture and values as those who reported the news. But in 1981 CBS, Inc., in its wisdom, decided to try a new and unsettling type of leadership. Sauter and Joyce were company men, executives who had climbed their way up the greasy corporate pole. Moreover, there were two of them, as if the company weren't quite sure that one of this sort would be enough. Officially, the president was Sauter, a rotund, bewhiskered man who seemed to be constantly posing as Falstaff. His inseparable second-in-command was Joyce; controlled, prissy, and immaculate, Joyce was known within the company as the Velvet Shiv.

During the two unhappy years that Sauter and Joyce ran the News Division together, I literally never saw them apart. It seemed to be part of their pose that they presented themselves together, Falstaff and the velvet shiv, cast by CBS as Management for the Infotainment Era.

The stories about their twinship kept us enthralled. Sauter drove a jeep. Joyce bought a Jeep. Sauter took up the trendy sport of fly fishing. Joyce became a fly fisherman. Sauter bought a new home outside New York in woodsy upscale Connecticut. Joyce bought Sauter's old home in the same neighborhood—and kept Sauter's old telephone number.

Their dual presence was distracting. I could not shake an image of my childhood, formed from a story I had read of Barnum's original Siamese twins, Chang and Eng. The story was that, although joined at the hip, they often quarreled, and that Eng had once become so furious he tried to throw Chang off a wagon. Whenever I saw them, I could not help wondering how it would be when Sauter finally threw Joyce over the side. True to my imagination, when it finally happened, Sauter was soon to follow.

From the day Sauter and Joyce came over from CBS's corporate headquarters to take over the News Division, it was obvious that changes were in the wind. Six months earlier Dan Rather had ascended the anchor chair, and things had not gone well. CBS had slipped Rather into Walter Cronkite's seat almost as if trying to pretend that Walter were still there. The producers did not brighten up the set, graphics, or format to complement Rather's younger look; Rather seemed out of place and ill at ease. The ratings of the "CBS Evening News" slid into an unaccustomed third place. All of us realized that the arrival of the Sauter-Joyce team meant changing the way things had been done on the CBS Evening News with Walter Cronkite. Most of us would have admitted that some changes were overdue.

By the late 1970s, "CBS Evening News" had become so archaic as to be, in television terms, almost quaint. But because it was still first in the ratings, most of us who worked there were deaf to the ominous footsteps of technology, close behind.

There was a tendency to put down the new advances in video as merely glitz. ABC had introduced fancy new laser and graphic effects in its sports coverage and then had adapted them to news. From our cozy perch atop the ratings it was easy to backhand ABC News's perky new look as the showboating of an also-ran.

But TV viewers were being conditioned to expect the pace of television to bounce along, filling the dead spaces and awkward transitions with pictures that peeled back, pivoted around, or zoomed in and out—all, perhaps, to the tune of a perky electronic sound. In effect, viewers' expectations were rapidly adjusting from reality to super-reality. But the Cronkite "Evening News" plodded along with its 1950s view of reality.

Satellites and lightweight video cameras had opened up the entire country to television coverage, but CBS had been slow to go there. For years, CBS had focused on New York, Chicago, Los Angeles, and especially Washington. That was where great events seemed to happen, and it was easy to get the pictures from there to the CBS News studios on West 57th Street by jet or telephone lines. So even after CBS had the technical capacity to cover the hinterland, the Evening News tended to drag its cameras to dreary congressional hearings and to foist the results off on the public as news.

Moreover, in those days the viewers were only receiving a fragmentary version of the hearings. That was before CBS had videotape cameras capable of blanketing public events as they do now, by simply recording everything on cheap, reusable tape. The film cameras of the mid-1970s posed two problems: film was far too expensive to roll through an entire day's hearings, and yet from a dead stop it took some of the cameras as much as seven seconds to pick up enough speed to take pictures.

The result for a rookie correspondent was agony. A plodding hearing would suddenly flare into an animated exchange between two antagonists; I would whisper "roll" to the cameraman, and seven seconds later, by the time my camera got up to speed, the combatants would be finished sparring and settling back in their chairs.

One day in 1973 I shot $300 worth of film in an effort not to miss an exquisite moment of Daniel Ellsberg's ramblings before a Senate subcommittee. My Ellsberg footage would have been enough to fill three whole evenings of the "CBS Evening News." But overkill proved a self-defeating strategy; the film took so long to develop that we had only enough time to edit and use the first part. CBS News was still shooting with film long after Roone Arledge's no-name crowd at ABC had switched to videotape.

As television changed and improved elsewhere, the "CBS Evening News" became one of the few television programs that managed to look old-fashioned. Cronkite, waxing avuncular amid his traditional anchor desk and familiar graphics, came across vaguely like the farmer out of "American Gothic," with his pitchfork and his dour wife.

It was almost, but not quite, a problem for CBS that Cronkite was also perpetually first in the ratings. I once asked a CBS News executive of that era if it wouldn't be prudent to start modernizing the "Evening News," toward the day when someone else would have to fill Cronkite's chair.

"Yeah, I think about that from time to time," he said. "Then I ask myself how I would like to have chiseled on my tombstone: 'He Changed the Cronkite Show, and It Went down the Tubes.' That satisfies my urge to change Cronkite."

So Walter Cronkite served as an anchor in more ways than one. His immense popularity retarded the natural pace of change, and while the rest of us at CBS News enjoyed the luxury of being number one, we knew there would be a reckoning, when Cronkite was gone.

Cronkite's departure was at first so unthinkable that many doubted the official story that he had become weary in the job as CBS's star anchor and had asked to be replaced, clearing the way for a younger man to succeed him. Most of us in the trenches took that as a parable, akin to Jonah volunteering to be swallowed by the whale.

The irony was that Cronkite had insisted on stepping aside, but that he regretted what came after. CBS's management had assured Cronkite that the anchor job was his—but if he really meant it about standing down, the seat would be offered to Dan Rather. Cronkite accepted that, planning to remain active on-camera as a sort of senior statesman of CBS News. But once Rather became the star anchor, Cronkite was infrequently seen on CBS. He complained bitterly to colleagues that he had been frozen off the air by Sauter, Joyce, and Rather, and that it was not the way he thought things would be when he volunteered to step aside.

I didn't know what the word "infotainment" meant when I first I heard it from a producer in the Washington bureau shortly after Sauter and Joyce took over the News Division.

"Yeah, infotainment," he said. "You know, information and entertainment—a combination. That's what the Big Guy wants."

Big Guy was what Van Gordon Sauter called everyone, and his underlings had picked it up fast. Nobody within my earshot ever called him that to his face (Sauter had a taste for the good life and a body that looked like closed parentheses), and after a few weeks, employees at CBS didn't say "infotainment" anymore except in the kind of mocking, private conversations in which the portly boss would also be called Big Guy.

Officially, the term "infotainment" was recognized to be an embarrassment. But actually, it remained the underlying technique for presenting the news at CBS, from Sauter's arrival in November of 1981 until his influence faded in the months before CBS fired him in September 1986.

In his pep talks to the staff, Sauter spoke of aiming at a mass audience by making the "Evening News" less like the *New York Times* and more like a well-produced video version of a tabloid. To the troops who went out and covered the news, it boiled down to two new marching orders: First, make the news appeal to the heart by capturing what came to be known as "magic moments," and second, make CBS News *look*, as much as possible, like entertainment TV.

The quest for Magic Moments in the news got everyone's attention fast, because Van Gordon Sauter regarded it as a virtual revealed truth.

Sauter had received his inspiration in the newsman's equivalent of Paul on the road to Damascus—on a back road in Mississippi, where he had gone during a youthful stint as a reporter for the *Detroit Free Press*, covering the explosive events of desegregation's freedom summer. It was the time in the dog days of 1964 when three civil rights workers were missing. Segregationist Governor

Ross Barnett tried to gloss it over by suggesting that they had fled to Cuba. Nobody believed it.

As Sauter told it later, he stumbled upon a Magic Moment that seemed to say it all.

He saw an old black man in a boat throwing a grappling hook into a deep pool where bodies might be. A television crew was filming the scene, and Sauter, realizing that he could never convey that Moment as well in print, became a convert to television news, with a mission to capture such Moments—and the ratings that went with them.

"Moments" became the key word at CBS News. Dan Rather took to saying things like, "I wonder at the marvels of the human spirit," and declaring that every broadcast should have Moments that "touch off tiny sunbursts of thought." His producers sported MOMENTS badges. Correspondents were sent jetting to faraway, mostly benighted places in search of poignant, photogenic Moments. The "CBS Evening News" became a showplace of pathetic victims, cuddly animals, and adorable children.

News stories on CBS tended to become two-minute morality plays, with heroes or villains and a tidy moral, to be summed up at the end. Unfortunately, many important events did not present clearcut heroes, villains or morals, but some CBS correspondents became expert at finding them nevertheless.

One correspondent ingeniously rose above the depressing story of a group of Vietnamese war orphans who had suffered irreversible brain damage in a plane crash. After two minutes of pictures showing unrelenting despair, he managed to end on an upbeat note by showing a picture of one orphan smiling, as the narrator cooed, "He feels a kinship with the others, and after all the trauma, that's something he treasures."

Correspondent Bob Simon strained so hard to find an uplifting Moment in the burying of the Vietnam War's Unknown Soldier that he lapsed into high-sounding videobabble. "This ritual," Simon inquired, "is it an act of remembering, or of forgetting? Are we honoring the men who vanished, or sealing, with a ceremony, a war that was lost?" (Background music: "Battle Hymn of the Republic") "There were always more questions than answers in Vietnam." (Guns salute.) "Whether it should never have been waged, or should never have been lost, what is being recognized is that the one man who cannot be blamed for what went wrong is this man, the man who died in Vietnam."

Correspondent Bernard Goldberg found one Moment so compelling that he played it twice in a single story. This video vignette pictured a fat, seedy prisoner in a New York station house, stumbling toward the lockup on charges of selling a stash of marijuana and sneering into the camera, "I'll be out in a few days. See you soon." Goldberg parlayed this infuriating Moment into a long, searing piece about crime and pillage in New York—while slipping into his narration a confession that "crime actually seems to be coming down in some major U.S. cities, like New York, which ranks only twelfth nationwide in terms of overall crime per capita." Nevertheless, he declared, "But if crime is a war in this country, a lot of people say the criminals are winning— no matter what the statistics say. And that's because of an escalation in places like New York of something that never shows up in the official reports, an escalation in the accepetance of crime."

Even when Moment-milking did not torture the facts, it exacted a price, in time devoted to flapdoodle instead of news. When the White House Christmas tree was lit in 1985 onthe same day 256 American soldiers perished in an air crash at Gander, Newfoundland, Dan Rather signed off with this peroration:

"Tragedy knows no season: but today's tragedy is especially painful. It comes at a time of traditional joy and celebration, celebration of rebirth of faith, celebration of a miracle of the flame that refused to be snuffed out: the trappings of joy all around us today for the season: the national Christmas tree lighting tonight by the president. But now, added to the traditional trappings, the unexpected symbols of grief, unfurled and half-staffed, on flagpoles and on faces, in a season of faith, remembering that those who died in the service of their country today were coming home from a mission of peace in the Sinai."

On ABC, Peter Jennings signed off more modestly by giving out phone numbers that anxious families could call for information.

The Moment mania also had its hidden costs, in credibility and in money. It made CBS News look more liberal than it really was, and this touched off the right-wing corporate takeover attempt that started CBS down the slippery slope of financial distress.

This happened because the first rush of Moment mania coincided with President Reagan's domestic spending cutbacks. The "CBS Evening News" responded with a torrent of pathetic victims—giving the impression that it was on an anti-Reagan crusade, when it was actually only attempting to wring as many heart-wrenching Moments as it could out of the affected farmers, steelworkers, and welfare families. But Senator Jesse Helms took it personally and unleashed his campaign to take over CBS and fire Dan Rather.

The Helms effort went nowhere, but it served to put the stock of CBS "in play" on Wall Street. This led to the more serious takeover efforts by Ted Turner and others, until CBS was forced to borrow heavily to buy back its own stock and then lay off employees to cut costs.

Moment-hunting was expensive. Every story was expected to have its special video eye-catcher, and nobody asked how much it cost to get it. During the trial of General William Westmoreland's libel case against CBS, a correspondent was assigned a story that seemed particularly barren of Moments—a sidebar piece on Westmoreland's effort to make CBS disclose its internal review of the case. Undaunted, the correspondent jetted off to Jackson, Wyoming, where he conducted the first known interview about journalistic confidentiality with a lawyer wearing a buckskin jacket and cowboy hat, silhouetted against a snowcapped mountain. The lawyer, Gerry Spence, had no connection to the Westmoreland case, and his analysis of the legal issue boiled down to this Moment/cliché: "What's sauce for the goose is sauce for the gander." Whatever the expense of such crosscountry reporting techniques, no effort was made to curtail them until the mid-1980s, when the News Division began to sink in red ink.

"Moments" became the journalistic tail wagging the dog at CBS. Some stories made the air because they contained heart-wrenching Moments. Correspondents sometimes hyped reality to match the emotions created by effective Moments. Careers went flat over stories that, while accurate, did not sing; whereas nobody, to my knowledge, ever got in Dutch because a poignant Moment created an impression that did not jibe with the truth.

The other side of Infotainment, the effort to give CBS's news reports the same look as prime time, created new standards for deciding whether a story deserved to be presented on the "CBS Evening News." When a correspondent proposed a story, an inevitable question would be asked: "How many elements does it have?" The key word was "elements," meaning that if the story did not lend itself to a series of quick, colorful visual changes, shot outdoors, away from Washington (and, if possible, in California), it was not a likely candidate for the CBS Evening News.

Researchers had discovered that television viewers were changing their habits because there were more channels to watch, and remote control zappers made it easy to change channels. People were becoming more easily bored and were quicker to switch. The antidote seemed obvious: to deter viewers from zapping your broadcast, make it move, bounce, and change—otherwise, the jaded viewer will shift channels.

For those of us doing daily television reports, that meant news designed for the short attention span, peppered with numerous, brief video "elements" so the pictures on the screen switched quickly and often. It brought in the era of the three-second sound bite, too quick to be boring, or, frequently, intelligible. Out of

curiosity, I went back into my scripts for 1975 and calculated that the average sound bite ran sixteen seconds.
By 1985, when infotainment was at its high-water mark,
the average time of a sound bite in my pieces was nine
seconds. That meant that some were so short as to defy
understanding.

In one story I explored the anguish of a divorced father in court, seeking a justification for child support
payments that gobbled up most of his weekly pay. The
judge's four-second explanation:

"That's your problem. Call the next case."

In another of my pieces, President Reagan explained
his position thusly on a complex issue of constitutional
law:

"I am for affirmative action. I am against quotas."

One byproduct of the effort to give the news the same
look as entertainment TV was to film a growing number
of CBS's news reports where many cop shows and sit-
coms were shot—in California. This became possible
(even though no more news than usual was *happening* in
California) because the "CBS Evening News" concentrated on covering themes and trends, with less emphasis
on events and facts. Using this approach, an impressive
variety of events that happened elsewhere could be reported from trendy California. Congressional approval
of the twenty-one-year-old vote; a birth in Australia
from a once-frozen human embryo; an anniversary of
the atom-bombing of Hiroshima; a U.S. Supreme Court
ruling on nuclear plant safety; asylum granted by the
U.S. State Department to a Chinese tennis star; the release of the wholesale price index by Washington
bureaucrats; an order by the Environmental Protection

Agency to phase out leaded gasoline—such stories were told in quick fashion by Dan Rather, then examined through filmed reports of the impact in California.

California's expanded presence on the "CBS Evening News" became a revealing difference between the eras of Walter Cronkite and Dan Rather. Between 1972, the year when I joined CBS, and 1984, when infotainment was on a roll, the number of stories done by correspondents in Washington was cut almost in half (from 614 stories in 1972 to 349 in 1984). The number of pieces done in California almost doubled (from 112 to 207).

To a substantial degree, the Cronkite Evening News had viewed the world through the prism of Washington, D.C. The Rather News tended to see it through California. Sauter's influence may have prompted the West Coast tilt—he had "gone Hollywood" when he ran the CBS station there and was married to the sister of the quentessential California politician, former Governor Jerry Brown—but the result served to underscore the airier tone of the "Evening News" under Dan Rather. The pumped-up quota of pieces from California inevitably produced such news items as the fiftieth birthday of King Kong, a town overrun by peacocks, a slump in the sale of jeans, satanism in music videos, a fad for firewalking, celebrity look-alikes, and the anniversary of Bozo the Clown. At the same time, the "Evening News" was serving up a frothy menu from elsewhere of cute pieces about chimps, penguins, sea lions, swans, chickens, turtles, squirrels, toads, and other critters—to the point that animal stories became a focal point of the intramural concerns about show business at CBS News. "Tax policy had to compete with stories about three-legged sheep,"

Bill Moyers said when he resigned in protest, "and the three-legged sheep won."

Moyers' departure underscored the most corrosive effect of infotainment on CBS News—its demoralizing impact on those who had gone to work there to practice journalism. The demoralization took various forms. Some of us did not look like prime time, and that led to what came to be known as "the purge of the old and ugly." Soon after the coming of Sauter, the "Evening News" picked an "A list" of correspondents, those favored to appear regularly on its newscast. Those not chosen included such CBS oldtimers as Bob Pierpoint, Ike Pappas, Marya McLaughlin, Jim McManus, Robert Schakne, and the dean of the CBS correspondents, George Herman.

Herman rarely appeared on the "CBS Evening News" after the "A list" was put in place. With so little left for him to do, CBS eventually tried to put Herman to work presiding over early morning stakeouts and conducting interviews to be inserted in others' TV pieces. Herman balked, claiming this was the equivalent of firing a television correspondent without cause. CBS backed down, and he spent the last four years of his career in the backwater of radio and off-hour TV.

One of the Washington correspondents left off the A list, Deborah Potter, was not old, but neither was she blonde or pert. In an effort to salvage her career, she had herself redone at Elizabeth Arden. The "Evening News" was unimpressed. Potter turned her efforts largely to the radio, where she put in several years of solid reporting, until infotainment fell into disrepute. Then she returned to duty on the "CBS Evening News."

When Dan Rather picked his A list, Bob Pierpoint became a victim of double jeopardy: at fifty-seven years of age he was getting long in the tooth, and there was bad blood between Rather and him. Pierpoint was a solid reporter who had served CBS with distinction in a number of assignments—including the second slot at the White House back in 1966, when CBS put the young and hard-charging Dan Rather on the beat as number one. Pierpoint let it be known that Rather came on a bit brash, and Rather spread the word that Pierpoint was one of his least favorite people. Fifteen years later, when Pierpoint failed to make the A list, nobody was surprised.

Pierpoint did not take it lying down. When the *Washington Journalism Review* took an interest in the A list, others at CBS discreetly clammed up. A reporter for the *Journalism Review* called Pierpoint, and he gave some heartfelt answers. Pierpoint was quoted as saying CBS was making a mistake to shrug off, for cosmetic reasons, the maturity and experience of its older reporters.

"We are being shoved aside," he told the *Journalism Review*, "and we hope that the quality of CBS News is not being shoved aside with us."

Pierpoint also kept pressing to get back on the "Evening News." He had been assigned to cover the State Department, and he argued to CBS executives that diplomatic sources were shirking CBS News because they realized that Pierpoint could not get their views before the public.

More than a year after he was omitted from the A list,

in late June of 1983, Pierpoint took his case directly to the "Evening News" staff. His office was next to mine, with only a low partition between, and he made no effort at privacy when he telephoned the "Evening News" desk and announced that he had a story to submit for that night's show.

A few minutes later, producer Brian Healy came into Pierpoint's office. Healy was a decent man and he delivered his message in a kindly voice.

"I want to be candid with you," Healy said. "They are down on you because you have said things that have caused this company problems.

"They do not want you to be on the air. So if you have some story that's really hot and nobody else can do it, they may put you on the air.

"But you have to be realistic, and so do I. If it's a story they don't have to have—or if somebody else can do it, then there's no chance, and we shouldn't waste our time."

I slipped out of my office, not wanting to hear any more.

My indignation at the downgrading of journalists based on presentability was tempered by the fact that I was led to believe that I had made the presentable "A" team. Dan Rather came to Washington for a special breakfast of the anointed; if a correspondent was invited, he or she was on the A list; "the old and the ugly" took breakfast at home. I was invited to break toast with the A-team. As one of the chosen, I found it possible to keep silent about the implications of blackballing journalists based on age and appearance. There was even a feeling of camaraderie and belonging that morning, as Rather laid out our marching marching orders under the new leadership of Sauter and Joyce.

My satisfaction was shortlived. There existed, it turned out, an "A-plus list," and most of us were not on it. The composition of those who were spoke volumes as to where CBS News was headed. It was to be a star system, featuring two types of stars. Some were standout correspondents with famous faces and such well-known names as Lesley Stahl, Bob Schieffer, and Bruce Morton. Others were video-savvy stylists, not good-lookers, but skilled at making stories appealing and interesting on television. Bernard Goldberg was the model for this type; with a round face and gray bangs, Goldberg resembled a latter-day Captain Kangaroo—but he had come up through the ranks as a television producer, and he had a knack for the emotional touches and visual highlights that made for high-impact pieces on TV.

Because the star correspondents were to be on the air so often, they would have to be generalists—fast studies capable of becoming instant experts on the way in from the airport. They could not be expected to report with the kind of detailed knowledge and sense of perspective that a specialist could bring to a story. It was a subtle recognition that style was overtaking substance at CBS News.

The new bosses at CBS News had in fact changed the concept of a news story. Traditionally, journalists had understood that news was what the public needed to know and wanted to know. Infotainment changed that by making the central focus "what will keep them watching our network."

Many of us found this unsettling on two levels. We

felt that it debased our profession and that our superiors were operating on assumptions that their predecessors would have rejected as unprincipled.

He was young, small, and curly-haired, and he was known throughout the Washington Bureau of CBS as Tom Shales' friend.

Because he had no experience working in television, he was given a job with the "CBS Morning News," presumably on the theory that it was already in such disarray that he would do the least damage there. He was allegedly a producer, but it takes years to get up to speed as a network producer from a flat-footed standing start, and he was impeded by obnoxiousness. The people who worked for the "Morning News" felt insulted, and they bitterly resented the nonproductive presence of Shales's friend in their midst.

They especially resented the reason why he was there.

"This guy doesn't know anything, he's a pain in the ass, and he stays on the phone to Shales all the time," was the almost-daily complaint of the producer in charge of the "Morning News" operations in Washington.

"But Shales has a crush on Dan Rather, and Howard Stringer wants to keep it that way."

Tom Shales of the *Washington Post* was, indeed, the nation's most influential television critic, and he was also given to writing gushing columns about the glories of Dan Rather. But his curly-haired friend was a burr under the blanket of the "Morning News" staff in Washington, and its chief ranted constantly about trying to get rid of him.

The complaint was that Howard Stringer, the executive immediately under Sauter and Joyce in New York, had insisted that Shales's friend be hired, and that after that Stringer refused—despite repeated complaints—to let him be fired. And the reason always given by the Washington staff was to preserve Shales's sunny view of Dan Rather.

The unkindest cut came when Phyllis George pulled her famous gaffe on the "Morning News," suggesting a little hug between a young woman and the man convicted of raping her. Shales led the charge in ridiculing Phyllis and the "CBS Morning News" but continued to gush over Dan Rather.

When the early layoffs came, they hit hardest at the staff of the "Morning News." At the Washington bureau, some staff members cried as dismissed colleagues cleared out their desks.

Tom Shales's friend was not laid off.

———

For me, the era of Infotainment induced a severe case of journalistic vertigo. I became disoriented and off balance because I no longer knew what a story was.

The object, we all understood, was to cover and present the news in a way that would attract ratings. But nobody knew the formula for that. Winning ratings was elusive enough in entertainment TV, but applying entertainment techniques to news was a leap into the dark. Our superiors constantly changed the recommended formulas and the marching orders, hoping to catch a trend and grab the public's attention.

There would be weeks when we concentrated on downtrodden farmers, times when we featured the homeless, periods of fascination with the rich and famous, and occasional stabs at investigative reporting. Many of us became uncertain and tentative about our work because our stories were repeatedly found wanting for reasons that had nothing to do with traditional journalism.

This disorientation eventually rattled news judgments at all levels of the operation. I got my most unsettling glimpse of its impact on management at the climax of the John Hinckley trial in June of 1982.

From the moment the case of Hinckley's attempt to assassinate President Reagan went to a Washington, D.C., jury on the evening of Friday, June 18, the CBS coverage effort became slightly crazed. The judge had assured those of us who had reported on the two-month trial that we would be given at least forty-five minutes' notice before the verdict was announced. Nevertheless, executives at the CBS News Washington bureau ordered a vigil in the corridor outside the empty courtroom. Throughout the weekend of jury deliberation, a solitary CBS clerk sat on the marble floor outside the courtroom door, while a colleague stood at a pay telephone around the corner, coin at the ready for the call to the network when the verdict was announced.

All of us who were reporting the story touched base at the courthouse at various times during the weekend, and there was much needling from the others about CBS's demonstration of journalistic overkill. I grinned and shrugged it off, but privately I had been worried for some time about the CBS Washington bureau's erratic reaction to the new signals from New York. Sauter and Joyce had been critical of the way CBS's oldtimers had done things, and there had been macho talk about "kicking ass and taking names." Because it was unclear what the new objectives were, this promoted an atmosphere of insecurity and fear.

I would have been more concerned if I had know about another fiasco that the CBS executives had engineered that weekend. They had assigned a courier to shadow John Hinckley's parents. The purpose of this was obscure, as John Hinckley, Sr., and his wife Jo Anne had made it clear they would have nothing to say until after the verdict, and CBS' courier was not equipped with a camera to take their picture.

Nevertheless, wherever the Hinckleys went during the dreary weekend while their son's fate was being decided, the man from CBS, on a motorcycle or afoot, followed. It ended in an ugly scene in a supermarket, where Hinckley's father confronted the CBS courier and shouted, "Why are you following us?" When the courier replied that he was obeying orders and would be fired if he didn't, Hinckley threatened to go public with his grievance against CBS unless the surveillance was stopped.

At that, the CBS brass called off the tailing of Hinckley's parents. This was admirable, except that after young Hinckley was found not guilty for reasons of insanity, the CBS honchos neglected to resume the coverage of the elder Hinckleys. Thus no CBS camera was present when Hinckley's father arrived home on the day after the verdict and gave an on-camera interview to ABC News.

The morning after ABC's exclusive interview ran on the air, Jack Smith, the CBS bureau chief, and Peter Kendall, his deputy, rushed up to me in the newsroom. The new bosses in New York were kicking ass and taking names. Kendall had an idea that would save us from the disgrace of the ABC scoop.

"Hinckley's been sent to Saint Elizabeth's [mental hospital]," he blurted. "In prison, they always let prisoners out for a while each day to exercise in the yard."

"You can charter a helicopter and circle around, and when Hinckley comes out to exercise, get a picture of him."

I looked at Smith; perhaps he had also been addled by too many reruns of *Escape from Alcatraz.* He gave me a do-something-even-if-its-wrong look and said nothing. I pointed out that Saint Elizabeth's was not a prison surrounded by a wall but a complex of several scattered buildings. We didn't know which one Hinckley was in. Also, I said, they might shoot us down.

"Then why don't you take a camera crew and march up to the door of the prison and bang on it and demand to see Hinckley," Kendall said. "Sometimes you can bluff your way into things."

I turned again to the bureau chief, to see whether this amounted to an order from the resident vice president of CBS News. Smith was not prepared to endorse such a daffy suggestion in the rapt presence of the entire newsroom, but he also seemed reluctant to associate himself with doing nothing. So he kept his silence.

I said I would try anything to get a Hinckley story that day, so long as it was not ridiculous or stupid. Then I left the newsroom, uneasily aware that I had witnessed a disturbing symptom of a new disease.

Two years passed before the effects of the infotainment era caught up with me in the form of a concrete setback.

For years I had done a once-a-week legal feature on the "CBS Morning News," the only regular weekly law report on network television. I avoided the big Washington issues, concentrating on legal trends that were changing the rights of citizens across the country. I was the first to tell network television audiences about videotaped wills, age discrimination rights, do-it-yourself computer wills, credit cardholders' rights, backyard pool liability, prenuptial contracts, right-to-die "living wills," liability for work-related stress, and many other legal developments.

It was a zesty combination of satisfaction and fun. I would first show a videotaped feature about the legal issue, then discuss some of the interesting sidelights with anchors Bill Kurtis or Diane Sawyer. Viewers recognized my pieces as different and special and told me so in many letters. When I negotiated my CBS contract with the Sauter-Joyce administration, I extracted a guarantee that I would continue to do the weeklies and that a special producer would be assigned to help me with it.

All went well until early in 1984, when CBS hired Phyllis George to replace Diane Sawyer. The chief producer for the Morning News in Washington was Mary Martin, a plainspoken, earth mother type. She returned from her first meeting with Phyllis in New York with this message to me:

"You'll never do another legal piece on the Morning News."

She explained:

"Can you imagine discussing a legal point on television with Phyllis George? She can't handle it. She'd look ridiculous, and they aren't about to take the chance." Mary explained that the Morning News planned to shift to simpler subjects that Phyllis could handle, topics that would hopefully appeal to the housewives-in-haircurlers set. Mary was my friend, but she laid it out straight—as long as Phyllis George was anchoring the "Morning News," I was out.

This was upsetting enough, because my contract guaranteed that I would do regular legal features on the "Morning News." I was more concerned by CBS's frivolous reasoning. CBS had decided to lower its approach to its viewers and had concluded that I no longer fit.

This seemed to be sending a message: the new currents of infotainment at CBS ran counter to my approach to covering the news. In reporting legal stories, I always operated on the assumption that the viewers were smart enough to understand the most complex matters if you presented them clearly—and that if you challenged viewer intelligence by requiring them to stretch their minds a bit they could handle it, and would appreciate you for it. My trademark became the complex legal issue presented on television in a way that ordinary people could understand. I had a knack for it, and it gave made me pleasure.

The television people who had taken over the News Division operated on the opposite theory, that the average television viewer was rather dense and that the way to reach the largest number was to aim low and talk down. This ignored the possibility that those who watch TV news might be different people from those who sat glued to "The Dukes of Hazard" or "Love Boat," and that news watchers who were treated as intelligent adults might appreciate it and stay tuned.

The "Morning News" had stooped lower than any other CBS News program, as if to test the thesis that the network that offered the most froth would win the highest ratings. Bob Ferrante, the executive producer of the "Morning News," insisted that the viewers were not interested in news. His credo was, "All they want to know each morning is that we're not at war with Russia and that nobody's invented a cure for death." Having reassured our audience on those basics, he said, we should devote the rest of our broadcast to the trends and problems likely to confront the viewers during the day.

The "CBS Evening News" aimed higher than that, but its emphasis on stories with soul and pace began to have, in a more subtle way, an effect on me similar to the arrival of Phyllis George. As the fluffier style picked up momentum in the early 1980s, fewer and fewer of my stories made it onto the "Evening News." I began to slight traditional stories and cast about for topics that would fit the jazzier mold. My news judgment became skewed. At times I was tentative and not aggressive about pursuing stories, for fear they would be rejected as too staid. I was unhappy, and not at my best.

By mid-year 1985 I knew I was in trouble, and I set a goal. Once a week I would prepare at least one iron-clad, irresistible story that would qualify as news under anybody's definition. I would muscle my way onto the air on the strength of pure journalistic quality, even if my stories fell below the desired standards of flash.

My first offering was a story on efforts by the Reagan Justice Department to abolish the court-ordered affirmative action plans that required racial quotas in public employment. The story had social significance, conflict, and even an element of man-bites-dog; several Southern mayors opposed the move to dissolve the once-hated court orders. I filmed most of my report in one of these cities, Norfolk, Virginia, where the white mayor explained how that old town in Dixie had decided that affirmative action was not such a terrible thing, after all.

The "Evening News" producers liked the substance of the story, but Norfolk came across on television like Pittsburgh with a Southern accent. The Grown-Ups had the story redone by Bernard Goldberg from Miami, which had the advantage of some striking outdoor pictures but one slight disadvantage—Miami happened to be a city not involved in the controversy.

I began to pander to the "Evening News" producers, with mixed results.

In one story I interviewed a porn movie star who had sued her agent for alleged racketeering activities. The point of the story was that the antiracketeering RICO law was being misused by litigants who were invoking it against each other in run-of-the-mill civil controversies. Using the porn queen as bait to get the story on the air, I also explained how the RICO law was being invoked against banks, law firms, and other un-Mafialike enterprises.

The "Evening News" concluded that, despite the presence of the porn queen, no story about civil lawsuit would make the viewers' palms sweat. So the story w bucked to the lowly CBS Morning News, where t thinkers in charge had gauged the mentality of show's audience and had concluded that its attent span was short. The result was an edict: no story could run longer than eighty seconds. By the time my story about the antiracketeering law was boiled down to eighty seconds, there was still some fetching footage of the porn queen but no comprehensible explanation of what she had to do with banks, law firms, or the racketeering laws.

I discovered that truth was no excuse for dullness.

The point was made in July of 1986, when the Supreme Court declared unconstitutional the automatic spending cut provision of the Gramm-Rudman deficit reduction law. The Court relied on the tortured reasoning that Congress had violated the separation of powers by giving the authority to trigger across-the-board spending cuts to the comptroller general, an official who theoretically could be fired by Congress. To me, the conservative Rehnquist Court had scuttled an innovative effort at fiscal control on a technicality, and I thought it important to explain how the Court had tied logic in knots to agree with the Reagan administration's position.

But the Grown-Ups decreed that I could not utter the words "Comptroller General" or explain the firing problem, on the ground that television viewers couldn't handle such detail. My resulting report—that the law was thrown out because it violated the separation of powers—was simple and easily to grasp. It also didn't burden our viewers with an understanding of what had actually happened.

I learned that straight news could be harmful to your professional health.

A young "Evening News" producer named Randy

Wolfe had developed an interest in legal stories, and he and I prepared a report on the successful efforts of the antinuclear movement to use litigation to bring the nuclear power industry to a standstill. It was a solid story, but it was deemed lacking in picture changes, short sound bites, and other video elements. There was harsh criticism from New York that the story was dull, and producer Wolfe was exiled to Chicago for reeducation in snappy TV news.

I discovered that much of what I had done for years was no longer considered entertaining enough to report to the public. There was a growing list of stories about the Supreme Court and the law that would have always made the "Evening News" in past years but that were bypassed, on the grounds that they were too dull to hold the viewers' attention.

An increasing portion of my effort went into sifting through the Supreme Court docket in search of whiz-bang fact situations that might make it onto the "CBS Evening News." In October of 1982 I thought I had found a sure winner in the case of Grendel's Den.

Grendel's Den was an eatery near the Harvard campus that had been denied a liquor license owing to the objections of a nearby Catholic parish. The dispute ended up in the Supreme Court.

As Supreme Court cases go, this one seemed made for the age of infotainment. There were boozy college students, a prudish priest, a famous liberal law professor, and a carefully muted question of Church and State. I had cannily concealed the constitutional issue amid scenes of noisy students and aggrieved parishioners; thus the legal point did not get in the way of a good yarn.

To me, Grendel's Den became the benchmark of legal reporting in the infotainment era. "If this one can't make it," I thought, "no Supreme Court case is a good bet."

Indeed, my piece on Grendel's Den was scheduled to cap the "CBS Evening News" on the Friday night prior to the court argument the following Monday.

But at the last moment, the Grown-Ups had second thoughts. They killed my saga of Grendel's Den in favor of a piece that featured a roomful of giggling young children playing a game that had suddenly become the rage of the kindergarten set.

When I asked, in agony, why my benchmark legal piece did not measure up, the response was not reassuring.

"It is Friday night," explained one of the "Evening News" producers. Viewers tend to be in a light mood as they anticipate the weekend, he explained, and CBS wished to end its newscast on an airy note, to suggest that the upcoming evening of TV would be equally pleasant. Despite its camouflage, I was told, my legal story set too heavy a tone to launch our viewers soothingly over into prime time.

He concluded, "We don't leave our viewers in that mood on Friday nights."

11

Rather Inscrutable

In covering the legal beat for CBS News, I reported on the most powerful court in the world, investigated some of the most insidious political scandals of this century, and covered many of the most sensational trials of the past two decades. Yet wherever I went, the question people asked most often was:

"What is Dan Rather really like?"

It was a natural question.

Viewers were rarely curious about the personal side of Walter Cronkite, who projected the reality that he was the same straight-ahead, no-frills journalist whether on camera or not. But Dan was a glaring exception to the bland-is-beautiful school of network anchors. Any viewer could see that he was intense and high-strung, and some felt that Dan was presenting himself in a fashion that was not really him. People sensed that Dan Rather was acting.

Some of those who asked about Rather suspected that

he was a closet liberal posing as an impartial reporter. These were mostly conservatives put off because Dan had gone after the Watergate story with such obvious relish and had once been uppity with President Nixon on television.

I found this easy to answer. I understood the reasons for Rather's prickly pursuit of the Watergate story, and it had nothing to do with political ideology. It was all about ambition and survival.

After working closely with Rather throughout the Watergate period, I couldn't recall a single political discussion between us. Dan's Texas-poor boy upbringing appeared closer to redneck populist than country club Republican, which led some viewers to smell a liberal. But I never heard him express an ideological thought. He was hot after the Watergate scandal because it was the story of a lifetime and he was an ambitious reporter.

What he did talk about were the intense pressures he felt from the Nixon White House to ease off the story. I sensed that Dan's bristling reaction was his own characteristic way of serving notice that he would not be awed or pushed around. To some extent, every White House reporter encounters this. When I was at the *New York Times* our White House correspondent, E. W. Kenworthy, Jr., used to bluster, "There is only one way to look at a politician—down." That seemed a bit defensive at first, but I eventually saw it as Kenworthy's overstated version of a White House correspondent's natural protective stance to avoid being awed.

In Rather's case, there were more specific reasons to be on guard. In 1971, even before the Watergate story broke, John Ehrlichman had suggested to CBS News president Richard Salant that Rather should be sent back to Texas. Relations between Rather and the Nixon White House went downhill from there, and Rather was not surprised when I picked up a strong hint in 1974 that the Republicans were actively on his case.

On March 19, Dan had tossed off his famous exchange with President Nixon at a forum in Houston, Texas. When Rather stood to ask a question and the audience clapped and jeered, Nixon asked Rather if he were running for something. Many people were scandalized when Dan shot back: "No, sir, Mr. President, are you?"

A few days later, I ran into George Bush, then chairman of the Republican Party.

"I'm concerned about Dan," Bush said, his eyebrows furrowed down into a look of distress. It struck me as an odd opener for a conversation, so I pursued the subject. Bush explained that he had been hearing that the CBS affiliates were up in arms over Dan's run-in with the president and that some station owners had written letters to top management protesting that Dan had gone too far. Bush didn't exactly say that he disagreed, but he did say that he hoped Dan wasn't in serious trouble.

I hadn't heard about the letter-writing campaign, so I phoned Dan at the White House to pass along what Bush had said. Dan was puzzled and taken aback; he hadn't heard of the letters either. He phoned Dick Salant in New York, and Salant confirmed that, indeed, a surge of negative mail was coming in from the affiliates, but he had been trying to protect Rather from the knowledge.

It was not lost on Dan that the chairman of the Republican Party knew about the letter-writing campaign when it was being kept a secret within the company. There was a popular saying in Washington during the

Nixon era that if you weren't paranoid you just didn't know what was going on. Dan Rather knew enough to be edgy about the Nixon administration's intentions toward him.

So when I was asked whether Rather was a liberal, I had a ready answer: that he was basically an apolitical journalist who was appropriately suspicious of all politicians.

The tough questions were those that did not imply that Rather was biased but that, on the air, he was not being himself. People mentioned Dan's smoldering on-air presence and his controversial escapades as evidence that Rather was struggling with his own identity.

Almost from the time that Dan took over from Cronkite, there was a similar undercurrent of concern about him among those of us who reported the news for CBS. The reason for the concern was that Rather's personality and style, and his occasional discomfort in his new role, seemed to reflect the changes that were overtaking CBS. Dan's theatrical leanings buoyed him along the new tides of infotainment at CBS, but he also seemed to vacillate and fret about what was happening. He was a beneficiary of the new order but was also burdened with its baggage like the rest of us, and we watched his doings with fascination.

As Dan's uncertain transition continued, the doubts around him grew. They played a corrosive role in the sagging morale among the correspondents and producers and became a constant topic of gossip among the troops.

Eventually, many of those who had been Rather's colleagues for years came to wonder, "What is Dan Rather really like?"

I would not have thought to ask that question back when Dan was the hard-charging White House reporter out to expose wrongdoing in a corrupt administration. That was something that a straight-arrow Texas lad could do on instinct.

As a scrappy, street-smart country slicker, Dan Rather seemed comfortably in character. Covering Watergate was a high-wire act, but Dan went about it with assurance and calm. The symbol of this in those days was Dan's reputation as a former marine. Rather had been in the Marines only briefly (he enlisted after college but was released four months later after he disclosed he had suffered recurring rheumatic fever as a child) and did not even mention Marine Corps service in his autobiography, *The Camera Never Blinks*.

But Dan's square-jawed persona was such that the marine image stuck. He, producer Ed Fouhy, and I were known around the office as the "three marines," and we sometimes lapsed into the kind of macho "Marine Corps" talk that former marines use to show off. Rather didn't overdo it (although he did occasionally quote his drill instructor's salty sayings among his colorful Ratherisms), but I often thought that if I were in a foxhole, I'd want Dan Rather beside me.

Rather was also crafty and ambitious, consistently beating the White House at its own game. It drove the Nixon men crazy.

One afternoon I got a tip from former Senator Albert Gore, Sr.,* who had good contacts in Washington and no

---

*Whenever I have identified a living person who gave me information in confidence, I have obtained that person's permission.

love for Richard Nixon. The president, Gore said, had a crippling case of phlebitis. I passed this along to Rather, who pored through recent Nixon film clips until he spotted a shot of the President walking with a limp. With that, Rather was able to muscle Nixon's doctor into confirming the story, which Dan broke on the "Evening News." The Nixon people had long suspected that Rather had a mole funneling information to him from within the White House. This apparent confirmation of that dark suspicion had them climbing the walls, much to Rather's delight.

After Dan moved up to the role of anchor and company heavyweight, he seemed to feel that the simple Texas lad image was no longer adequate. He appeared to be groping for a new persona that was a better fit. As a consequence, both on camera and off, Dan often seemed to be posing.

Rather's aw-shucks personal style did not always translate well in his more exalted situation. His modesty and acts of kindness sometimes seemed strained and inappropriate.

As a Washington reporter, Dan had a polite and pleasant habit of saying "thanks" to colleagues for their work; as the network's star anchor, he overthanked his "incredibly caring, loyal and talented" staff by running a large ad in the *New York Times*. When correspondents Lesley Stahl and Marya McLaughlin got a scoop, Rather sent champagne. When he worked with camera crews, he fetched armloads of coffee and donuts. Once, after radio editor Anne Reilly did a minor touch-up job on a Rather commentary, a vase of flowers arrived, with an effusive note of gratitude from the anchorman. Reilly thought it was so overdone she hid the flowers in a coat closet. People knew that Dan meant well, but his oversized manner of expressing it made them squirm.

Dan had never made a secret of his desire to emulate the founding spirit of CBS News, Edward R. Murrow. But after he became the network's star anchor, he seemed intent on sharpening that image. Rather became a Murrow-like figure from Texas, a sophisticated rustic with a common touch.

The mix did not quite seem to work. Rather had his suits tailored at the same Saville Row shop where Murrow had been outfited. Yet he went out of his way to spout good-ol'-boy sayings, as if to remind viewers that he was just a Texas boy at heart. A Senate race winner would be announced by, "You can pour water on the fire, call in the dogs, the hunt is over." Or an unlikely effort would be put down with "that dog won't hunt." A presidential election would be summed up with, "If the day were a fish, Walter Mondale would throw it back in." Or a candidate's chances would be as unlikely as "a stick with one end."

On election night 1978, when Rather was still being groomed for the star anchor job, he outdid himself in sprinkling down-home sayings into his narration of events. Two candidates "were going at each other with everything but hand-axes." Disconsolate Democrats in Iowa "would like to dig a hole and become a radish." One candidate's lead was "as shaky as cafeteria jello." Late in the evening, Rather declared it to be "cardiac time" in Kansas, but vouched that Kansans were stout of heart: "They have a saying in Kansas that church isn't over until the deacon says amen. Nobody's saying amen in Kansas."

At the end of the broadcast, as a weary Rather swept up his papers and left the anchor set, a scrap of paper remained. A lingering employee could not resist discreetly picking it up.

It was a note to Dan from his secretary, one gleefully passed around among Rather's colleagues. The note said that Mickey had called in with the following from Texas; it then listed a series of colorful sayings. His colleagues had heard Rather "spontaneously" reel off many of those same good ol' boy expressions to the viewers that night. They also knew that Mickey Herskowitz, a sports columnist for the *Houston Post,* was the ghostwriter who had helped Rather write *The Camera Never Blinks.* There was much chortling over the notion that Rather's "spontaneous" good ol' boy-isms were fed to him by a ghostwriter who gathered the material as a sportswriter in Texas.

Rather's various public escapades also served to exacerbate the qualms about him that had been growing in many of his colleagues' minds. (Rather seemed prone to inexplicable scuffles in public places; he told a pushy interviewer, on-camera, "Fuck you. You got it?"; he took to signing off his broadcast with the word "courage." All this was before his overheated interview with George Bush and his disappearance from the anchor chair for six minutes.) After each incident, there would be a good deal of what-will-he-do-next speculation among the people of CBS News, and it seemed to have an unsettling impact on the staff.

Lem Tucker was one of the CBS correspondents least inclined to conceal his feelings, and he let them all hang out one afternoon in 1987, shortly after Rather's famous disappearance from the anchor chair. Tucker had been working with a producer in a videotape editing bay of the Washington bureau when Rather scurried in to broadcast a bulletin about an anticipated break in the Iran-Contra scandal. But the expected announcement was repeatedly delayed, leaving Rather sweltering under the studio lights, waiting for the signal to go on the air.

Periodically Tucker would wander out of the editing bay into the fringes of the studio, where he would watch Dan Rather. Each time Tucker wandered away, the editing staggered to a halt. Finally, the exasperated producer tracked Tucker down and confronted him about his disappearances.

"What the hell is wrong with you, Tucker? You've seen Dan Rather before. What are you doing, looking at Dan Rather?"

"Don't you understand," Tucker exclaimed excitedly, "that this guy, sometime, someplace, somewhere, is going to go stark, raving mad!" Tucker's voice was rising, and heads swiveled around among the studio crew.

"If it happens when he's around me," Tucker added, "I don't want to miss it!" The bulletin was finally delivered, with Rather's usual finesse—but not before several others had gravitated over to stand with Tucker, watching.

By the mid-1980s, the cumulative effect of the incidents of flakiness involving Rather was having a visible impact on his colleagues' attitude toward him. If Rather's name was mentioned in any sort of an unusual context, people would roll their eyes and shrug their shoulders. When Dan did something odd or ill at ease on the air from New York, someone in the Washington newsroom would shout, "Courage!" Someone else would answer, "Meadow!" They were contesting whether

Rather was attempting to project his macho or sensitive image, as reflected in what he said were his two favorite words. (When Rather had been asked why he signed off his broadcast a few times with the word "courage," he told a reporter that was one of his favorite words, along with "meadow.")

It all amounted to what seemed to be an unspoken consensus among the ranks that CBS's star anchor was— well, a bit of a phony. This had the subtle effect of encouraging the sense at CBS News that reality could be puffed, slanted, and tweaked a bit to make it more interesting. It helped create the atmosphere in which the excesses of the infotainment era crept in—excesses that would have seemed out of place with Walter Cronkite in the anchor seat.

There was another reason why a shaky Dan Rather was unsettling to the personnel of CBS News. Rather made himself a power center in CBS's management to an extent that Walter Cronkite never had, and this created potential tensions between Dan and the correspondents who were technically his peers. Cronkite could wield clout when he considered it necessary, and this gave a great sense of security to those in the ranks, who felt they could go to Walter for relief if management did something truly outrageous. But Dan was so closely identified with management that he became part of the problem.

Rather fell into the habit of hobnobbing with Sauter and Joyce a great deal during and after office hours. When Sauter let his hair down, he had a way of speaking unfavorably of CBS's older personnel as "yesterday people," while approving the younger, video-savvy employees as "today people." Stories of Rather's silence while

Sauter put down the "old guard" made edgy telling among some of the aging correspondents who used to work closely with Rather. It also became notoriously well known that anyone unfortunate enough to get on Dan Rather's bad side was in for a bleak tenure at CBS News.

Rather exhibited sensitivities that verged on the paranoid. Correspondent Rita Flynn once protested to Rather that a story she had developed was delivered on the "Evening News" by one of the A-list correspondents. Rather was so offended that Flynn virtually disappeared from the "Evening News" and finally asked to be released from her CBS contract so she could move to ABC. Another correspondent, Robert Schakne, was quoted in a magazine article as saying he had managed to get on the air, despite not being one of Rather's A-list favorites. Schakne was immediately removed from his beat and soon elected to take early retirement from CBS.

A major drawback of Rather's unusual power was that he used it to enhance his "Evening News," sometimes at the expense of other CBS broadcasts. The producers of the "Morning News" complained frequently that correspondents neglected the morning broadcast, the better to reassure Rather and his staff that they were devoted to the "Evening News."

Every correspondent knew well the experience of Martha Teichner. She had once told Rather she liked to do long, time-consuming pieces—which he took to mean that Teichner preferred working for the weekly "Sunday Morning" show to his own nightly news. Rather became so critical of Teichner to his staff that the atmosphere around her turned stone cold. Her career hit the skids and recovered only when Rather's associates persuaded him that he might be accused of being anti-woman if he did not let up.

It did not occur to me that my strategy for broadening my career at CBS could ruffle Dan's sensitivity about the "Evening News." I was doing my best to adjust to the jazzy "Evening News" style, but I was also trying to carve out a new role by anchoring "Face the Nation," "Nightwatch," and other shows whenever possible, and by doing regular legal features on the Morning News.

The stories about Dan's increasingly thin skin didn't concern me because I had told him about my efforts to structure a broader career for the future, and he had given no hint of disagreement. In any event, we went back so far that if Dan Rather had any problem with me, I assumed he would just tell me about it.

12

Going Pains

"**Y**ou are a pirate!" I shouted, to my lawyer back in Washington.

I was standing at a public telephone in the Denver airport, and I was gloating. My attorney had just given me the bottom line of the new pay package he had negotiated for me with CBS. My reaction was a remark I never imagined this Texarkana boy would be in a position to say: "I would have done it for a hundred thousand dollars less."

It was true.

My lawyer's message, that wintery day in 1982, was that Sauter and Joyce had given away the store.

Under my old contract, a three-year deal covering 1979 to 1982, my salary had topped out at $100,000. That was more than I had ever expected to earn, certainly as a reporter. When I had left law practice in 1965 to write about the law for the *New York Times*, I had insisted on, and received, the same pay I had made as a lawyer,

$19,000. That was then top dollar for a newspaper reporter, and Managing Editor Clifton Daniel was fairly prickly about paying it to a rookie reporter for on-the-job training.

I would have been worth it, writing about the law. But it happened that the week I left my job practicing law for the secretary of labor to write about it for the *New York Times*, violence broke out over civil rights in the South. Because I spoke the language, the *Times* dispatched me to cover the story, where I was hopelessly in over my head. My assignment was to report on trouble in Bogalusa, Louisiana, where blacks were boycotting white-owned businesses, and in the Selma, Alabama, area. Klansmen there had murdered a white woman named Viola Liuzzo, who had come down from Detroit to take part in a voting rights march. Both situations involved suspicious, close-mouthed antagonists on both sides, and a newly minted reporter with no sources did not stand a chance of cracking the stories.

The mismatch was so obvious that a hardbitten civil rights reporter, Jack Nelson of the *Los Angeles Times*, took pity and invited me to go along with him for the first couple of weeks. What followed was a series of sizzling front-page stories, as I shadowed the craftiest reporter in Dixie around the backwoods of the South. Not noticing that my string of "exclusives" always appeared on the West Coast the same day, Clifton Daniel announced to his staff that "our high-priced young lawyer is earning his pay down there," and I was safe until I returned to Washington, where I knew how to do my job.

Seventeen years later, with CBS, I was earning five times as much. But life had steered me into a business where people were being paid outlandish salaries, so I had high hopes for another good raise. In my rosier moments I dreamed of earning $185,000 in the final year of my new contract. But I knew that in the cold light of reality, I would sign for $150,000.

CBS had just agreed to pay me $255,000. That would be my salary in the final year of a four-year contract that would start at $185,000 the first year and stairstep up in hefty raises each year.

The size of the overpayment was surprising, but not the fact that Van Gordon Sauter had been generous with CBS's money. His strategy was to infuse the values of entertainment into TV news, and he seemed to associate that with Hollywood-style pay scales. Also, Sauter enjoyed playing the flamboyant media mogul; it would have been out of character for the Cecil B. De Mille of network news to play the part of Scrooge. The curious thing about Sauter's largess was that most of us could not have gone anywhere else and earned anything like what he agreed to pay. The going rate for law correspondents at the other networks was probably less than $150,000, and no job openings existed.

None of us questioned these fabulous salaries at the time, but the results would come back to haunt CBS soon enough. By the time the Sauter era crashed amid layoffs and acrimony, there were more million-dollar-a-year journalists on the CBS payroll than on the other two networks combined. The media gossips put the CBS figure at eight: Walter Cronkite (who was being paid *not* to anchor), Mike Wallace, Bill Moyers, Charles Osgood, Diane Sawyer, Phyllis George (who collected her million one year from Kentucky, after being benched by the

"CBS Morning News"), Don Hewitt, the producer of "60 Minutes," and, of course, Dan Rather. Rather had been making about $2.2 million when Sauter and Joyce arrived, but they cannily raised it by about $800,000 a year—which was approximately the total salary that Peter Jennings made around the corner at ABC.

Delighted as I was to tag along behind such company, a memory flashed across my mind that was to recur with increasing frequency in the coming years. It was a piece of advice given me by one of the revered uncles who had left Arkansas and done so well.

"Always be underpaid," the revered uncle had said, "Always be underpaid." It had been some thirty years since he said it, and it made me nervous that I had not recalled that bit of wisdom until I learned of my raise that day in the Denver airport.

In fact, I had already begun to worry about the viability of the legal beat in the age of infotainment. Sauter and Joyce were playing down Washington news in general, but the law beat took a double hit because it turned out almost perversely bad video. The Supreme Court was normally not the stuff of which Magic Moments were made, but even had it been, no cameras would be allowed inside to capture them.

My plan was to use my new contract to broaden my role while I was still hot. Negotiating what turned out to be my Christmas-tree contract, I extracted promises from the Sauter-Joyce regime that promised an expanded role for me on the television network. I was guaranteed regular appearances on the "CBS Morning News," and CBS promised that if George Herman should pass from the scene as moderator of "Face the

Nation," I would succeed him. It seemed to me that I had hedged against the future fashion shifts in TV—so I found it irksome that my uncle's advice continued to nag at the horizons of my mind.

The nag had to do with a reality of television: in TV, the only way to earn your pay is to be constantly on the air. That proved increasingly difficult for me to do, as CBS turned more and more toward infotainment.

———

After he stepped down as the anchor of the "Evening News," Walter Cronkite used to tell one of those stories that was too good to be true. According to Walter, his fame vanished swiftly after he no longer appeared in America's living rooms each night. The ultimate proof of his anonymity came, he says, when a man approached him on the street and asked:

"Didn't you used to be Walter Cronkite?"

I assumed that Walter made it up, because it was too perfect an example of the thoughtless cruelty that people can sometimes inflict. But as I began to fade from prominence on CBS, things were said to me by strangers that made me start to put more stock in Cronkite's tale.

One man came up to me and asked, "How come I don't see you on TV any more?" Another put it more politely; "Why don't they use you as often as they used to?" Another man (women never did this) simply said, "Where've you been lately?"

Nobody meant to be cruel, but I worried constantly about my inability to stop the slide of my career, and it hurt to have strangers confirm that things were as bad as I thought them to be. I usually mumbled something about legal news not being in style and that I was hoping to move into other areas of reporting at CBS.

One day in the Atlanta airport I began to get the familiar look from a man who was trying to remember my name, and I had a premonition that he was going to ask the ultimate question. He came up to me, and the words began to flow:

"Excuse me, but didn't you used to be . . ."

I flinched.

". . . on CBS?"

It was close enough. I concluded that Cronkite had been telling the truth.

———

One day Eric Sevareid told me a story about Edwin Newman. At NBC, Newman had always played a respected role as an experienced, sophisticated correspondent. But he was thought to lack star quality, and despite hard work and ambition, Newman was never given a chance to break into the front ranks of the stars of NBC. After a while, he rarely appeared on the air.

Those who knew Newman felt that he came to a decision: if they would not let him broadcast, he would take their money and write. Newman played a modest but respected role at NBC for years, during which time he wrote several graceful, intelligent, best-selling books about language and writing.

"If they won't let you work, perhaps you should accept the situation and write," Sevareid concluded.

It was a tempting course to take. I had tried everything I knew to fit into the new regime at CBS—including some things I would rather forget. Nothing seemed to work. But as appealing as it was on a rational level to fade into the background and write books, I couldn't bring myself to give up. I continued to press for a wider role at CBS.

My break seemed to have arrived with the renaissance of the Sunday morning talk shows. David Brinkley changed the face of Sunday television when he made "This Week with David Brinkley" a big hit on ABC. Obviously, CBS would have to pump some life into "Face the Nation" in order to compete. I had bet my future that this would happen some day, and there it was in cold print in my contract: "Should (George) Herman not be the anchor of 'Face the Nation,' Graham will be his successor."

In the spring of 1983 CBS announced that "Face the Nation" would be restructured. The announcement said that George Herman would be removed as its anchor and that his successor would be . . . Lesley Stahl.

Sauter and Joyce were hard to reach in the weeks that followed, and by the time I arranged a meeting, Sauter had been promoted out of the News Division into the higher reaches of the company. Thus when I went to New York in October of 1983 to confront the new president of CBS News, it was the velvet shiv himself, Ed Joyce.

My mother had persuaded me early in life that you catch more flies with honey than with vinegar, and I was determined to proceed with sweet reason. I said I understood that CBS had to do what it thought was best about "Face the Nation," but that we had made a deal; CBS's promise was an important part of my future. I would be satisfied, I said, if CBS would offer me some other new assignment that would take the place of the one I had lost.

"We're not going to give you anything," Joyce said. "Why?"

"Because that's not 'Face the Nation.' It's a totally different program. It has a different format. It just happens to have the same name."

In fact, Sauter and Joyce *had* planned to change the name and had intended to focus on softer news, "lifestyle" topics far removed from the traditional Washington political fare. But when Walter Cronkite learned that the new program had prepared mock shows on the subject of "The Contraceptive Sponge" and "The Academy Awards," he saw it as another lamentable break by CBS from its tradition of hard news. He was a member of the board of directors of CBS, Inc., and he persuaded the board to turn Sauter and Joyce around on their plans for the Sunday morning show. The CBS board decreed that the program would continue to focus, for the most part, on Washington news, and that it would continue to be called "Face the Nation."

When Joyce insisted that it was really something else, I couldn't resist quoting a familiar Ratherism—that if it walked like a duck, quacked like a duck, and looked like a duck, it was a duck. The velvet shiv was not amused.

Joyce had his heels dug in, so I left the matter in the best posture I could manage. I said I had a deal with CBS, that it represented an important part of my future, and that I could not believe that CBS would not make an effort to live up to its side. I told Joyce I would assume that he would come up with some new assignment and that, if it was anywhere within reason, I would be satisfied.

I was worried enough to go from there into the studio

to consult with Dan Rather. Dan was the most sure-footed corporate politician I had ever known. In the Byzantine world of the CBS hierarchy, his judgment was far better than mine. I told him of Joyce's insistence that "Face the Nation" wasn't "Face the Nation" and explained that I wasn't sure it was wise to crowd someone known for his adroit use of the executive stiletto. This was a matter of importance to me, I said, but I also saw no purpose in committing professional suicide in a losing cause. Would I do better to let this drop, or stick to my guns?

"Ed's new in this job, and he's trying to make an impression as a tough guy," Rather said. "You seem to be in the right about this, and I think Joyce should come around."

"Hang in there," Rather advised.

It soon developed that Ed Joyce was overwhelmed by the job of running CBS News. As long as he and Sauter had been a team, Sauter's expansive personality and style had served as a cushion between them and the unhappy organization that they directed. But once Sauter left, Joyce was exposed as a rigid and unpleasant man presiding over an institution that wished him gone.

A cold and distant man by nature, Joyce's response to the growing hostility around him was to avoid personal contact with his subordinates. Instead, he wrote notes. This alienated Dan Rather, who was particularly furious when Joyce circulated a memo criticizing the operation of the "Evening News" instead of talking it out with Dan.

By the spring of 1984, only six months after he became president of CBS News, Joyce had retreated into his office. He became a reclusive figure, "The Phantom of 57th Street," a subject of curiosity and increasingly open jibes from his subordinates. Joyce's office was on the first floor, fronting on a corridor that everybody used as they entered the building. There was lively speculation as to how Joyce got in and out without being seen.

"He's got a ladder," was Bill Kurtis's theory, suggesting that Joyce came and went through his office window. It was a measure of Joyce's isolation that Kurtis openly peddled a theory in the corridors of CBS that the president of the News Division had become CBS's version of Howard Hughes. Nodding toward Joyce's closed door, Kurtis would say:

"He's in there, growing a fingernail."

Far away, most of us in Washington did not realize how withdrawn Joyce had become. Later I was told by Margery Baker, then a top producer on the "Morning News" and later a vice president of CBS News, that she had tried without success for a year to get in touch with Joyce to discuss a career problem. But since I did not know that others were running into the same stone wall, I could not understand why Joyce continued to ignore CBS's violation of my contract. When he did not return my calls I tried a change of pace—calling daily for a while and then at long, irregular intervals. Having schemed to provoke a response, I stewed about his silence. I consulted with lawyers about a possible lawsuit (they said CBS could legally ignore its promises about assignments, so long as it paid my salary) and slipped deeper and deeper into a funk. As my morale slumped, so did my job performance; it was a self-fulfilling nightmare.

Frustrated that I could not get through to Joyce, I tried to pass the word to him through his subordinates that I was waiting to hear from him. This was obviously risky, but I could not bring myself to let it drop. One day I received a call from David Buksbaum, a CBS News official in New York who was known as "Dan Rather's man."

"You should know that Joyce is ranting about your claims that he owes you something," Buksbaum said. "He insists that 'Face the Nation' isn't 'Face the Nation' any more, and he's furious with you about it."

It was well known around the Washington CBS bureau that since Dan Rather had moved to New York, Buksbaum had become his close confidant. But I did not pay enough attention to office politics to pick up on Buksbaum's reputation for never doing anything that didn't have Rather's blessing. I assumed that if Rather had changed his mind about his advice to "hang in there" he knew me well enough to tell me himself. I dismissed it as a bit of well-intentioned gossip-mongering and let it go at that.

By this time a year had passed since the meeting in Joyce's office; I had not seen him since, and he had long since stopped taking my calls. I wrote him a long letter, pouring out my frustration and unhappiness over the stalemate and imploring him to let me "sit down with you in the near future and work this out."

There was no response of any kind.

————

It was punishingly hot and muggy the way Washington can be in August, and the movers were sweating buckets as they muscled our furniture into our new home. But my wife Skila and I were in light spirits that blistering day in 1985. This was to be our last move, at least for a long time.

We had bought an old house and restored its beauty, and the process of moving in reinforced a sense of reassurance that had begun the week before. My lawyer had received a letter from CBS saying the network was prepared to negotiate a new contract with me.

We had decided to make no demands and let CBS come to us. My lawyer suspected that they would offer no raise and might even push for a pay cut. I was ready to go along because I wanted peace with CBS. I had come to understand the downside of being overpaid. The new contract would, by its silence, signal my surrender over "Face the Nation." There would be no promising new assignments—an unspoken recognition that my career had leveled off and that I would gravitate into the ranks of the correspondents who were not put on the air when the network was parading its stars.

Edwin Newman would have understood.

Skila and I were in the second afternoon of our move when the telephone installer appeared. I used the new phone to check in with CBS. There were three messages from my lawyer, marked "URGENT."

"I've been trying to reach you for two days!" he cried. "A terrible thing has happened. They are not going to renew your contract!"

A lawyer from CBS had phoned with a curt message: CBS would not offer me a new contract when the current one expired in six months. The translation of the lawyer's notice was to surface later in the week in an article leaked to *Variety*, a show-biz tabloid that Sauter and Joyce often used to float their version of events. Under the headline, "Graham Sought Raise," the article said, "Graham reportedly notified CBS News management, including Edward M. Joyce, prez of the division, that he wanted a raise. But at that moment, sources said, word came down to lower expenses. Graham may be caught by bad timing." The article concluded that Joyce and Sauter "may use this episode to send the lean budget message throughout the division."

The velvet shiv had settled a score and sent a message, all in one swift stroke.

I decided not to tell Skila what had happened as she breezed cheerily in and out of the house, directing the placement of the final pieces of furniture. The move into her dream house was one of the happiest days of her life, and tomorrow would be soon enough to tell her that we probably could not stay. My lawyer had said that I could make a fight of it, could go over Joyce's head to his superiors, who would not appreciate the duplicity with which this had been done. But I was sick at heart at what CBS had become and had decided that it was time to leave.

The thought depressed me so much that the gloom showed. Late that night, after we went to bed in our newly furnished house, Skila demanded to know what was wrong. There was no way to shield her.

That night, for the first time in a quarter of a century, I cried.

———

With six months to find a new job, I had expected a comfortable transition to a new career. It didn't work out that way. As a fifty-five-year-old specialist in broadcast legal journalism, starting over proved to be more complicated than I had thought.

For openers, the leaked story made me damaged goods in the television industry. When you present yourself for employment and the word is that you were canned from your previous $255,000 job for demanding a raise, the psychology is not good. This exposed me to the victim's perspective of trying to stuff the journalistic toothpaste back in the tube. Several newspaper writers who had already repeated the false *Variety* story assured me they would set it right (Howard Stringer at CBS confirmed that I had not asked for a raise)—but they did it by weaving the correct version into subsequent stories, where almost nobody noticed.

I also developed more tolerance for the bruised ego of the formerly successful person, newly unemployed. The trendy term for it—"lowered self-esteem"—had been tossed around a good bit in stories about former take-charge executives who had turned to mush when they couldn't find new employment. I had run into this while reporting on age discrimination and had felt that some of the one-time boardroom tough guys were indulging in self-pity.

But from the sharpened perspective of the middle-aged jobseeker, I discovered a revealing truth: a successful person is usually one who has simply found his niche in life. If he's dislodged from that in his middle years, it is almost impossible to reach that level again anywhere else. I came to understand that being a supplicant for a job when all concerned know you are on the way down does not enhance esteem—self- or otherwise.

One development that seemed to shuffle the cards

again for me was the growing awareness that Joyce was on the way out. CBS News, which had set out to bring the nation entertainment, was finally doing it in a big way. The public watched transfixed as a series of highly publicized fiascos unfolded. In September of 1985 CBS News suddenly told seventy-four of its employees—many of them veterans of many years' service—they were through. They were to clear out by the close of business the next day and turn in their keys, or the locks would be changed. The next month, in an inspired grandstand play, the boss of "60 Minutes," Don Hewitt, offered to buy CBS News from the network. He said Dan Rather, Bill Moyers, Mike Wallace, Morley Safer, and Diane Sawyer were in the deal with him as an entre-preneurial venture—but the implication was that CBS News was in such chaotic shape that only amputation could ease its pain.

No one was surprised when CBS tried to calm things by kicking Joyce into a meaningless job upstairs. There was some amazement that Sauter did not get the boot with him—and more when Sauter was brought back as president of CBS News. This shuffle inspired one corre-spondent to remark to *New York Times* reporter Peter Boyer, "They've just thrown out the symptoms and in-stalled the disease."

In one of the countless rehash sessions among the CBS correspondents, someone mentioned a rumor that Sauter would also have lost his job but that Dan Rather had gone to bat for Sauter with CBS's top management. The story was that with Dan's backing, Sauter had nudged Joyce over the side and had taken the vacant job himself.

When I expressed some surprise that an employee like Rather would have a hand in picking his boss, I was hooted down. No personnel change of any importance, I was told, went forward without the Rather blessing. I began to realize that I had been naive not to have realized that.

About this time I began to observe a "reverse pinhead effect" at CBS. This was CBS' version of a mode of institutional behavior that I had first observed when covering J. Edgar Hoover's FBI. According to legend, after a get-acquainted meeting one day with a group of new FBI recruits, Hoover snapped to one of his aides, "Who's the pinhead?" This question traumatized Hoover's staff, who had not noticed which recruit piqued the great man's displeasure and were afraid to ask. Checking each man's hat, they found that three recruits wore a size six and seven-eighths. The story is that the word went out about these three "pinheads" among the recruits, and each fell into such disfavor that none completed the training course and became G-men.

As billionaire Laurence Tisch began to move in as the new boss of CBS, he was, in many ways, the corporate equivalent of J. Edgar Hoover. Tisch was tough, remote, and such an enigmatic figure that CBS executives who scrambled to please him were at a loss which part of the apple to polish. Shortly after Tisch began his takeover in New York (declaring at every step that he had no takeover in mind), I noticed a warming of the atmosphere toward me. Formerly cool and distant vice presidents and their underlings began to speak and smile.

The rumor mill quickly churned up the reason. Laurence Tisch, it seems, had mentioned me in a way that touched off a "reverse pinhead" phenomenon in the CBS bureaucracy. According to the story, when Tisch was being introduced to the multitude of vice presidents at CBS News, he turned to one fawning executive and grumbled, "With all of these executives reporting to each other, I don't understand why CBS can't afford Fred Graham."

Rumors flew that CBS would ask me to stay. In due course, Sauter was sacked, and CBS made an effort to close the rift between Sauter's video-generation executives and the Old Guard, of which I, regrettably, was one. Some of my contemporaries went to Dan Rather to ask him to intervene on my behalf. He telephoned me and said he would. I was thankful, and said so.

But the final week of my contract arrived, and nobody in authority had asked me to continue to work there. At midweek I prepared what everyone judged to be my last broadcast for the "CBS Evening News," then passed the word that I would spend the next day clearing out my office and would be gone on Friday.

As I signed off at the end of my story, a producer turned to an executive in the control room, and remarked, "Well, that's Fred's swan song."

The executive gasped, "You mean, nobody told him?"

The next morning a phone call interrupted my packing and summoned me to the office of the Washington bureau chief, Jack Smith. Smith was famous for his managerial style. When the first round of layoffs struck and caught everyone unprepared, Smith had broken the bad news to a young reporter named Eileen Shields by telling her to clear out of the building by the end of the day. Later, when Smith heard that "Face the Nation" might interview the British singer Boy George in a program about changing sex roles, he screamed, "What's this about interviewing Lloyd George!" When correspondent Jim McManus jogged from the scene of the tragic Air Florida crash near Washington's National Airport to a motel a mile away, barged into a startled guest's room, and called the CBS control room to offer a live eyewitness account, Smith replied, "Can you get to a telephone?"

On the morning of my audience, Smith was bubbling with good cheer. CBS, he announced, had decided to give me another chance. The pay would be $150,000—$105,000 less than I had been receiving—and the contract would be for one year, three less than the usual tenure.

I had one question. Why had they waited so late to tell me?

"Oh, Howard Stringer was supposed to do that," Smith chortled. "He forgot."

I said I'd take it, and left. The next day my contract expired, and I worked for a few weeks without one until CBS got around to presenting me with my one-year extension. I gratefully signed it.

In the year that followed, 1986, many of the wounds healed at CBS News. Laurence Tisch may not have known much about television, but he knew everything about money. Tisch demonstrated an acute awareness that Wall Street was not going to boost CBS's stock price so long as the News Division was constantly in an uproar. Tisch came to the Washington bureau, declared that he was an ardent admirer of television news, and fell asleep in the control room watching Dan Rather. Still, when Tisch later delivered what most of those present took to be a promise that there would be no more layoffs at CBS News, a roomful of correspondents applauded, and believed.

With Joyce and Sauter gone, the tension went out of my relationship with CBS News, but the scars remained. Early in 1987, CBS offered me a new four-year contract, under terms that could best be described as unenthusiastic. The pay would be $150,000, and unlike all my past contracts, there would be no raises during the four years. If I needed further hints of the damage to my career, it came when the Iran-Contra scandal erupted. My assignment was to provide pieces for the benighted "Morning Show" that had replaced the "CBS Morning News"; Phil Jones would deliver the Iran-Contra pieces in the evenings.

In the Washington bureau one night I glanced at the NBC monitor. Edwin Newman was reading a one-minute "Newsbreak," a job younger reporters often performed to get their faces on the screen during prime time. The sound was off, but I stopped for a moment and watched Newman. It seemed to me he looked sad.

———

Roone Arledge understood the value of intrigue in seducing a desired employee from a rival network. Secret lunches, late-night telephone calls, and the ritual conference in a suite at Washington's grand old Mayflower Hotel—these gave a spark of excitement and importance to the campaign by Arledge and his second-in-command, David Burke, to persuade me to switch to ABC.

It had happened back in the fall of 1978—a time when the idea of jumping ship to ABC did not stir the imagination. CBS News—and I—were flush with our post-Watergate successes and very much on a roll.

But as the new president of ABC News, Arledge had set out to create excitement, and he used it effectively in his acts of piracy against the other networks.

"Because we're third, ABC is where the opportunity is!" That was Arledge's pitch, and it made some sense. ABC would be growing, he reasoned, and there would be much more room for advancement than at CBS, where the bench was so strong. At ABC I would be much more than the law correspondent; there would be documentaries, regular appearances on the "20/20" program, and other special projects. I would also be free to do occasional documentaries for public television—a pleasure that CBS had refused to consider. The pay would be a princely sum for that time—$130,000 per year for three years, compared to the CBS offer of $90,000 the first year, $95,000 the second, topping off the third year at $100,000.

At the time, it was easy for me to turn down Arledge's magnificent offer.

I had made it a matter of pride, in my life, to go with the best. It had been that way with Yale, the Marines, Oxford, and the *New York Times.* It was also that way with CBS, the broadcast news organization with the highest ideals, the finest correspondents, the most honored traditions. I decided to stay with CBS.

During the depressing decline of CBS News that began a few years later, I found myself thinking back many times to Arledge at the Mayflower Hotel, making his case for ABC.

It was small comfort to recall that even Roone Arledge had not had the foresight to argue that I should not be swayed by CBS's premier position among news organizations because it would soon vanish away.

It was important to me that my style of departure from CBS would underscore my preference for my hometown station over the once-high-and-mighty network. Also, I wanted—in a modest way—to get even. So as the day approached for me to respond to CBS' four-year offer, I entered into secret contract negotiations with the management of Channel 2. My plan was to sign a contract with Channel 2 and then break it to CBS that it was no longer competitive in the world of television news.

I reckoned without the garrulous general manager of Channel 2, who, in his enthusiasm, told a local newspaper that it was "ninety percent certain" that I was coming home to Nashville to anchor the news. The wire services picked the item up, and it appeared in the New York press the next day. Unfortunately, this was the first week in March 1987—just as CBS News was preparing to carry out the massive firings that Laurence Tisch had so eloquently implied would not take place.

Having learned that I was on the way out the door, CBS beat me to the punch. Faced with a quota of 215 jobs to eliminate, the CBS executives saw me as a "free cut," a person who was leaving anyway and could be listed as a fired employee, sparing someone else the pain of unemployment. Thus I was denied my little satisfaction and was also treated to one last, sorry episode at CBS.

That incident was a sacking of network news personnel so emotional that a scene very much like it was used as the dramatic climax of the movie *Broadcast News*. There was a haunting, ironic aspect to that; the moviemakers had observed the turmoil at CBS, but they had written and filmed their fictionalized firing scenes *before* CBS's layoffs actually took place.

In the summer before the March 1987 firings at CBS News, the movie people moved in on the Washington bureau. It was as if those who were making *Broadcast News* could sense the dramatic potential in the tensions at CBS. Actress Holly Hunter came to observe the frenzied exertions of Susan Zirinsky, the CBS News producer who became the model for Hunter's Academy Award–winning role in the film. An actress named Lois Chiles had been cast as the brassy female correspondent, despite the fact that Chiles was not blond. Chiles bleached her hair and came to observe Lesley Stahl. James Brooks, the director, sat around the CBS News bureau, watching.

Then they left and produced the movie. Its final scenes—filmed, edited, and prepared for release months before the massive firing at CBS—eerily foretold what happened later at CBS News. In the movie, people were called in and told that after years of service they were being let go. Those who were spared consoled the losers and tried to conceal their own relief. Some people cursed, and others cried. People huddled in small knots of sympathy or relief, placed hushed calls to spouses, and walked about with boxes of personal effects. When it happened to us in reality, it took place much as the moviemakers had predicted.

But when I was called into the front office for the

ritual sacking, a wrinkle was added that even the doom-saying movie makers did not predict. From my point of view, the dismissal ceremony was just a formality that management chose to perform with a colleague who was departing anyway, in order to save a job for someone else. I was a bit surprised that the heavy-handed Jack Smith was not doing the honors, but still I was relaxed and casual as Smith's young deputy, Joe Peyronnin, began to recite the terms and conditions of my termination.

Suddenly I realized that CBS was trying one last, outrageous act. The young assistant was saying that I would receive severance pay for only one year—not for the fourteen-plus years that I had worked for the company.

"How," I asked, "can CBS say that I'm entitled to severance pay for only one year, when everybody knows I've been here for almost fifteen years?"

Peyronnin squirmed, looked away, and invoked the messenger's defense. He was only carrying out orders. The decision, he said, had been made higher up. After placing a call to New York, he explained that I had lost my rights to my accrued severance pay the previous year when my contract briefly ran out.

"Technically, that means you've worked here only one year," he said, "not fourteen." He looked miserable.

I suddenly felt as miserable as he looked—but for different reasons, because I knew my rights had been protected in advance. I was sickened that CBS had managed to end what had once been such a proud relationship on such a sorry note.

My attorney, who was considerably less sentimental than I about CBS, had anticipated such a maneuver.

When my contract had lapsed briefly the year before, he had obtained a letter from the CBS legal department. The letter said I was entitled to severance pay for my full fourteen years.

I fetched the letter from my office and presented it to the unhappy young executive. He made an ashen-faced call to New York and quickly switched signals. A mistake had been made; I would receive full severance benefits.

I went home and began to prepare for the move to Nashville.

By the summer of 1988, a year and a half had passed since the agonizing last days at CBS and my move to Nashville. Events that had been confused and blurred had begun to settle into focus.

Two revealing CBS books had been published—one by Ed Joyce and another by *New York Times* TV writer Peter Boyer. Both said that no significant decision was ever made at CBS News without Dan's prior concurrence.

I decided to have a talk with Dan Rather. I wanted to ask if he had approved my dismissal. If so, why—had I offended his sensitivity about devotion to the "Evening News"? Why had he not told me what his role had been?

At the 1988 Democratic and Republican national conventions that summer in Atlanta and New Orleans, I tried to locate Dan. I prowled around the CBS compound, hoping for a chance encounter. Once I brought a CBS executive meeting to a stunned halt by poking my head into the wrong doorway. I tried to arrange a meeting through Dan's secretary.

Everyone was cordial, but it didn't work out. Friends

at CBS told me that Dan had become more remote and withdrawn, isolated by a bodyguard and a crushing load of work and appearances. For the cleansing conversation between two old friends that I hoped to have, this was not the time and place.

After the political conventions I began to telephone Dan at his office. I was told he was snowed under but wanted to talk with me, so I always left my number, with a promise to leave my recorder on whenever I had to be away. I called about once a week, and once I found a message from Dan's secretary on my recorder saying he was returning my call. On my sixth call, I explained that I very much wanted to talk with him about my forthcoming book but that I did not want my calls to become troublesome. Dan, I knew, could reach Yasser Arafat, Bishop Tutu, or indeed, Billy Graham on short notice—he could certainly reach me if he wanted to talk. I told his secretary this call would be my last, but that I, or my recorder, would always be waiting in Nashville to receive his response.

For once, I got through to Ed Joyce right away. Our telephone conversation was businesslike and to the point.

Did Joyce tell Dan Rather in advance that he intended to fire me?

"Of course," Joyce replied. "Nothing significant happened during that period of time that Dan was not fully informed about, that he was not a complete player in."

The reason for his action and Rather's agreement, Joyce said, was my "lack of productivity" for the "Evening News." What about my persistence on the "Face the Nation" issue? "That used to irritate me," Joyce admitted.

That seemed to leave only one question to ask. Why, if Dan Rather was unsatisfied with my output for the "Evening News," did he never say a word about it to me?

"I was often amazed," Joyce answered, "at Dan's ability to have a conversation with someone and walk away and have a totally different conversation on the same subject with someone else."

Dan Rather's call never came. My final word from him remained a warm note, written shortly after I left CBS, saying, "We miss your good work, and we miss you as a person. . . . Stay in touch."

13

WORN

When Channel 2's station manager first contacted
me about coming home to anchor the news, the
station's call letters were so unfamiliar that I could not,
at first, get them right. Friends and relatives would ask
about my new station, and the first few times it came out
"W-O-R-N." It was not just that the call letters WKRN
were so remarkably forgettable, but that the station's
down-at-the-heels reputation made WORN seem to fit.

WKRN's past was so humble that it gave new meaning to the term "room for improvement." It began in 1927
when a couple of good ol' boys who owned a service
station in a town north of Nashville swapped five barrels
of oil for a radio transmitter and began broadcasting
from the room upstairs. They were the Draughon brothers, Jack and Louis, visionaries who had moved into
broadcasting early and who might have become communications barons, but for one fact—they were tightwads,
skinflints who were perpetually content to be outdone

by competitors who were not as cheap.

The pattern was set from the day in 1936 when the Draughons moved south with their station, WSIX (the SIX was a play on the address of the service station) to become the third radio station in Nashville.

From the start, it was Cadillac and Lincoln versus Uncle Willie's Tin Lizzie. As young as radio was then, Nashville already had a station with a stately tradition— WSM ("We Serve Millions"), a powerful, clear-channel NBC affiliate owned by the respected National Life and Accident Insurance Company. WSM had, with one brilliant stroke, created a presumption in Nashville that to listen to any other station was an act of civic disloyalty.

WSM had pulled this off by creating "The Grand Ole Opry," a Saturday night showcase of country music, which set Nashville apart as the pickin' and singin' capital of the world—and established WSM as an object of local pride. The second radio station was second only by comparison. It was WLAC, a CBS affiliate owned by the Life and Casualty Insurance Company, with a tradition of excellence in programming and news. The Draughon brothers' 250-watt radio station trailed along without a network connection until, shortly before World War II, it joined NBC's second-string "blue" network—later to be reborn as ABC.

When the 1950s came, Nashville's three network-affiliated radio stations marched forward into the television era, their traditional mismatch firmly in tow. WSM-TV went on the air in 1950 as an NBC affiliate and had a three-year head start by the time my future station began to broadcast from an old summer cottage in the hills south of town. CBS, with nowhere else to go, teamed up with my station-to-be. But as soon as WLAC-TV got on the air, CBS prudently dumped my station and switched, leaving WSIX no recourse but to return to the undistinguished ranks of ABC.

WSIX-TV went on the air in 1953, and its news operation became a legend, even in its time. It consisted of one astonishing man named Jim Kent, whose versatility was a monument to the frugality of Jack and Louis Draughon. The visionary Draughon brothers, years ahead of their time, lived in mortal fear of being sued. They would trust no person but Kent to have a hand in delivering the news, and they would broadcast only material that had come direct from the AP wire, or had already been published in a newspaper.

That meant that Jim Kent was not only the anchorman but also writer, announcer, sportscaster, weatherman, and—to the extent the station's news philosophy permitted it—the reporting staff. But for Kent, that was only a start. Following the trend of the day, the station had a live children's program in the afternoon. The Draughons would have no one less than Jim Kent play the star role of "Sea Captain" for the kiddies. Thus the viewers of WSIX received their early evening news from an anchorman who had barely had time to remove the greasepaint from his role as a buoyant clown. After the news, Kent devoted his spare time to performing promotional spots and commercials.

Louis Draughon, who ran the station, was a man who drove in from a country town each day with his lunch in a sack. He paid rock-bottom wages and saved money by buying the raw chemicals that went into the film-developing solution and having his studio crew mix their own. When he built the structure where the station still holds forth, he included almost no windows. Draughon cannily housed his station in a bunker so his employees wouldn't be tempted to waste their time gazing out—and so that, if television didn't last, the premises could be easily turned into a warehouse.

With only three TV stations in town, there was money to be made in frugal third place, and by the time the Draughons sold their station in 1966, its news operation had cemented a public reputation as a contented also-ran.

In a community less committed to tradition, pulling a third-place TV news operation up from obscurity might have seemed a modest challenge. But Nashville had a custom of loyalty to its sources of news. Nashvillians had been reading the *Tennessean* with their morning coffee since Andrew Jackson read it in the White House. They had read the *Banner* in the afternoon since just after the Civil War. This did not mean that an also-ran TV news operation could not gain acceptance, but it did imply that to do so it would have to earn a tradition of its own.

A turnaround seemed possible when WSIX-TV was purchased by the General Electric Corporation, as well-heeled and free-spending as the Draughons had been parsimonious. The prospects were that the station, renamed WNGE, could finally compete.

But GE proved that while money talks, it does not necessarily make sense. It turned out to be crucial that General Electric was a manufacturing business run by engineers, and not a media company run by broadcasters and journalists. A decade later, the *Columbia Journalism Review* conducted a study of the nation's local network affiliates' news operations: Based on the amount of air time devoted to news, WNGE was rated dead last. It turned out that more was needed than just money. Indeed, GE brought to the station some peculiar problems of its own.

In Nashville, General Electric demonstrated that a good, big corporation cannot always whip a good, little one; the two locally owned TV stations consistently ran circles around faraway GE. Managing a funky Nashville TV station was not considered the road to glory among all GE executives. The company changed general managers too often, and they were a mixed bag, including the man who had once been the voice of the Green Hornet on radio. Before long, the employees became so sullen they voted to unionize and won featherbedding concessions from GE that put the station at a further competitive disadvantage with its nonunion competitors.

Soon after General Electric entered the Nashville television market it demonstrated an unfortunate weakness for progress through gimmickery. The federal government had initially assigned Channel 8 on the VHF dial to the station purchased by GE and had given Channels 4 and 5 to its two competitors. In a technical sense, this put WNGE at a disadvantage, as the lower-numbered channels, with their wider wavebands, reached farther out from Nashville into the rural countryside. The widest and most far-reaching band of all, Channel 2, had been assigned to the public broadcasting station in Nashville.

This inspired GE to cut a deal with the PBS station that was a triumph of hope over common sense. General Electric swapped channels with PBS, so that my future station became Channel 2. This was intended to give the station a fresh start, a new image based upon a lower-numbered channel. In return, my station gave the PBS station (now broadcasting on Channel 8) $800,000 in cash and services up front, plus a commitment to broadcast the PBS programs from our tower free (a service worth $60,000 per year) for the next ninety-nine years.

The catch was that by adding the extra distance, the station's longer signal reached mostly into cow pastures and into Kentucky, where people watched their local station. Closer to home, the switch to Channel 2 muddied the reception of many Nashville residents, whose roof-top antennas had been designed to receive Channel 8. But most damaging, the change of channels ignored the importance of habit in television viewing. The former owners had spent years enticing the public to tune in Channel 8; now it had to be done over, for reasons that the average viewer would never understand.

GE's switching of channels to its own disadvantage was symbolic of an impatience that became the station's trademark. It became addicted to the "quick fix" approach to news improvement, hiring and firing anchors and news directors in a frenetic search for a winning formula.

In the seven years before I arrived, there had been nine news directors. They came and went at a disorienting pace, each making changes that compounded the dislocations. Channel 2 tried hiring the former star anchors of both competing stations. Both flopped at Channel 2. It then signed on a handsome and flamboyant newsreader often described as "a dead ringer for Ted Baxter." Once, while reading a story about an explosion, this anchor repeatedly referred to the use of "din-a-mite," as the studio crew and director went through wild antics in attempts to call his attention to the correct pronunciation. There were other anchors, good and bad, at a rate of about one every year and a half for the dozen years prior to my appearance on the scene. Always, Channel 2 remained a distant third in the ratings.

General Electric finally gave up. In 1983 it sold the station to Knight-Ridder, a media company with a more settled journalistic reputation. But Channel 2 (rechristened WKRN) had developed a tradition of impatience; it had never stuck with anything long enough to achieve success through patience and perseverance. There were some signs that Knight-Ridder had fallen into the quick-fix tradition. WKRN's management had just cleaned house before I was hired, relieving yet another news director and anchorman. For that reason I insisted on a four-year, no-cut contract. Channel 2 would be forced to stick it out with me for four years, and I was confident that in that time I could prove myself to the viewers of my hometown.

From my viewpoint, what Knight-Ridder was undertaking in Nashville was part of a healthy national trend. Many cities formerly had bedraggled local news stations that had never seriously attempted to compete. To me, one of the most promising developments in American journalism was that these perennial losers were being bought up by large newspaper and television chains, setting the stage for a stimulating wave of news competition in local TV.

All agreed the new competitiveness was a good thing, but nobody knew whether bringing aging network correspondents home was a sound way to conduct it. I would help determine that.

14

Getting Heads Together

Triumphant homecomings probably all have their queasy moments—at least, that was true of my return to Nashville in April of 1987 to anchor the news.

Channel 2 threw a welcome home party, and the governor and mayor came—I had to take a night off from boning up on the teleprompter to attend. Phone calls flowed in from former classmates and old acquaintances—most were real estate agents and stock brokers. During my twenty-five-year absence, Music City had matured into a bustling, prosperous metropolis—we sold our Washington home for an extravagant sum, rolled the proceeds into a Nashville house, and paid more.

Above all, I was enjoying the process of learning my new role—on the other hand, I had yet to come to terms with "happy talk."

If there is one universally denounced symbol of the shortcomings of local television news, it is happy talk. Everyone deplores the often mindless and sometimes silly and distracting chatter that goes on between local news anchors. News buffs condemn it as a struggle for charm without substance, trivializing the news. Everyday viewers often object that the anchors don't manage to make it funny.

Even so, happy talk remains a fact of life, because two or more people sitting together saying things into a camera must occasionally say something to each other. Local TV news usually offers a larger cast of characters than the lone network anchorman because local newscasts don't have as many filmed stories to put on the air. (Usually not that much has happened on the local scene, plus the stations haven't had the facilities and reporters to dig up more.) So local TV is forced to confront the viewers with more faces, talking. The result is the predictable male and female news anchors, weatherperson, and sportscaster and the television imperative to make their conversations appear normal. It has proven desirable that this talk be at least civil, preferably pleasant—or perhaps, even happy.

Like everyone who has never actually had to make happy talk, I felt that the solution was simple. I would bring it charm with substance. My ad libs would be instructive, even educational. I would provide meaningful happy talk.

The prospects for this in Nashville seemed promising. My co-anchor at Channel 2 appeared to be the perfect meaningful happy talk partner.

Anne Holt was one of the most remarkable people I had ever met. She was young, willowy and beautiful, with the kind of high-spirited intelligence that in the South is associated with sassy rich girls. Her style was classic iron-magnolia; pert and smiling on the outside, tough and disciplined underneath.

But in fact, Anne had grown up among the cotton patches of the west Tennessee Delta, picking cotton in the same dusty fields that produced the author of *Roots*, Alex Haley. Her father was a sharecropper who had thirteen children and a formula for launching them beyond the cotton patch: make them obey, work them hard, send them to college. There are no photographs of Anne before she made the high school yearbook, because her family could not afford a camera. But by the time she graduated from the University of Tennessee, Anne looked and acted like Audrey Hepburn would if she had been born black.

After I completed two weeks of practice on the teleprompter, all agreed that I should rehearse with Anne for a few more weeks so that we would become comfortable with each other before I actually went on the air. As we began our nightly rehearsals, it seemed to me that Anne and I were perfectly matched to produce meaningful TV. The gray-haired white guy and the black Audrey Hepburn could do it. She could supply the charm, and I would lay on the substance. We would be dynamite.

After the first week of dry runs, I began to sense that years of experience reporting the news did not necessarily add up to appeal as a local anchor. Driving home each night after frustrating efforts at projecting charm and authority, I felt my first twinges of doubt.

In a perfect world, it would have been enough that Channel 2's new anchor was the most experienced and knowledgeable journalist on the local scene. But this was television, and both it and its newest local practitioner fell considerably short of the perfect norm. I instinctively looked at the wrong camera. I missed my cues. I read other anchors' copy. My on-camera visage, intended to be authoritative, fell between worried and terrified. And my meaningful happy talk came across as pompous lectures.

The first hurdle was Rule One of television—knowing which camera was on.

It turned out that the seemingly easygoing chit-chat of local TV was in fact highly complex and heavily choreographed. The presence of four performers delivering the news requires three cameras moving about the studio, changing shots and angles as the participants talk to each other, and—they hope—to the camera that happens to be on at the time.

Channel 2 had compounded the complexity of this. In an effort to conceal the essential boredom of talking heads, Channel 2 had attempted to turn its newsroom into a real-life television studio. The newsroom had been floodlit and wired for sound, so that anchors could move about the room, chatting with reporters, the sportscaster, and the weatherman in their natural habitats. It was phony realism, which television always attempts at its peril. In this instance, it overstrained the fundamental illusion underscoring all television—the use of technology to make unnatural acts appear natural.

Camera angles and picture composition were constantly changing, as three cameras glided around the studio taking alternating shots. The challenge was to be in the right spot, looking at the right camera, and saying the right things while making casual, preferably coherent chatter.

To accomplish this nightly triumph of contrived casualness, the producer (the TV name for an editor) and director (the person responsible for making it look good) plan each shot in advance. A shot-by-shot rundown is drafted, beginning with the first word of the broadcast and extending to the last. The resulting document could be a cross between the plan for the Normandy invasion and the diagram of a screen pass to the tight end. Using numbers, colors, and letters to designate who is speaking, from which spot, and to whom, a coded series of symbols are printed onto sheets of paper that accompany the anchor's scripts.

For my rehearsals with my co-anchor we always used scripts from the actual newscast earlier in the day. One rehearsal broadcast began, for instance, with a story that came to be known locally as "The Case of the Headless Preacher."

It was vintage Nashville TV.

A fundamentalist preacher had apparently decided to fake his own death, leave his family and parishioners, speed away with a mysterious lady on a motorcycle, and take up a new life elsewhere. According to the district attorney's view of events, the preacher befriended a homeless drifter, lured him to the church, dispatched him with an axe, chopped off his head and right hand, put his own clothes on the corpse, set the church afire, and roared away on a motorcycle. This was a less than foolproof scheme. The preacher had departed with $50,-000 of the church's funds, was much larger than the headless corpse, and was known to have done part-time work as a butcher.

Within a few days after the fire the police had declared the incident a murderous ruse, and the preacher had meekly reappeared to stand trial. But meanwhile, Channel 2 had broadcast a vivid story of the tangled events and had passed the script along to me for my nightly rehearsal with Anne Holt.

Understandably, the script of this story was not simple. But compared to the script, the coded instructions for the anchors were pure Greek.

According to the script, Anne would say:

"Tonight there are more pieces to the puzzle . . . but some of the pieces do not fit, and the picture still isn't clear."

And then Fred was supposed to say:

"Investigators continue their search for a missing Nashville preacher who they hope holds the key to a bizarre and baffling murder. Firefighters found the headless body of James Matheny inside the burning Emmanuel Church of Christ Tuesday morning. Since then, an intensive search has been underway for church pastor David Terry. Channel 2's Art Sasse joins us now for an update on the mysterious case. Art, I understand that Reverend Terry has been reported missing by his wife."

The coded instructions told me that, while reading the above, I was to do as follows:

AH/FG R2,3 (2), set/pkg; R3 (2z); R3,5 (3); R5 (1k); Tag R5 (1k); R3,5 (3) (question); R5 (1); R3,5 (3).

Translated roughly, that meant that I was supposed to, meaningfully: (AH/FG R2,3 [2] set/pkg)—Look into camera 2 as Anne Holt began to announce the news package, which would be introduced by the reporter from the set; then, so as not to appear uninterested in what Anne was saying, turn to look at her as she continued; and then swing back to look into camera 2 as my turn to read approached. (R3 [2z])—Read my first two sentences as camera 2 rooms in close on me. (R3,5 [3])—Look down at my script as I read the words "an intensive search," as a signal to the director to cut to camera 3 for a shot of me and reporter Art Sasse, and then swing around to my right and look at reporter Sasse, standing behind me in position red 5, and—despite the fact that I am no longer looking toward the teleprompter—complete my lead-in to Sasse. (R5 [1k])—Try to recover my composure, while Sasse reads his introduction of his story into camera 1, waits as the pretaped package is played, and then (Tag R5 [1k]) reads his tag into camera 1. (R3,5 [3] [question])—Read into camera 3 the question to reporter Sasse that Sasse has scripted in advance and presumably knows how to answer. (R5[1]—Breathe easier, as Sasse answers the question. (R3,5 [3])—Thank reporter Sasse and, casually, glance at camera 3 while bailing out with a debonair, "Anne?"

All this was to be done while appearing authoritative and relaxed. It was in fact accomplished with a look of white-knuckled confusion—and with a momentary flashback of Walter Cronkite, only his script between him and his stationary camera, being avuncular.

My plan had been to make up for my technical shortcomings with what might be termed a thinking person's happy talk. Instead, I learned that television technology does not lend itself to spur-of-the-moment profundity.

Because camera shots are planned and laid out in advance, it often happened that when inspiration struck I was on camera alone, with no one in sight to share my insights. Usually the cameras were not positioned so that they could suddenly include Anne in one of my philosophical moments. Moreover, it was hazardous to force it.

During our rehearsal one evening Anne ended a report on the Supreme Court on a note that I found intriguing. The battle plan called for me to speak next, so I turned to Anne and, drawing on my long experience on the legal beat in Washington, I added an incisive remark about the likely outcome of that case.

It happened that I was on camera alone and that my next scripted story was the predictable report of that night's slaying, with the killer's picture flashed on the screen over my right shoulder. As a result, the camera saw me turn, gesture meaningfully, and intone my thoughts about the Constitution into the murderer's ear.

So much for spontaneity. My vision of happy talk was crashing into television technology—casual remarks between local television anchors usually had to be well planned. They would not work unless the director's shot schedule called for the participants to be on camera together, and this pairing normally took place just before a commercial, or before weather or sports. That is why conversations between anchors degenerate into mindless chit-chat on many local newscasts, often despite the best intentions of the participants: it is difficult to be profound while leading into a report on high school football or the prospects for rain.

During my early campaign for significant discourse on TV, one additional complication surfaced: Anne Holt was deaf in one ear—the ear turned toward me.

It came as no surprise to me that Anne had no hearing in one ear. My parents lived in Nashville—and several weeks before, when I broke the news to my eighty-one-year-old father that I would be leaving CBS, moving back home, and taking up local anchoring, his first response was:

"Anne Holt is deaf in one ear."

This turned out to be an item of local lore, like the fact that Minnie Pearl had graduated from a snooty women's college, that Johnny Cash had been to prison, and that illegal gambling went on in Printers' Alley.

Anne joked about it, claiming that she deliberately always sat with her deaf ear toward me. In any pursuit other than television that would have been the end of it, as her right ear did quite well. Unfortunately, anchors must wear a tiny transmitter in one ear to receive instructions from the control room, and hers, naturally, was worn on the right side. The result was that she heard the control room loud and clear, but she and I were sometimes in less than perfect communication.

This was exacerbated by another circumstance that I had neglected to mention to my new employers—I did not hear so well either.

In my own mind I attributed this to Marine Corps training years before, when a powerful explosion had gone off uncomfortably near my head. But since it seemed to get worse as I slid deeper into middle age, I suspected, in dark moments, that it might be related to the same condition as the failing eyes.

For whatever reasons, in the early weeks my new partner and I found ourselves working out a unique hearing-impaired system of anchor-to-anchor communication. We devised a set of surreptitious hand signals, reinforced by our own special huddles at strategic moments. When the weatherman was holding forth across the studio, or when for some other reason we were off camera with our microphones switched off, we learned to put our foreheads close together and half-lip-read, half-whisper "spontaneous" repartee to swap later. To outsiders it would have looked odd, but it forced us to think ahead, and there was a symbolism about it that felt right.

One hazard that comes with the territory of anchoring is the inevitable rumor that the two anchors do not get along. Sometimes they don't. I had seen that at the "CBS Morning News" with Bill Kurtis and Diane Sawyer (who started off in sync but soured as the ratings fizzled), and Kurtis and Phyllis George (whose off-camera relationship ranged from indifference to contempt.) Co-anchoring is a relationship that lends itself to friction, because people with substantial egos must rely on each other to look good. When the ratings flourish, even anchor teams with bad personal chemistry manage to paper it over on the air. It was that way with Chet Huntley and David Brinkley during the glory days of NBC's Huntley-Brinkley show. But more often a sour relationship shows on the air, and viewers switch to more congenial channels. The most famous case in point was Harry Reasoner and Barbara Walters, who briefly poisoned the atmosphere, and the ratings, as co-anchors at ABC.

But many anchor teams are unselfish and friendly, even under adverse Nielsen conditions. As a veteran contributor to the low-rated "CBS Morning News," I had seen this firsthand and often. It was that way with

Phyllis George and Bob Schieffer, who replaced Bill
Kurtis on a temporary basis and had no ego involvement
to overcome. Lesley Stahl and Hughes Rudd managed it
in the happy assumption that their futures lay elsewhere. Before that, Rudd gave grandfatherly support to
co-anchor Sally Quinn, who had been thrown on the
"Morning News" unprepared and needed all the help
she could get.

Rumors started soon after I arrived in Nashville that
Anne Holt and I were on the outs. There was never any
basis for it, but it got into the media gossip columns and
then into the letters-to-the-editor pages. Anne had a loyal
following. Her fans did not want to see her slighted for a
hotshot newcomer. The rumors quickly passed, but I always felt that there would never have been any if the
camera had caught us just once in one of our head-to-
head exercises in special communications.

Meanwhile, my employers at Channel 2 resorted to a
move that has become instinctive with worried local stations. They sent me to a media consultant.

Media consultants—sometimes known as "news doctors"—are either the Attila the Hun or the Louis Pasteur
of television news, depending on whether you report the
news or manage it. On-camera journalists regard them
with fear and loathing, because media consultants are
viewed as itinerant pseudo-experts who periodically
come to town, cluck around over the sagging ratings, and
recommend that somebody be fired. It is the video version of the basic objection to all management consultants—they are paid to find fault, so they tend to do so in
order to justify their existence. Most galling to the journalists is their perception that the consultants are so daz-

zled by the cosmetics of television that they encourage management's latent instincts to stress appearances over quality.

One legendary operation by a consultant was the firing of the anchor team at Los Angeles's CBS station after an ingenious electronic gizmo disclosed that, when these journalists were on the screen, viewers' palms did not sweat. Patrick Emory, one of those who failed the sweat test and lost his job for allegedly being too bland, went to the NBC affiliate in St. Louis—where he was canned three years later because a different team of consultants decreed that his style was too abrasive. Another consultant's coup was the discharge of a Chicago TV weatherman who was deemed to be "too dull," only to have the station deluged with more than 14,000 letters of protest. The station sheepishly hired him back.

But the case that nailed the "news doctors" most convincingly was the celebrated sex discrimination suit brought by anchorwoman Christine Craft. Craft testified that her employers at a Kansas City TV station fired her (as it turned out, just before the latest ratings showed her newscast moving into first place) because a media consultant said the viewers considered her "too old, too unattractive, and not sufficiently deferential to men." An outraged jury awarded her $500,000, but a cooler-headed court of appeals threw the judgment out on the ground that whatever offense the station committed by following the consultant's advice, it wasn't sex discrimination.

The witch doctor view of media consultants is largely undeserved these days. Consultants have learned to play down the pseudo-scientific aspects of their craft. Many of them are former TV journalists who have sound advice to offer. Moreover, viewers' reactions to television *are* such a complex psychological mix that only people who aspire to be experts can claim to comprehend them.

In my case, expert assistance was considered advisable. I was sent to the euphemistically labeled "charm school" of the largest and most notorious of the consultants, Frank N. Magid Associates. The Magid facility, in an unmarked building outside Iowa City, Iowa, had all the warmth and openness of the headquarters of the CIA. But its methods turned out to be far less sinister than television folklore had suggested.

My handlers were a former television news director and a speech teacher, who concluded that (1) I couldn't see, and (2) I was too laid back. They advised my employers to buy larger teleprompters (they did) and told me to wave my arms more and overact.

Both pieces of advice were sound. Television communication is the art of making an unnatural act seem normal. The camera's view is so intimate that ordinary speech comes across as flat and wooden. To appear to be speaking naturally, an anchor's delivery must include glances, gestures, inflections, and energy that fade into normalcy on the cold face of the TV screen. The secret is to learn to do it while retaining your natural conversational style—to act, while still being yourself.

This can come hard for a journalist whose first interest has always been substance. But in truth, the message will not get across if the viewers are put off by the messenger. I concluded that the consultants were right and concentrated on waving my arms. (It turns out that the camera shots are usually so close that the arms don't show, but the gestures help, anyway, to loosen the speaker's delivery. So television viewers are spared the full reality of all of the consultant-taught arm-waving anchors that appear on their screens each night.)

I tried hard, and the consultants reported back (with more reserve than I thought necessary) that "Fred has made a good start." Their conclusion: "He is capable of making the adjustment to an anchoring role."

The Magid endorsement was less than rousing, but my employers had little choice. They had decided to offer the community experience and authority, in hopes that quality would bring its own rewards. Here was a principle anyone in journalism could applaud—but in the form of a middle-aged, gray-haired anchorman, it was an experiment that could easily turn cold.

WKRN-TV, and I, took the plunge. Nothing further was to be gained from intramural practice sessions before phantom audiences. In mid-May it was announced that Channel 2's new anchorman would go on the air.

15

Anchors Astray

"Hi, Fred—think it'll rain?"

I beamed back at the man across the street, waved as if I were running for sheriff, and bellowed out that we sure did need rain, but the chances looked slim until the weekend. I had been anchoring the news at Channel 2 for several weeks and had become accustomed to the fact that everybody recognized the local anchor; most called him by his first name—and some mistook him for the weatherman.

I had also come to understand that people related to the local anchorman in assorted ways.

Strangers phoned to offer remedies for my cold, to ask my age, to seek relief from injustice, and to solicit help for worthy causes. People I had never met greeted me by my first name. On Mule Day, as the wagon bearing me and the other Channel 2 anchors rattled through the streets of an outlying town, the families along the parade route chatted with me as if I were a respected city cousin. Once, after I wrote an article for the newspaper, a man sent an admiring letter which began, "Didn't know you could write." Another man, irked at a remark I had made, called while I was still on the air to say that my wife was dying in a hospital emergency room. My place in the community resembled that of a politician—I was soliciting the people's votes in the Nielsen ratings, and they felt entitled to pass judgment on me.

It was all part of settling into the culture of the local television anchor, a life style that exists among only 3,500 people in the world—the men and women who read the news on the local television stations across the United States.

In most countries television news is delivered as if designed to stamp out charisma. Usually, the news is broadcast from the nation's capital by a government bureaucrat. Sometimes, reporters take turns reading the news, each with an assigned night. In England, France, and a few other places some TV news readers (a more accurate term than the American word "anchor," which CBS invented to describe Walter Cronkite) have become celebrities, but they are remote, national personalities. Only in the United States has the scramble for ratings by local television stations mass-produced the combination of media celebrity and community figure known as the local TV anchor.

A few years back, Charles Kuralt expressed a widespread view when he described the typical local anchor as the "continuing disgrace of this profession," who "wouldn't know a news story if it jumped and mussed his coiffure." But not long after, Kuralt became a network anchorman himself.

Anchors make an inviting target because they are essential to the delivery but not the substance of TV news. The result is a blend of showmanship and journalism that can lead to excess.

There was the former fashion model turned local anchor in New York who interviewed Henry Kissinger without knowing who he was; the handsome New England anchor who ordered the camera moved ever closer, the better to "make love to those women right through that lens"; the Boston station that advertised that it had discovered its new twenty-three-year-old hunk of an anchorman "in a motel room in Denver"; and the freshly hired anchor who descended by helicopter into his new station, sprang to earth in a blue sequined jumpsuit, and announced, "Thus begins the assault upon the Miami market!"

Station executives who should have had a sharper sense of self-preservation have contributed to the competitive frenzy. There was the Baltimore station that filmed its anchor living out his childhood fantasy of playing motorman on the Chicago subway; the Los Angeles station that ran promotional ads of one anchor skippering a sailboat and the other affectionately stroking a kitten; and the San Francisco affiliate that caught the public's attention with full-page newspaper ads of its anchors in dog masks and cowboy costumes. The stimulus behind these shenanigans is simple—attractive anchors pull in viewers, and nobody can say what makes anchors attractive.

In my case, I felt the chances were good to achieve ratings with dignity. Channel 2 had brought me aboard to counterbalance the popular Anne Holt with a male anchor who had authority and maturity. Maturity I clearly had, and the authority part could be expected to come with exposure. In the meantime, the station would have no motive to spoil the process by pushing me into undignified escapades on the air.

Other factors leaned my way. People were pleased that a noted son had come back from the big city. Strangers greeted me on the street with "Welcome home!" I had to learn to act surprised when a succession of well-wishers reinterpreted Thomas Wolfe with, "you *can* go home again!" A former colleague from CBS, Nelson Benton, had become a case study in how-not-to-do-it when he tried to become an anchor in Baltimore. The station ran promotional ads featuring his White House press credentials and implying that Baltimore was fortunate to have such an eminence step down to its level. He lasted less than a year.

Channel 2 did better by me. It ran old snapshots of me playing on a local high school football team and arguing a case in a Nashville court. The message came through that I was coming home, not stepping down.

In one respect this identity went too far; I was the only anchor in Nashville with a Southern accent. For years, the neutral network-style manner of speech had been fashionable on Nashville television. One newspaper complained that my style was too "down home." A lady was so put off she wrote the station that I "should be presenting the news in a very small town, not a city like Nashville."

I was also blessed that Nashville had a "hard news" tradition that placed a premium on my skills as a straight-ahead newsman. There is a conservatism about Nashville that has spared it the tabloid TV so rife in local television news elsewhere.

Experts have an axiom about local TV: "Bad news drives out good news." They can point to a string of cities where one station took the low road with "flash and trash" TV and scored so well in the ratings that soon all its competitors were copying the *National Enquirer* in an effort to keep up. Some viewers complain and others tune out, but the record shows that those stations that try to fight back with quality usually lose.

In Los Angeles, the ABC and NBC stations fattened their ratings on a heavy diet of "news" about soothsaying, psychology, witchcraft, UFOs, and kinky sex. Finally, the last-place CBS affiliate was forced out of its hard news format into a semitabloid approach. Washington, D.C., used to be the national capital of hard news; when one station grabbed the ratings lead by featuring fires, crimes, and gore, the others played catch-up. Now the unofficial credo of Washington TV is: "If It Bleeds, It Leads."

Tabloid TV is trendiest in the big cities, but it appears to be spreading. Each year the Magid Company lists for its clients the popular TV news series that had been broadcast around the country. In 1988, the Magid list included "Men Who Love Boys," "How To Marry a Millionaire," "Men Who Dress Like Women," and "Sex with Your Ex."

Nashville is so straightlaced that no TV station has yet dared to go the tabloid route. But there is also a raunchy side to the town, born of country music, redneck values, and uninhibited politics that makes it a fertile town for news. In my first few months back down South, I found Nashville a newsman's delight.

The mayoral election in 1987 was won by a former

congressman who had left Washington just ahead of the posse. By giving up his seat he had rendered moot the House Ethics Committee's investigation of how he got rich on a representative's pay. One of the most respected members of the Tennessee legislature, which sits in Nashville, had won his seat while serving a term in prison. A prominent city councilman caused barely a ripple when he denounced "this movie about queers" and tried to keep a gay TV production off the cable system on the grounds that "anything other than heterosexual behavior is demented and sick." At about the same time, another council member introduced a bill to ban sexual activity in all 200 city-owned buildings, which included housing projects and a home for the aged. On another occasion, the city council solemnly voted down a council member's bill to construct a landing pad to welcome UFOs from outer space. Meanwhile, a 375-pound exconvict, who was leading the effort to win a referendum to legalize off-track betting, accused an opposing preacher of soliciting prostitutes. Unfazed, the cleric produced documents to prove that on the day of the alleged indiscretion he was in the Holy Land, preaching the Gospel. Every Nashville election produced distractions of this caliber, and Nashville had elections all the time—there were six different election days in the first year after I returned home.

A few months into the job I was beginning to feel comfortable at it, but I was also discovering a hard truth—the shortcomings of others can bring down disaster upon even the most smoothly functioning anchor. This was especially evident at Channel 2, which had more than its share of shortcomings.

During one broadcast, in stunning succession a lightning bolt hit the tower and knocked out the graphics, a camera went dead, and the teleprompter operator fell asleep. Finally, with the show mercifully only three minutes from its end, the control room crew mistakenly began showing an eight-minute piece on the Tennessee National Guard. The technicians recovered just in time to give the viewers a final glimpse of me, slumping despondently into my anchor chair, wondering if this would affect my listing in *The Directory of American Scholars*.

Even the studio floor contributed to the disarray. It had a wavy contour, so that as the cameras glided across one particular spot they took on a slightly nautical roll. Pictures shot while moving across that area often resembled the view from a destroyer's porthole. Also, Channel 2 was the only television station in Nashville that did not own a satellite truck. On stories out in the hills, that made it difficult to compete. It meant that our reporters had to film their reports early and careen down the backroads to Nashville, while the opposing stations reported live from the scene.

We were always at a disadvantage in terms of personpower (Channel 2 had as many women reporters as it did men). We tried to cover the community with a staff of nine reporters, about half the number fielded by the mighty Channel 4. Several of the reporters at Channel 2 would have stacked up with the performance level in any newsroom, but I noticed a subtle difference between the backgrounds of the local TV reporters and their counterparts in the world of print.

Newspapers these days attract graduates of the most distinguished universities, while television reporters tend to be from smaller, less high-powered colleges. The reason is that every Yale grad knows how to write and can sign on with a newspaper and do something helpful the first day. It might take him or her six months to learn enough about pictures, sound, tape editing, and on-camera ego to be a functioning television reporter. The result is that TV reporters tend to come from technically oriented colleges that teach such things, and graduates of the famous universities are largely missing out on the glories of careers in local TV.

This encourages an atmosphere around television studios that is considerably less reserved than the average print newsroom.

Our weekend weatherman, an aspiring rock guitarist, forecast the weather as an expedient to pay the bills. He would dash in for the late news between sets of a music gig, throw on a sport coat that appeared to have been made from a horse blanket, and stand before the weather map in jeans, bare feet, and thongs. The cameramen carefully shot him from the waist up.

WKRN's weeknight weatherman was a sawed-off dynamo from Arkansas named Tom Siler, who in previous years had presented himself on air as the "Weather Wizard," complete with bulging eyes and crystal ball. In deference to the more dignified tone now being cultivated at Channel 2, Siler no longer cast himself as the Weather Wizard during my tenure, but his efforts to tone down his act met with mixed success. Even at his more subdued pace, he had a windmill style at the weather map that gave him the appearance of a man fighting bees.

This was disarming to me in the studio because I could see that the weatherman was not standing before a weather map at all. Actually, he was pirouetting and pointing before a blank wall. All weathermen use this technology, called chroma-key, which involves a blank wall, usually colored green, with the electronic maps and charts programmed so that they superimpose on top of that shade of green. The weatherman can never wear that hue of green or the weather map would magically appear on that part of his clothing. It also means that when the weatherman points to places on his map, he is actually gesturing toward a wall that looks like a pool table, while peeking at himself on a TV monitor off camera to make sure that he's pointing at the right places.

Orchestrating the weather map is as tricky as rubbing your stomach and patting your head at the same time, and it has to be done while changing the graphics with a button attached to a wire running out of the weatherman's sleeve. Our feisty little weatherman did it while ad-libbing into the lens without the benefit of a teleprompter for two flawless performances each night.

Often it was the little things that reminded me I was a long way from the network. In the commercial breaks, instead of stately ads for IBM and Prudential-Bache, there would be plugs for soybean herbicides, used cars, water beds, and Opryland. In the field, rather than the two-person camera crew and producer who always accompanied a CBS correspondent, there would be a sole shooter carrying the camera and lights and me lugging the tripod. Before I went on camera at CBS, I was made up by the same classy lady who had applied the powder that Richard Nixon had sweated through on the night John F. Kennedy drubbed him in their first debate. At Channel 2, they issued me a makeup kit and I did it myself.

One day Michael Dukakis came to Tennessee to campaign, and I arranged a sit-down interview. We had a pleasant chat afterward, and he said he missed my legal reports on the network. I made modest noises and then stated a good case, I thought, for the proposition that, under the circumstances, I was where I ought to be.

I was mercifully not present later in the day, when Dukakis held a news conference. A reporter from one of the other stations badgered Dukakis for allegedly taking Tennessee for granted and demanded to know why, "even though you didn't choose (Howard) Baker or Lamar Alexander (as his vice-presidential running mate), do you think Tennessee is a shoo-in?" Dukakis, ever the politician, did not inform the reporter he was running as the Democratic nominee, while Howard Baker and Lamar Alexander are Republicans.

In theory, local stations and their networks are equals. A network has no authority to order its affiliates to cooperate on news coverage, and the relationship between the two is generally one of mutual indifference. Networks rarely trust a local station to cover a news event, preferring to send their own camera crews and correspondents from afar. Some local stations won't even let the network's news teams in the door, considering them bothersome and arrogant.

But occasionally an incident serves as a reminder that, deep down, even the local people consider the networks the big leagues.

On the day that Oliver North and his codefendants were indicted by a Washington grand jury in the Iran-

Contra scandal, ABC News reached toward Nashville. Ted Koppel planned to devote his "Nightline" program to a comparison between Iran-Contra and Watergate. That meant interviewing Fred Thompson, the Nashville lawyer who had once served as Republican counsel at the Senate Watergate hearings. Since Channel 2 was the ABC affiliate, Thompson would appear before one of our cameras, to be interviewed by satellite from Washington.

Thompson showed up just as I was preparing to anchor our late newscast, and we wallowed in Watergate a bit. Then Thompson went into the studio next to mine, to await his time with Koppel. I told him I would stick around until after he was through. Maybe we could have a nightcap.

Late in my broadcast I was grooving along, following my instruction sheet and moving smoothly between the three cameras, managing—so far—always to look at the right one. Then I got to a part that instructed me to swing to the right, look up, and read into camera 1.

When I looked up, camera 1 was gone. All I saw was a gaping blank space and a thick black cable snaking across the floor and out the door leading to Fred Thompson's studio.

In one thunderstruck moment, I realized that the psychology of network superiority had done me in. Channel 2 had two studios, but only one set of cameras. Koppel had needed to interview Thompson early. Our control room should have told the network it would have to wait, but awe had prevailed over self-interest. So as I gaped, slack-jawed, into the open space, my designated camera was next door, broadcasting Fred Thompson back to the network. A secondary camera on my flank, which had been pressed into service, was taking the too-familiar picture of my ear.

I stumbled through the rest of the broadcast and went home, skipping the nightcap.

———

By mid-June of 1987, after three months on the air, even I could tell my campaign for meaningful happy talk was not going well. The plan had been to weave some of my knowledge and experience into the conversation at the anchor desk. The results suggested that either I was not adroit at doing it or that "meaningful happy talk" was a contradiction in terms.

During my anchor training in Iowa, the Frank N. Magid Company handlers had come up with a technique for injecting my own thoughts and personality into the format. The voice coach suggested that when a scripted news item caught my attention, I could add "a dollop" of my own insights as I tossed the conversation to Anne Holt for her next story. In theory she could either respond to my thought or proceed, but in either case, I would have contributed content and texture to the broadcast.

When I first tried it on the air, reality surfaced. The story concerned a lawsuit filed by the State of Tennessee to determine the constitutionality of a federal highway regulation limiting heavy trucks on local stretches of interstate highways. This item struck me as legalistic and not very informative, so I added, turning to my co-anchor, that this appeared to be a ploy by the state to get out of enforcing a federal rule that was unpopular around here.

She looked at me, said, "That's interesting," and proceeded to read a story about a local child's liver transplant.

My comment had, indeed, contributed some substance to the newscast. But it had also created an awkward moment and had put my co-anchor on the spot. She had nothing to say about the constitutionality of a federal highway regulation.

Over the next few weeks, Anne demonstrated an effective way to avoid appearing unlearned in response to my stabs at meaningful happy talk. She invariably smiled sweetly, said "That's interesting," and then went on with the show. It turned out that Anne Holt could say "That's interesting," six different ways, none of which sounded interested.

Before long, the two "news doctors" were summoned from Iowa to facilitate meaningful happy talk between Anne Holt and me. They sat us down and explained how we could contribute to the substance and flow of the broadcast by occasionally adding a fact or a comment to the stories as we shifted to a new subject, rather than just taking turns reading scripts off the teleprompter. They said our newscasts too often seemed mechanical and sterile. The solution was to work more content and spontaneity into the process.

"Take a few chances," they advised.

My co-anchor listened politely. Then, having heard them out, she spoke with a quiet intensity that came across as a ladylike declaration of independence.

"I've been in this market eleven years, and I didn't become a success by taking chances," she said.

"My reputation is not one of being flippant, or speaking out when I ought to be silent. I haven't been here this long by saying something stupid. If it's stupid enough, you might not be around to be stupid again."

"I have seen a lot of you guys come and go," she said. Anne was looking at the two media consultants, but I had a feeling I was included. "I have a reputation to protect, and I am not going to take chances. If Fred wants to take chances, let him do it."

"I am only going to react," she concluded, "when it is appropriate."

Nobody said so, but that was the end of meaningful happy talk between Anne Holt and me. There was simply nothing in it for her. The viewers had come to rely upon Anne to deliver information in a pleasant and precise manner. They did not necessarily expect her to be able to discuss news events in a casual way. Anchoring normally did not demand that, and my co-anchor was not a news buff by nature; she had initially studied speech and drama in college, had switched to broadcasting to avoid teaching, and sometimes grumbled that her husband was "a news junkie who sits glued to CNN all the time." She accurately saw that, although the public does not want to be read to by frauds and dunces, most people are satisfied to receive the news in a pleasant manner and might be put off by unscripted observations on matters of substance.

Aside from the demise of meaningful happy talk, the summer of 1987 raised other questions about my attempt to bring content to local news through anchoring.

Another target of my extemporaneous efforts had been the uplifting approach of too many of Channel 2's news items. Our reporters were hard-eyed skeptics of politicians and cops, but where businessmen, preachers, unions, civic leaders, little children, and almost any other noncriminal elements of the community were concerned, our newscasts often took on a boosterish tinge. The result was a hooray-for-our-side tone frequently unjustified by the facts. I took to adding a dollop of offsetting information at the conclusion of some of these reports.

Unfortunately, some of my remarks were clumsily stated, and even when not, they tended to come across as gratuitous put-downs. My intent was to add balance to overly rosy reporting; the result was to rain on everybody's parade. I managed to offend such diverse groups as lawyers, gays, supporters of the symphony orchestra, supporters of Jesse Jackson, and (despite my own military service in Korea) Korean War veterans.

I soon learned that nice is a quality that an anchor abandons at his peril. Some of Channel 2's audience felt that I was performing in an unanchorly fashion. Letters characterizing my work ranged from "a distinguished and professional journalist of competence, sincerity, and naturalness in his delivery" to "a seedy old character," "a clown act," and "a joke."

Some of the negative reaction even found an audience in-house. When the producer of our late news broadcast was fired, he sued the station. Part of the theory of his case was that his performance suffered because I was such a bad anchor. He later abandoned the lawsuit, but not before I began rehearsing my testimony. I was relieved not to become famous as the first anchor forced to defend his performance under oath.

By degrees, I began to concede to myself what more knowledgeable people had tried to tell me—that anchoring is basically a function of reading, and it can't be much more than that. The opportunities aren't there.

Most anchors write very little of the copy they read. This is not because they're inept or lazy, but because in most cases it doesn't matter. Introducing someone else's report about a scandal or murder is so mechanical that there's no way to make it sing, and so long as these "intros" are written the way the anchor normally speaks, it makes no difference who writes them.

There is a bit more room for input when the anchor is to read the entire story, either as an on-camera copy piece or a voiceover story told with pictures. If the news item is based on wire service copy or reports from the network, the anchor can rewrite it himself and at least have the satisfaction of knowing that it is accurate and complete.

From such meager possibilities, the anchor's satisfactions can be lean, indeed. I tried to expand my input in ingenious ways.

As a way of drawing attention to some shortcomings of local officialdom, I created a weekly "Dubious Moments" award, an accolade that I bestowed upon the most memorable official gaffe of the week. Nashville had a raw and primitive side to its government that was a fertile hunting ground for Dubious Moments.

There was the city councilman who proposed to fight AIDS by licensing tatoo artists. There was the assistant district attorney who admitted, when he granted probation to a prisoner with AIDS who promised to refrain from spreading the virus, "I don't know how we'll monitor this." There were the guards at the state penitentiary who failed to prevent the escape of a prisoner confined to a wheelchair. There were the deputies at the city jail who didn't notice when prisoners sneaked into the jail-

ers' offices and ran up a phone bill of $220 calling dial-a-
porn services. There was the judge who ruled that for-
feiture of a pistol was the proper punishment for a man
who, because he had "had a very bad day," fired seven
pistol shots into a malfunctioning gas station pump.
There was the lagging candidate for Nashville's seat in
Congress, whose campaign perked up after an irate husband released tapes of the politician sweet-talking the
constituent's wife. The sweet-talking candidate won the
election.

One thing I knew I could do respectably was report
stories, so I tried to impress the home folks by going out
into the community to cover the news. The problem was
that, while I made the point that I was a first-class reporter, it fed a growing suspicion that I was miscast
when swapping chit-chat with the weatherman.

I discovered that knowing how to report a story is
almost irrelevant to being a successful anchor. Television stations are forever trying to slick the viewers by
pretending that their anchors can actually go out and
report the news. It may have some effect when people
suspect that the anchor is a fraud, but for the most part,
viewers are satisfied if the anchor is likable and relaxed.

My reporting persuaded me that most anchors who
venture out to cover stories do it to persuade themselves
that they are still journalists. One pleasure of local news
is that the events are close enough really to matter. That
made it rewarding when I reported on lax punishment of
local unethical lawyers, on off-duty policemen who were
guarding illegal gambling halls, on premature parole of
chronic sex offenders, and on top police officials who ran
private security businesses on the side. After I reported
that Tennessee was one of only four states that did not

require its lawyers to contribute to a fund to repay clients who have been swindled by their own attorneys, the State Supreme Court created such a fund. But as much fun as all this was, it didn't improve the process of anchoring.

I tried taking over the writing of many stories on national and international affairs. Many local stations include almost no national or international news in their early evening shows because the network news comes immediately after and provides all that. That is why house fires and homicides dominate so many early evening local TV shows—they are the equivalent of the "local" section of the daily newspaper, and that is basically the news there is to tell.

But the late local newscasts are more cosmopolitan. The network has no late news show to upstage them with national and international reports. So we always offered a strong dose of worldwide news. I usually wrote and read it because I had more experience reporting on these matters than anyone else at our station. It was satisfying, but I also recognized the irony of returning to my hometown and finding that I was most useful doing what I had done at the network.

After a time I found that the small satisfaction I got out of writing copy was not enough. I recalled that John Chancellor of NBC had once told me he had the same experience. He had turned his energies to the editorial process, helping select the stories to be covered, deciding how the news would be presented. I had sought a similar arrangement when I signed with Channel 2 by having myself designated "anchor and senior editor." The "senior editor" part proved meaningless.

It was not that my younger colleagues at Channel 2 did not want my advice. Rather, I was not there at the right time to give it. A local anchor works late into the night. He is not in the newsroom in the morning, when news decisions and assignments are made. I did what I could by phone in the mornings, but by the time I appeared in midafternoon, I best contributed to the success of the broadcast by powdering my face.

I soon learned that the graveyard shift dominates a local anchor's life style. Swapping the bright lights of Washington for the neon of "Nash Vegas" made no difference, because a TV anchor sees no city lights at all. The most dramatic change in my social life was not missing embassy dinner parties but working in a windowless studio while everybody else was on the town and arriving home after my wife had gone to sleep.

Mealtimes at CBS had been enlivened by a time-hallowed policy—any correspondent who treated a news source to lunch was permitted to charge both meals to the company; correspondents who dined alone footed the bill themselves. The logic of this encouraged correspondents to patronize fancy eateries where—if no knowledgeable officials were available—friends and associates could be wined and dined as CBS news "sources." The system created some hazards for CBS's White House correspondents. Occasionally, both claimed to have treated the president's press secretary to lunch at Sans Souci on the same day. But in general, it engendered an appreciation of fine food and drink among network correspondents that was the envy of Washington journalism.

As a local TV anchor I made more money than most

CBS correspondents, yet dined at places that served pizza and fried chicken. Why? Because local anchors have only enough time to grab a bite between the early and late newscasts and consider it forbidden to have wine with the meal. It is easy enough to appear foolish on television while sober. Nobody I knew in local TV shortened his odds by having a drink.

This created an unpretentious routine. Anne Holt and I often ate fast food together in establishments where the meal was ordered at a counter, eaten with a plastic fork, and purchased for less than five dollars. We did observe some standards; at McDonalds we ordered from the car and ate in the privacy of the newsroom.

Our "fast-fooding" together contributed to an ironic turnabout in the rumor that we were at odds. Channel 2 had erected two huge billboards along the Interstate bearing oversized pictures of Anne and me and the new station slogan, "Something's Happening Here." Some people misinterpreted that, and for a time the story floated around town that Anne Holt and I were an item.

By the six-month anniversary of my welcome home party, mid-October of 1987, I began to nurse dark doubts about my Tom Paine rationale for returning home to local television. My theory had been that people would see they were getting something beyond the usual fare. In due time, that was supposed to bring success.

But after a half-year of nightly broadcasts, I was beginning to suspect that the best an anchor could do was create the *illusion* of adding substance. I found myself recalling a saying among TV oldtimers: "The main thing an anchorman needs is integrity, and once he learns to fake that, he's really got it made."

My efforts not to fake it had clashed with the rigid

conventions of local news. When we retained the traditional boy-girl, happy talk format, while I attempted to
reform the role of the anchor, we struck a false note. At a
stronger station, the audience might have stuck with us
until I got it right. But in 1987 Channel 2 was swimming
against the tide. ABC's prime time audience shrunk by 6
percent from the year before, so we had to persuade a
growing number of viewers to switch to our station at
news time, just to stay even.

Despite that, when the Nielsen ratings came in from
the July 1987 sweeps, Anne and I had gained a precious
point over the year before. I was beginning to feel at ease
in the anchor seat, and it showed.

I was improving, but I was not Peter Jennings, and I
never would be. I did, however, have some of Ted Koppel's qualities—I was a good interviewer, fast on my feet
without a script, and I had a firm grasp of the issues.

Channel 2's management decided to play to my
strength. Anne Holt and I would continue to plug away
late at night—but at dinnertime I would anchor a new
newscast, with a co-anchor chosen for her hard news
credentials. We would modify the traditional local news
format in favor of a mini-version of ABC's "Nightline."
For a portion of each broadcast we would focus on a local
issue, with an in-depth cover story and a live interview.
During the rest of the half-hour we would give short-
hand treatment to the usual fire-and-police stories, and
would report on developments behind the headlines—
both serious and light-hearted—that interest and affect
the average person.

We would attempt to reinvent local TV news in our
community. We would also, I knew, have to attract ratings, or I would be looking for a new career.

16

Reinvention

On the night my new program went on the air, there was an omen. In retrospect, the sign could have been taken two ways. I took it to be a good omen.

Shortly before air time, with the studio lights up and opening night jitters just beginning to wind down, one of our three cameras went out. The elaborate game plan, pointing out which camera to address and when, was obsolete.

A crash on takeoff seemed to be in store for my new co-anchor and me. She was a pleasantly attractive, predictably blonde young woman named Cyndee Benson who had even less anchoring experience than I did.

Cyndee was a living rebuke to the bubblehead stereotype of blond TV anchorladies. She was a driven reporter who bit her fingernails to the knuckles and ran marathons in her spare time. Cyndee had turned to anchoring to keep her career rising as she indulged in her passion for reporting. Channel 2 had been able to hire her from a Cincinnati station by promising that she could report as well as anchor and by pointing out that our innovative format would give the anchors more to do than just read. Her presence meant that both of us had strong journalistic credentials—but also that neither of us was seasoned to deal with swooning cameras on opening night.

But the jive-talking, yuppie director proved to be the kind of scrambler who could make fancy footwork look easy. He quickly scribbled down new instructions, employing two cameras instead of three, and talked us through the broadcast using our earpieces. This is tricky business, because when the earpiece whispers "Camera 2!" the anchor must—while trying to give the appearance that he is thinking for himself—remember first to look down at his script and then turn to the designated camera. The glance down is the universal signal to the control room to switch cameras. It is done because if the anchor simply turned from one camera to another the turn would always come a second or two before the control room's reaction and would result in the dreaded shot into the anchor's ear. The most authoritative anchors develop this signal into an art form, glancing down with a look of thoughtful scholarship, as if unwilling to proceed without a prudent check of their notes.

It can be confusing to have a stream of chatter in the ear while attempting to speak naturally into a camera. Television directors know this and normally use the earpiece only to nag the anchors when they are running overtime. It is never done as presented in the movie *Broadcast News*, when a producer talked an empty-headed anchor through a bravura performance during live coverage of a military emergency. Our yuppie director whispered in our ears that first night just often enough to keep us faced in the right direction and let it go at that.

Our debut went off without a hitch. The discussion format allowed us to talk around the script problems without undue awkwardness. The mayor came to the studio for a live interview and was obligingly testy when I confronted him with complaints that he had been substituting publicity stunts for policy. My closing commentary concerned a subject that I could discuss with some authority—the need to create a system of small claims courts in Tennessee.

Champagne was poured at the anchor desk after we went off the air. Nobody mentioned that, viewed differently, it could be seen as a bad omen that, just before Channel 2's experimental new program made its debut on the air, a camera went dead.

We were well served to focus on the brighter side of things. Viewed objectively, this was going to be a hard push. We had decided to jettison the accepted format, starting from scratch against two entrenched competitors.

For years, Channel 2 had been too timid to field a newscast at the traditional 6 P.M. local news hour. Anyone who fancied news at dinnertime tuned in one of the two other stations. Only those who preferred "The New Newlywed Game" dialed up our channel.

So when Channel 2 threw down the gauntlet in mid-February of 1988 by thrusting Fred Graham and Cyndee Benson on the air at six, it challenged the ingrained habits of viewers on all three stations.

No one will ever know of the angst that rippled

across middle Tennessee those first few evenings, as Channel 2's viewers flipped on their sets to enjoy the latest smirking episode of "The New Newlywed Game," only to find me interviewing the mayor, or talking earnestly about small claims courts. The Nielsen and Arbitron companies provided some fascinating hints as to what must have taken place.

It happened that our new show went on the air midway through a period known as the February ratings "sweeps," which, along with similar ratings periods in May, July, and November, are hallowed times in television news. These are the months when Nielsen and Arbitron sprinkle the nation's households with little diaries, mailed to a cross-section of viewers, who use them to report back what they are watching on TV. The ratings are based on these reports, and advertising rates are based on the ratings.

In a perfect world, the ratings periods would be unannounced and thus would reflect the normal state of television viewing. But in the real world of television, the ratings companies assume that bribery and corruption would be rampant in efforts to discover the ratings times, and thus they are announced in advance. The resulting scramble is far from normal, even by the standards of television.

I have often wondered what the average, unsuspecting television viewer thinks, when, four times a year, his community is suddenly presented in the news as reeking with corruption, satanism, prostitution, alien beings, crooked politicians, and sex-crazed nuns. It is a time of stories about incest, teen-age suicide, child molesting, battered spouses, and sex addicts, bearing such titles as

"Sex in the Pulpit," "Frisky at 50," and "Is Elvis Really Dead?" and promoted by ads that blare, "Are Juvenile Sex Offenders Getting Away with Murder and Spreading Dread Diseases?"

All this competing hype cancels itself out, of course. Thus the ratings do present a fairly accurate, hour-by-hour picture of how many people were watching which television stations.

The ratings revealed that WKRN's new format sowed chaos during the sweeps of February 1988. Most of the "Newlywed Game" fans were apparently so stunned they switched off their sets. Our ratings for two of the nights during my first week were an astonishing 2 percent of the households in the area. That is within the survey's margin of error; conceivably, there were times when nobody was watching at all. In the second week, our ratings inched up to 5 percent. If we were to do well enough to stay on the air, that would eventually have to triple.

My game plan was based on my feeling that conventional local news was predictable and shallow and that we could succeed by offering a more innovative alternative. The strategy was to counter-program the competition. The other stations used almost identical boy-girl happy talk formats. Their news featured the photographable events of the day, ranging from politicians' publicity stunts to who got arrested, shot, or burned out.

If we could position ourselves so that the competition split the happy talk audience while we attracted viewers who wanted an alternative, we might skim off the 15 percent of the households that would make us a solid success. To swing this, I hoped to make our new program clearly different—more informal, less predictable, and more thoughtful than the competition.

In place of the other stations' obligatory coverage of each day's mishaps and photo opportunities, we squeezed such routine fare into a series of rapid-fire headlines. That gave us time to explore an issue every day in enough detail to make it interesting. There would be a filmed background report, and I would interview one or more people who were movers and shakers on the issue. We delved into the growing pollution of TVA lakes, tax exemptions for church-owned minister's residences, the fleeting impact of the mayor's highly publicized crackdown on drugs, a depressed mountain county where the major industry was cannibalizing cars stolen in Nashville, the local right-to-die movement, brutality charges against the Tennessee walking horse industry, and a wide range of other civic and political issues that came along.

To lighten up what was often a fairly earnest start, we loaded the final two-thirds of each broadcast with weather talk, society news and gossip, hunting and fishing, health tips, and entertainment. My role was to try to maintain a tone of thoughtful informality. In local television, the anchor is usually an authority figure with no authority. My situation was different because the format had been tailored to fit me, and I was clearly senior to my youthful co-anchor. I tried to make each broadcast informative, informal, and unpredictable—and, therefore, different.

Once, in an unguarded remark to the television critic of the morning newspaper, I said I was *glad* that my new station was in last place; with so much room for improvement, our progress would be obvious to all.

She flicked me a glance as if I had dropped in from another planet, and then, with a live-and-learn shrug, she let it drop. But her shrug stuck with me, and in the weeks after our new program went on the air, I began to see the hazards of my method of reinventing local news.

Sometimes our topic-of-the-day proved too dull, or too narrow, to hold the viewers' interest. When that happened, rigor mortis began to set in before we could change the subject. Sometimes my interviews flopped; the interviewees occasionally froze, or filibustered, or spoke as if their words should be chiseled in stone. The rough-and-tumble courtroom instincts that had served me so well in network interviews were out of place in courteous Nashville. In that smaller community, where there was a limited supply of people to interview, this could cause problems. After a couple of skirmishes with the mayor, hizzoner let it be known that he would not be available for future interviews on my show.

In place of the traditional humorous "kicker," our broadcasts signed off three days a week with commentaries by me. Most of them carried a sharp edge. It set us apart from the sweetness-and-light style of the competition, and it was fun. But I developed a growing suspicion that it worked against the first need of an anchorman—to be liked.

As part of my ambition to do well by doing good, I threw open our news program to the opinions of the viewers. I hoped to take some of the sting out of my commentaries by dropping one each week, instead reading the most provocative letters from our audience.

The idea had everything. It gave viewers a chance to

have their say; it promised to increase audience interest in the show; and it relieved me of having to write so many commentaries.

I announced it with great fanfare and waited.

Nobody wrote. Or, almost nobody.

There were only the predictable letters from convicts, preachments from religious fanatics, and some complaints about the departure of "The Newlywed Game." There seemed to be two possible explanations for the dearth of letters, one of which I put out of my mind. It was possible that some quirk of video psychology discouraged viewers from writing in about what they saw, contrary to the behavior of newspaper readers. It was also possible that almost nobody was watching.

I repeated my solicitation of the letters. A few trickled in, but not enough to fill the once-a-week time slot, not the right kind anyway.

My appeals took on an increasingly pleading tone. "Our address is . . ." "If *you* have an opinion you'd like to share with our viewers, our address is . . ." "We *invite* you to write us at . . ." "*Please* write us at . . ."

Desperate, I turned to provocation. My plan was to use my commentaries to bait the viewers into lashing back. It was not that I took bogus positions, but I stated them in the most uncompromising terms I could muster.

I said it was time for Tennessee to have an income tax, denounced a bill in the legislature to ban abortions for young girls, advocated confiscating the cars of drunk drivers, and criticized setting aside city contracts for minorities and women. I lambasted our station for its leering coverage of men arrested for soliciting young boys. I advocated fighting AIDS by giving clean needles to drug addicts, establishing birth control clinics in public schools, decriminalizing marijuana, and creating a red-light district to draw the prostitutes and pornography shops from otherwise decent sections of the city.

The flow of letters rose to a trickle.

Finally, I delivered a witheringly sarcastic critique of the Geraldo Rivera show, which had a loyal audience on our station in the late afternoon. Some spoilsports among our viewers had grumbled because "Geraldo" had replaced the wholesome "Little House on the Prairie" and suggested that "Geraldo" was less than uplifting after-school fare for children just home from school. I tore into "Geraldo" as a "sometimes sleazy, sexually explicit program" that was inappropriate for children— but I added that Geraldo Rivera's program "is to real life as professional wrestling is to fighting" and concluded that any children who watched it would know not to take it seriously.

My only letter came from a lady who wrote, "I agreed with everything you said. I like Geraldo, too."

As the time for the May 1988 ratings sweeps approached, I became edgy about the first real audience judgment on our new newscast. With our trial period behind us and most viewers familiar with what we had to offer, these ratings would tell us whether we were within striking distance of a viable program. If we were being watched by about 10 percent of the households, then we could dig in and improve, bit by bit, until we had a respectable audience. My assumption had always been that with almost three years yet to run on my four-year contract I had time to prove my worth to enough viewers to make a go of it. But it would be reassuring to know that we were off to a promising start.

Then it occurred to me that there had been another omen, this one involving the trends in TV popularity.

The two news programs most like the format of our new show were Ted Koppel's "Nightline" and the Mac-Neil-Lehrer Newshour on PBS. Channel 2 thought so little of "Nightline" that it delayed broadcasting it each night for an hour, while it showed back-to-back reruns of M*A*S*H. MacNeil-Lehrer was the only newscast that consistently managed lower ratings in Nashville than we did our first week. On many evenings, its ratings were only 1.

On the other hand, the hottest thing that summer on Channel 2 was "Geraldo."

———

As nightmares go, mine was short. But it qualified as a nightmare because it kept recurring in my dreams, and it was scary. In it, a hand reached out to a television set and turned the switch to "off."

The hand always belonged to Charles Munro, one of the "news doctors" from the Magid Company, but still too nice a man to be cast in a recurrent nightmare. Yet there he was, night after night, because it was Munro who had uttered the sinister line that stuck so vividly in my mind.

"The most serious competition to the late local news," he said, "is 'off.' "

Local television news, Munro had explained, was being ambushed by an unexpected threat—a news glut. Throughout the day, the average citizen was being soaked with news: from the morning television talk shows, from the car radio, from local TV newscasts, and from brief television newsbreaks during prime time. Saturated with news, people were turning off, especially in the late evenings.

"Television viewers used to have the habit of staying tuned for a touch of news after the entertainment programs ended," Munro said. "It was the old notion of wanting to make sure the world hadn't come to an end before turning in for the night. But people don't feel they have to do that anymore. If something important enough had happened, they'd have heard about it."

A trend seems to be settling in, Munro said. At the end of the prime time network schedule, multitudes of people are reaching out and turning their sets to "off." In some cities, the total audience for the late evening local news shows had slipped 40 percent since just the year before.

It *was* a nightmare, because just two years earlier, when I had made the decision in 1987 to return home, all the indications were that local news was immune to the erosion that had eaten away at the networks.

Ted Turner's news-when-you-want-it Cable News Network was gnawing away at network news ratings, but cable didn't provide local news, so local TV news operations seemed safe. Not long after I made my move, however, the first *local* twenty-four-hour cable news operation started a test run in New York's bedroom suburbs on Long Island. That sent a chill through local news, even though the experts calculated that only the dozen largest markets are big enough to support round-the-clock local cable news. For the rest of the country it was a strong hint that local cable-system operators may soon begin to stitch together shoestring news operations (perhaps in cooperation with local newspapers), with just enough news presence to come on the air several times a day, and scramble for a slice of the local TV stations' audience and advertising money. It will be the one-man-band routine of the Draughon brothers' Jim Kent all over again, with the losers being over-the-air stations such as Channel 2.

Even without direct competition from cable, at about the time that I returned to Nashville, local TV news ratings across the country began to slide. The reasons were very much the same. With so many channels to watch, some people skipped the news. Those who still watched became restless, and distracted. "Zapping" became the rage during local TV broadcasts, which were all so much alike that some viewers learned to "construct" their own news programs—watching one channel's anchors and reporters at the top of the show, then zapping to another channel to catch the friendly weatherman, and on to the next station, for its genial jock sportscaster. The advertisers got onto this and mounted such counter-strategies as splitting their commercials, running a fifteen-second spot at the start of a commercial break and the same one again at the end, in an effort to catch the zappers coming or going.

For local newscasters, it added up to a steady shrinkage of the audience—and of the advertising dollar. Nashville was depressingly typical; as competition heated up between the three news operations, we were each hustling for a larger slice of a shrinking pie. In the two years since I had come home, the number of people watching Nashville's local newscasts had declined for the first time since television was invented.

In my darker moments I began to doubt my earlier belief that the competition going on in TV news in many communities was destined to lead to a better-informed public. Perhaps, instead, it was the beginning of a struggle to determine which local news operations would survive.

A small item from a local newspaper began to haunt me.

It reported the hospitalization of a young Nashville woman who had been shot in the head with a .38 pistol by her live-in boyfriend after she persisted in constantly zapping the TV set from channel to channel.

The boyfriend explained what it was that drove him over the edge:

"She just kept flipping the channels."

In mid-June of 1987, the PBS network called me from Washington about doing some anchoring from Capitol Hill. It was a time when the notion of legalizing drugs had become trendy in the media, and the House Select Committee on Narcotics Abuse and Control was planning two days of high-profile hearings. PBS wanted me to anchor its gavel-to-gavel television coverage.

I thought it would be good public relations for Channel 2 if I appeared on the air again, coast-to-coast. One evening in the newsroom, I approached our news director about the idea. Would it be a problem, I asked, if I took a couple of nights off from the Channel 2 anchor desk to do a little moonlighting in Washington for PBS?

His eyes popped open, in one of those speechless moments that say more than words.

Then he said, "Let's go into my office and talk."

The reason for the speechless moment and the private talk was that my invitation to make a brief return to coast-to-coast broadcasting had forced the station's hand.

I would be perfectly free to anchor for PBS in Washington, the news director told me, because I was being taken off the anchor desk at Channel 2—not just from the new early evening broadcast, which had started out so badly, but also from the newscast that Anne Holt and I anchored after prime time.

Channel 2 had reverted to its tradition of panicking and switching too soon.

A few days before, the May ratings had been published, and they were not good. Where we had dreamed of a possible 10 rating for the new early show, it had pulled in only a 5. For the late newscast, the ratings had remained almost flat since I arrived. There was an irony to this, because my contract called for bonuses ranging up to $5,500 a year for each share point added to the two newscasts I anchored. I caught a mild burst of flak about this from Steve Bell and Sylvia Chase, two former ABC correspondents who had also become local anchors. They told a media magazine they would have no part of such a materialistic arrangement—but as it turned out, I was in no danger of being compromised. Due to the basement ratings of my early newscast, if my incentive clause had been double-edged, I would have owed the station money.

In addition to the bad news on the ratings, I had become a victim of the perennial villains of broadcast news, the media consultants.

Only two years earlier, the news doctors from the Magid company had come to Nashville, convened "focus groups" of local citizens to comment on Channel 2's newscasts, and concluded that a more authoritative anchorman was needed. As a result, I had been hired, and the Magid people had given their blessing. When my presence did not provide a quick fix, in May of 1987 Channel 2's management had invoked the wisdom of media consultants again. This time, however, the station had snubbed the Magid Company. It had called in a fresh team of news doctors for a second opinion—and that is what it got.

Media consultants' wisdom may be no more valid than that of witch doctors or palm readers, but for those who have paid handsomely for their opinions, a consultants' report such as the one submitted to Channel 2 would have to catch management's attention. After the people in the focus groups were shown a randomly selected tape of each of the two news shows that I appeared on, more than six out of ten did not like me as an anchor. They backed it up with such comments as "too old," "a hick," "tries to be cute, but doesn't make it," "overdresses," and "overpaid."

The remark about my income revealed more than just that I had created some bad vibes among average folk by once more violating my wise uncle's advice. It underscored one of the flaws in the consultants' system. There was no effort to find out how much of the negative reaction might have been formed months before, when I made my stumbling debut on the local tube. Since then, I had become steadily more comfortable in the anchor seat, where success is largely a process of wearing well. The problem with the consultants' work, valid or not, was that it gave the station an occasion to cut off my opportunity to "wear well."

Everyone in television news has heard the adage that the key to success is to adopt a plan and stick with it. I felt that when Channel 2's management agreed to pay me for four years they would resist the panic to take me off the air. I lated fourteen months, about the average for an anchorman at Channel 2.

In such a fast and erratic world, knowledge is never complete.

None of us knew that, at about the time the tapes were being picked at random to play for the consultants' focus groups, other tapes were selected in the same fashion to be judged for Emmy awards. Months later, Channel 2 won its first Emmy award for the best late night newscast in our area. The anchors were Anne Holt and Fred Graham.

There was a final irony to my undoing at the hands of the media consultants. I had been given my chance to come home as an anchorman because one bevy of consultants had concluded that the incumbent anchorman at Channel 2 could never summon the authority to make the station a success. The demoted anchor remained on the staff, and when the new team of consultants proclaimed that I would not do, they opined that the original anchor would be a promising replacement. Channel 2 took the new consultants' advice and returned him to his former position.

A personal failure is always hard to accept, but this one also deflated a larger vision. After my experience, few network correspondents were likely to think quite so seriously of returning home to anchor local TV—and the stations might be less likely to want them.

There was also bad news in the consultants' findings for the type of upscale news format that we attempted.

Many viewers found the in-depth stories too long, the interviews boring, and the emphasis on politics and government too heavy. Despite all our efforts to reinvent local TV news, viewers seemed to be telling us that they felt more comfortable with the familiar rituals of happy talk.

It was decided that the people of Channel 2 would be called into the newsroom to be told about my demotion before it leaked to the public somewhere else. I agreed to appear and calm the waters by telling my colleagues that I was not bitter, and that the show should go on.

Several days later, the local entertainment tabloid would blanket its front page with a photograph of me looking woebegone, topped by the headline: "How Much Hard News Can a Guy Take?" But I did not feel put upon by the hard landing at Channel 2, even on that day when I bowed out in the newsroom. Partly, this was due to an ingrained Presbyterian fatalism that tends to keep my pulse low when the bottom drops out. This time, it took the form of a shrug and the thought: "That's show biz."

But I also realized that if I had been betrayed by developments in television news, the deed was done at CBS; by the time I reached Channel 2, I was an unindicted co-conspirator in the mishaps that took place.

That had not been true years before, when, during my first year in law practice, I mentally began the switch toward print journalism. My career change began one sweltering August afternoon as I measured skid marks at an intersection on Nashville's Gallatin Road. That day, as I stretched my tape measure along the tire tracks in preparation for my defense in a car wreck case, I experienced a seizure of *deja vu*.

I realized I had measured skid marks at that intersection before.

It was a hazardous spot, and once before I had represented an insurance company whose policy holder had come a cropper at that corner. For an instant, a vision flashed across my mind of a lifetime spent returning to that intersection to measure burned rubber, in a joyless crusade to channel dollars to my insurance company, instead of someone else's. I knew it was an exaggeration, but just of degree, not substance. At that moment I realized my career in law was a goner.

When I settled on print journalism as the alternative, it was for the right reasons—the fun of reporting, the excitement of breaking a big story, the thrill of observing important events. But mostly, it was to satisfy my childhood urge to "give a penny," to try to serve by informing the public. As a reporter, I assumed (wrongly, it turned out) that I could not expect as much money as my law practice would have produced, but the other considerations made the decision to change careers not even a close one.

Later, when I switched to CBS News, the move to television did not seem to undermine those reasons. I believed it was possible to have at CBS the same satisfactions that brought me to the *New York Times*. Perhaps there was a grain of self-delusion in the belief that television would double my salary and not expect me to do a little soft-shoe if times got lean. But money lubricates credulity. It was easy to assume that the news organization of Edward R. Murrow, Walter Cronkite, and Eric Sevareid would never risk its reputation by fudging on news standards.

That was why, when CBS turned to infotainment,

there was such a painful sense of betrayal. We had signed on to be journalists, and they had changed the rules on us, in mid-career. When the driving purpose shifted from informing the public to inflating the ratings, those of us who had come there under different principles felt betrayed.

But when I went to Nashville, there had been a much more realistic meeting of the minds. Everybody understood that I was coming home to raise Channel 2's ratings; if the ratings did not go up, I would be out. That did not bother me, because it never seriously entered my mind that I might fail. I believed that we would improve the quality of the news broadcasts, and the ratings would follow. When things did not work out, the cause was not betrayal, but miscalculation. I had been wrong to assume that my no-cut contract would induce Channel 2 to control its panic and give me a full chance. I had also been naive to believe a person could contribute substance and content to the news as a local TV anchor.

As my colleagues began to drift into the newsroom and I mulled over what to say, the anguished young man's accusation on the occasion of my departure from print journalism drifted back from over the years: *Why did you sell out?*

At the time, I had laughed at the assumption that a move to television news was a journalist's handshake with Faust. In an era when most people got their news from TV, that struck me as elitist, patronizing, and depressing.

But as I prepared my swan song, seventeen years later, from a struggling local TV station, it was time to ask that question of myself. Had I sold out? Knowing what I know now, would I have switched to television news, even without the oversized salaries?

Absolutely.

Without hesitation.

With the benefit of hindsight, I would take a deep breath and brace for a fast ride—but I would do it again. For the fun of it, for the excitement and the influence, but mostly for the challenge. Television is the people's medium, and if journalism is going to continue to reach the grass roots, much of it will have to be done through the tube. Despite the disarray of the networks, the taint of sensationalism, the appeal of tabloid-TV, and the fender-bender tendencies of local news, serious journalists must find roles in television news, or surrender the most potent medium to trash and sleaze.

I had not come up with the formula for how to do this—particularly in local TV news—but I was not sorry I had tried.

As I stood to face my colleagues, I toyed with the idea of giving them the whole story behind my return to Nashville—all but the Tom Paine part. But to say such things in a farewell speech by a fired TV anchor would have sounded presumptuous and overblown.

Instead, I told them that I was disappointed and sorry to see it end; that it was a decision I would not have made—certainly not until we had given it more time to work—but that it was management's decision, and they had made it in good faith.

I explained that the decision makers had concluded that my presence as anchor was serving as a drag on the efforts of everyone else. If so, I did not want to hold back the recognition that my colleagues deserved for the improvement they had made and the good work they were doing. It was important, I said, that Channel 2 was no longer the rag-tag news organization that it used to be. There had been steady improvement and I was proud to have been a part of that process.

I said that I would stay on for a while, doing commentaries and special projects. After I got my bearings, it would probably be time to move on.

"I had a chance to succeed at this," I said. "Everyone tried. My colleagues supported me. The station made an honest effort.

"I tried to make it work, and I'm just sorry that it did not. What we attempted to do was worth all the efforts that we made.

"I have no regrets."

17

Friendly Robots

There had always been one aspect of Secretary of Labor Willard Wirtz's vision of the march of automation that I found hard to swallow. It had to do with friendly robots.

Wirtz was a Harvard liberal, a former law partner of Adlai Stevenson, and a darling of the Brie-and-Chablis wing of the Democratic party. The fashion in those circles was to View with Alarm, but to Face the Future with·Confidence. Wirtz was a natural for the viewing-with-alarm part, but his crewcut bristled at the obligation to find a silver lining in automation. He developed what I privately called the "friendly robots" thesis.

A typical Wirtz speech would be 90 percent lamentations over the ravages of technology on America's workforce. Then would come the friendly robots part. Through gritted teeth, he would claim to believe that technological disruptions were "not only inevitable but necessary if we are to remain competitive," and would profess that "the bargain a machine strikes with a man is that it takes one job and offers another." The purported moral was that after technology undercut people's jobs at one point, it would create new and different ones in other places.

To me, the friendly robot theme was always a bit forced. I especially thought so later, when electronic wizardry began to whittle away at the CBS workforce. My skepticism hardened as the proliferation of TV channels eventually put the squeeze on me. It culminated in 1989, when the Knight-Ridder Company decided that the path to riches was no longer in owning local television stations. Knight-Ridder put all its TV properties up for sale and snuffed out my fading career in local television by selling Channel 2.

But in other places the sunny side of the upheaval in television was beginning to glimmer through. All those new television channels needed to fill the video screen, and who had more experience in doing that than the refugees from the shrinking networks?

So many veterans of CBS News had departed that they published a newsletter to keep in touch. It revealed that most had shifted to careers in cable TV, independent productions, videocasettes, and free-lancing. Many of them had started businesses of their own, churning out video to fill the many hungry television channels. They discovered there was life after CBS, and it offered more variety and independence than the monolithic network had ever allowed.

For me, television's friendly robots held out a promise known as "narrowcasting." This is the prospect that, as the number of TV channels continues to increase, some of them will focus on narrow audiences with special interests, much as magazines have done.

Soon after my contract with Knight-Ridder ended, practitioners of narrowcasting came to me and began to make their case. They said the whittling away of the networks' monopoly had made possible splinter television enterprises aimed at smaller audiences with more specialized tastes. They held out the ultimate plum for a TV legal journalist—a full-time law channel on cable TV.

With the nation's courts increasingly opening their doors to cameras, the law channel would specialize in bringing the most interesting and significant ones into peoples' homes on a daily basis. This would be a video-age restoration of the old American tradition of going to the courthouse to sit and watch the trials. After hours, the law channel would employ various means to feed the enormous public appetite about courts, lawyers, litigation, and the law. There would be legal news, tips on consumer rights, legal talk shows, and other programs related to the law.

My role would be going back on camera to talk about the law, plus taking charge of all the law channel's programming content. To me, this seemed an affirmation that the winds of technology had brought television almost full circle in one journalist's working career—from the days when the pinnacle of a legal correspondent's aspirations was presumed to be a network, to the time when the highest form of TV legal journalism would be a cable channel devoted to the law.

The irony was not lost on me that such a channel could easily lapse into the excesses of infotainment—and that this time, I would be in charge. Decisions would have to be made as to what trials to cover, how much sin, sex, and gore to include on the menu, and where to strike the balance between audience appeal and responsibility and good taste.

Even as I agreed to sign on to direct the course of the new law channel—which is not scheduled to appear on the screen for at least a year—I felt the sharp edges of my resentment begin to soften toward the former purveyors of infotainment at CBS. There will be future lines to be drawn between what the public wants to know and needs to know, and this time I will be drawing them, with a respectful eye toward the bottom line.

But there will also be a new opportunity to reveal and explain on television the fascinating world of the law. With the luxury of speaking to an audience with a special interest in the subject, the talk will be—without the need for gimmicks or contrived machinations—well, meaningful. And in my mind at least, it will also be happy.

Acknowledgments

Those who deserve the most thanks from me are the majority of my former colleagues at CBS News, who maintained standards of journalism and decency through a difficult time. Many of them helped me with this book, and I owe them a special debt of gratitude. They know who they are, and I do them a greater service by allowing them to receive their satisfaction from these pages than by mentioning their names here.

A number of people at Channel 2 were helpful with information about the history and technology of the station. Among those who went out of their way to assist were Anne Holt, Charlie Scott, Jan Wade, Toni Plummer, Gary Womack, Charlie Dunaway, John Denson, Tom Siler, Bill Lord, Deb McDermott, and Art Elliot.

Several people in busy jobs gave time and thought to helping me. They include David Wigdor of the Library of Congress; Toni House, public information officer for the Supreme Court; Charles Munro of the Magid Com-

ACKNOWLEDGMENTS

pany; Ernie Schultz, president of the Radio-Television News Directors Association; and several former colleagues from the Supreme Court press corps—Nina Totenberg, Ron Ostrow, Carl Stern, Aaron Epstein, and Lyle Denniston.

By a great stroke of luck, the nation's most comprehensive collection of tapes of network news broadcasts is located in Nashville at the Vanderbilt University Television News Archive, and its staff operates as if it is running a foster home for struggling book writers. With the help of Scarlett Graham, the Archives' director, and John Lynch, Dorothy Hamilton, and others there, I was able to review years of CBS broadcasts and compare them with the contemporary coverage of ABC and NBC. My statistics on the decline of CBS coverage of Washington, D.C., and the increased coverage of California were obtained from the indexes published by the Vanderbilt TV News Archive.

This book became inevitable when Sterling Lord read the outline and said, "I think it's terrific!" Sterling, my agent, had managed to contain his enthusiasm about some of my other literary ideas. I am fortunate to have a friend who reserves his praise for when it is justified. I am also blessed that another old friend, Don Lamm, president of W. W. Norton & Company, liked my book—and that a new friend, Ed Barber, my editor at Norton, helped me make it better.

I was aided in my research by Bobbie Ohs, a fellow broadcast journalist who was then learning her trade at the School of Journalism at Middle Tennessee State University.

Among those who read all or part of my manuscript

Acknowledgments

and added their perspectives, knowledge, and good judgment were Barbara Matusow, Jack Nelson, Paul Leeper, Alan Novak, Peter Tufo, and Skiles Harris. I was fortunate to have as a critic an old friend who is the only politician I know who can write—Lamar Alexander. Beginning with my earliest drafts, he insisted on a saga written with a common touch. I was also aided, advised and encouraged by another old friend who writes, David Halberstam.

Skila, my wife, was my most helpful adviser in this, as in all things. Her presence meant everything in the writing of this story—but much more in the living of it.

Index

347

INDEX

Index

349

INDEX

Index

INDEX